Finally. The church has waited too long for an exegetical excavation and application of the Bible's teaching about ethnicity, Christ, the cross, and our new humanity. Jarvis Williams serves us all by helping us to see more clearly the implications of Paul's theology of the cross and reconciliation. Heartily commended.

Thabiti Anyabwile
Senior Pastor, First Baptist Church of Grand Cayman
Cayman Islands

Jarvis Williams has provided a much needed contribution to the work of racial reconciliation and Christian unity. I applaud the work for its foundational biblical and theological commitments. Williams informs both head and heart, while challenging us toward faithfulness in our thinking and our living. While seeking to dispel numerous misunderstandings, both old and new, he invites readers to participate in vital kingdom work. It is a genuine joy to recommend this volume, which hopefully will have a shaping influence on both church and society for years to come.

David S. Dockery
President, Union University
Jackson, Tennessee

One New Man: The Cross and Racial Reconciliation in Pauline Theology by Jarvis Williams takes the ongoing evangelical dialogue on racial reconciliation into some helpful new directions. With meticulous detail Williams presents racism as the consequence of the fallen human condition. For a solution Williams turns to Paul's theology of the reconciling work of Christ on the cross and the new humanity that results from it. This work may be a little heady and technical at points. But it is a thesis that takes us much deeper in our consideration of the perversion of the human condition, and the solution is far more substantial than some of what has come down the evangelical pike.

Ken Jones
Pastor, Greater Union Baptist Church
Compton, California

Jarvis Williams brings considerable exegetical skill and personal experience as an African-American scholar to bear on the critical issue of racial reconciliation in the American church. His book offers the reader an approach to the subject that is rarely found—a thorough exegetical study of the biblical passages on the teaching of reconciliation.

Kenneth A. Mathews
Professor of Divinity, Old Testament
Beeson Divinity School, Samford University
Birmingham, Alabama

Jarvis Williams's book on racial reconciliation is an important contribution to a sadly neglected issue in our churches. The book is characterized by careful study of relevant biblical passages and suggestions for application. Particularly important, in light of the current cultural climate, is the author's distinction between ethnic diversity and racial reconciliation. The church, he argues, must not be content with diversity; it must push forward to a biblically distinctive, Christ-centered and Spirit-led embrace of one another in love.

Douglas J. Moo
Blanchard Professor of New Testament
Wheaton College, Wheaton, Illinois
Chair, Committee on Bible Translation, NIV

One of the saddest realities of American church life is that too many of our congregations are racially and socially isolated. One of the most joyous realities of the contemporary American church is that God is calling out young leaders who are willing to seek to change this. Jarvis Williams is a brilliant, young New Testament scholar. He also has a burning passion for churches that picture the gospel in their racial makeup and witness. Read this book and ask the Spirit to show you your place in helping the church model the "one new man" of the gospel of Jesus Christ.

Russell D. Moore
Dean, School of Theology
Senior Vice President for Academic Administration
The Southern Baptist Theological Seminary
Louisville, Kentucky

Racial reconciliation—and not just racial diversity, as Williams argues—is fundamental to the gospel. Accentuated by passion and personal experience, Jarvis Williams engages in a rich biblical and theological exploration of this important issue facing the church today.

Preston M. Sprinkle
Associate Professor of Biblical Studies
Eternity Bible College
Simi Valley, California

The apostle Paul is clear: our vertical reconciliation with God occurs as he reconciles horizontally those who have been at enmity with one another, who then are reconciled together, as one new man, to God in Christ (Eph 2:14–18). So, to miss horizontal reconciliation is to miss something central to the gospel itself. Jarvis Williams demonstrates in a clear and compelling way that racial reconciliation is no nice optional "extra" to the substance and proclamation of the gospel but is at the heart of that message of the cross itself. Williams evidences both exegetical care and theological acumen in his discussion of key Pauline texts that should inform significantly our views of racial reconciliation. And the practical impact of this book is monumental. There are few issues of our day more urgent to "get right" than this one, and we owe Dr. Williams a deep debt of gratitude for the excellent treatment he has here produced.

Bruce A. Ware
Professor of Christian Theology
The Southern Baptist Theological Seminary
Louisville, Kentucky

one
new
man

The Cross and Racial Reconciliation
in Pauline Theology

Jarvis J.
Williams

B&H
ACADEMIC
Nashville, Tennessee

ISBN: 978-0-8054-4857-3

Published by B&H Publishing Group
Nashville, Tennessee

Dewey Decimal Classification: 261.8
Subject Heading: CHURCH AND RACE RELATIONS \ RACE
RELATIONS

Printed in the United States of America

1 2 3 4 5 6 7 8 9 10 11 12 • 17 16 15 14 13 12 11 10

VP

For my beloved son

Jaden Alexander Williams

whose very existence reminds me of the
beauty, the power, and the joy of racial
reconciliation

contents

list of abbreviations

AB	Anchor Bible
ABC	*Anchor Bible Commentary*
BAR	*Biblical Archaeology Review*
BBR	*Bulletin for Biblical Research*
BECNT	Baker Exegetical Commentary of the New Testament
BHT	Beiträge zur historischen Theologie
Bib	*Biblica*
BJRL	*Biblical Journal of Religious Literature*
BN	*Biblische Notizen*
BThSt	Biblisch-theologische Studien
CTJ	*Calvin Theological Journal*
CBQ	*Catholic Biblical Quarterly*
CD	Cairo Genizah copy of the *Damascus Document*
CQR	*Catholic Quarterly Review*
CSR	*Christian Scholar's Review*
DSSSE	*Dead Sea Scrolls: Study Edition.* Edited by F. G. Martinez and E. J. C. Tigchelaar. New York, 1997–1998.
EKKNT	Evangelisch-katholischer Kommentar zum Neuen Testament
ETL	*Ephemerides theologicae lovanienses*
EvQ	*Evangelical Quarterly*
EvT	*Evangelische Theologie*

ExpTim	*Expository Times*
HDR	Harvard Dissertations in Religion
ICC	International Critical Commentary
Int	*Interpretation*
JAAR	*Journal of the American Academy of Religion*
JBL	*Journal of Biblical Literature*
JETS	*Journal of the Evangelical Theological Society*
JSNT	*Journal for the Study of the New Testament*
JSNTSup	Journal for the Study of the New Testament: Supplement Series
JSOT	*Journal for the Study of the Old Testament*
JTS	*Journal of Theological Studies*
LXX	Septuagint (the Greek OT)
MNTC	Moffatt New Testament Commentary
MT	Masoretic Text (of the OT)
NAC	New American Commentary
Neot	*Neotestamentica*
NIBCNT	New International Biblical Commentary on the New Testament
NIBCOT	New International Biblical Commentary on the Old Testament
NICNT	New International Commentary on the New Testament
NIGTC	New International Greek Testament Commentary
NTD	Das Neue Testament Deutsch
NTS	*New Testament Studies*
NT	New Testament
NRA	New Revised Standard Version with Apocrypha
OT	Old Testament
PRSt	*Perspectives in Religious Studies*
PNTC	Pillar New Testament Commentary
PTR	*Presbyterian Theological Review*
Presb	*Presbyterion*
RelEd	*Religious Education*
SBL	Society of Biblical Literature
SBJT	*Southern Baptist Journal of Theology*
SNT	Studien zum Neuen Testament
SNTSU	Studien zum Neuen Testament und seiner Umwelt

SNTSMS	Society for New Testament Studies Monograph Series
SP	Sacra pagina
STJ	Second Temple Judiasm
STL	Second Temple Literature
THKNT	Theologischer Handkommentar zum Neuen Testament
TNTC	The Tyndale New Testament Commentaries
VD	*Verbum domini*
WBC	Word Biblical Commentary
WMANT	Wissenschaftliche Monographien zum Alten und Neuen Testament
WTJ	*Westminster Theological Journal*
WUNT	Wissenschaftliche Untersuchungen zum Neuen Testament
ZNW	*Zeitschrift für die neutestamentliche Wissenschaft und die Kunde der älteren Kirche*

acknowledgments

S imon J. Gathercole was absolutely correct when he stated in the preface of *The Pre-existent Son,* his second monograph, that completing a second monograph is more difficult than writing a doctoral thesis since one's *Doktorvater* and his examiners do not give the manuscript the guidance and rigorous scrutiny throughout the writing process that they gave the thesis. After writing this book, I certainly agree with Gathercole. This is my second monograph, but my first monograph since the publication of a revised version of my doctoral thesis "Maccabean Martyr Traditions in Paul's Theology of Atonement," now published as *Maccabean Martyr Traditions in Paul's Theology of Atonement: Did Martyr Theology Shape Paul's Conception of Jesus's Death?* (Eugene, OR: Wipf & Stock, 2010). Because of my graduation from Southern Seminary's doctoral program in December 2007, the beginning of my full-time teaching post at Campbellsville University in January 2008, my heavy teaching load each semester, the birth of my son in June 2008, and the purchase of a new home in September 2008 (all of which happened as I was writing this book), this book has been a challenge and a joy. Similar to my doctoral thesis, I owe thanks to many scholars and friends who have helped me shape this book in several ways, although I have space to thank only a few. All deficiencies in this work are my own fault.

I must first thank B&H Academic for accepting this book for publication and for standing behind it every step of the way.

I especially thank Terry Wilder, who supported this work and my initial idea for the book from day one. Terry did everything in his power during the early stages of the proposal to ensure its publication. I am eternally indebted to Tom Schreiner, my *Doktorvater*, both for writing the foreword and for the profound impact that he has made on my life throughout the years. When I first showed him the proposal for this book in the fall of 2007, it was only an idea I had been thinking about for years that began to develop more precisely during the final stages of my doctoral thesis. After reading the proposal, Tom encouraged me to pursue publication. Only eternity will reveal to him how much I truly love and appreciate him, how much he has shaped my understanding of exegesis and Pauline theology, and how much he has helped my reading of the Bible. I owe thanks to Micah Carter, my dear friend, for carefully reading most of the manuscript and especially for his incisive critique on chapters 4 and 5. Micah's analysis of my work has made the manuscript a little more accessible for readers outside the academic guild. In addition to his analysis of the manuscript, Micah offered me much encouragement in the writing of this work. His friendship is priceless. I owe thanks to the scholars and pastors (whose names you can see both within and on the back of the book) who graciously read the manuscript and kindly endorsed it. I sincerely admire each endorser and am honored that each one has attached his respected name to my work.

I owe thanks to Pastor Michael Caudill (known by his parishioners simply as "Brother Mike") and to the members of the Hindman First Baptist Church (HFBC) from 1996 to 2000, where I actively served as a member during the previously mentioned years. Pastor Caudill (a Caucasian) and Hindman First Baptist Church (a predominately Caucasian church in Eastern Kentucky) physically modeled for me the Pauline idea of racial reconciliation, by the abundant love that they showed me (a new Christian at the time). Regardless of my race, they expressed their love when I became a Christian and when I became the first African-American to join HFBC church in the church's history in a community that was and is very segregated and extremely racist. Pastor Caudill not only gave me immeasurable love and treated me with the same level of acceptance as he treated any white member, but he also forcefully preached against racism when a few members left the congregation due to my membership. I am forever grateful to Pastor Caudill and HFBC for many reasons, one of which is their practical grasp of the Pauline message of racial reconciliation in a social context that does not grasp it.

I owe thanks to Campbellsville University (CU) where I am privileged to teach. I am especially grateful to my dean in the School of Theology, John E. Hurtgen, and to all of my colleagues in the School of Theology who (in spite of our theological differences and different academic interests) constantly support my scholarship and my efforts to help foster a love for biblical scholarship throughout both the School of Theology and the university community. I am immensely grateful to Dean Hurtgen for graciously providing me with the freedom to pursue at CU what God has called me to do. I am not only thankful for Dean Hurtgen's constant encouragement and support of me and of my work, but I am also thankful that he gives me the freedom to pursue my calling to and love for scholarly research, writing, publication, and other scholarly endeavors at an institution that holds teaching and instructional effectiveness in the classroom in high regard.

I owe thanks to Daniel Motley, my research assistant at CU, for carefully checking the abbreviations, the footnotes, and the bibliography for typographical errors and for ensuring that the footnotes and bibliographic citations harmonized. Daniel's meticulous work caught several mistakes. His work is greatly appreciated and is to be commended. I also offer thanks to all of my students at CU from 2007 to 2009 who participated in discussions and lectures related to this book. I think especially of an introduction to New Testament course in the fall of 2009, where the class and I had a stimulating discussion for the entirety of the class about the issues of race, racism, and racial reconciliation in light of Ephesians 2. The discussion proved to be very profitable both for them and for me, and their insightful comments about race, racism, and racial reconciliation from their perspective as ethnically diverse university students reinforced to me the need for this book. I owe thanks to Ian Lawrence for carefully reading the entire manuscript on such a short notice. He found mistakes and made helpful recommendations.

Finally, and certainly not least, I owe a myriad of thanks to my family. First, I owe many thanks to Ana, my sweet and beautiful wife of eight years, for her continued love, prayers, patience, and support. I am privileged to call Ana my wife. I love her so much. She works extremely hard to ensure that I have balance in my life, and she reminds me often that there is much more to life than scholarly research and writing books. If it were not for her, I would truly lock myself away in a room with books and a computer and endlessly give myself to scholarly pursuits without taking time to enjoy God and life in this world.

Second, I owe thanks to my beloved son, Jaden Alexander Williams, who was born during the early stages of writing this book. As I wrote chapters 3, 4, and 5, Jaden was only a few months old and was always with me in my study at home. He was either in my lap trying to destroy the keys on my computer keyboard, in his bouncy laughing away, in his swing screaming, or in his playpen making various noises. Jaden was very helpful throughout much of the writing process in that he caused me to be very efficient with my time and provided me with many (as he thought) needed study breaks by laughing, screaming, crying, and needing feedings and diaper changes. Jaden has brought much joy into the lives of his mom and me. When I look at him, I am often reminded of the beauty, the power, and the joy of racial reconciliation. It is, therefore, with great joy that I dedicate this book to my beloved son, Jaden Alexander Williams, whose very existence constantly reminds me of these things.

Jarvis J. Williams
Louisville, Kentucky

foreword

I am not denying that we as evangelical Christians may be able to learn some truths about racial reconciliation from those in the secular world. Also, I freely confess that Christians who have preached the gospel have too often been on the wrong side of the issue so that their words and their actions have promoted racism. As Christians who believe the Bible's teachings, we have many sins to confess with respect to racism. Even though I am not a big proponent of apologies for what past generations did, I think the Southern Baptist Convention (of which I am a member) rightly apologized in 1995 for its role in U.S. slavery. It was imperative to clarify that we do not endorse the sins of the past, even while we confess that we ourselves are not entirely free from the sins of racism and prejudice.

It is helpful here to review some of the sins confessed in the resolution adopted by the Southern Baptist Convention:

WHEREAS, Our relationship to African-Americans has been hindered from the beginning by the role that slavery played in the formation of the Southern Baptist Convention; and

WHEREAS Many of our Southern Baptist forbears defended the right to own slaves, and either participated in, supported, or acquiesced in the particularly inhumane nature of American slavery; and

WHEREAS, In later years Southern Baptists failed, in many cases, to support, and in some cases opposed, legitimate initiatives to secure the civil rights of African-Americans . . .

WHEREAS, Racism has divided the body of Christ and Southern Baptists in particular, and separated us from our African-American brothers and sisters; and

WHEREAS, Many of our congregations have intentionally and/or unintentionally excluded African-Americans from worship, membership, and leadership; and

WHEREAS, Racism profoundly distorts our understanding of Christian morality, leading some Southern Baptists to believe that racial prejudice and discrimination are compatible with the Gospel . . .[1]

The resolution then continues more specifically, saying, "We lament and repudiate historic acts of evil such as slavery from which we continue to reap a bitter harvest, and we recognize that the racism which yet plagues our culture today is inextricably tied to the past," and "we apologize to all African-Americans for condoning and/or perpetuating individual and systemic racism in our lifetime; and we genuinely repent of racism of which we have been guilty, whether consciously (Psalm 19:13) or unconsciously (Leviticus 4:27)."[2]

Furthermore, in this resolution Southern Baptists asked for "forgiveness from our African-American brothers and sisters" and committed themselves to "eradicate racism in all its forms from Southern Baptist life and ministry."[3] This resolution reminds us of past sins. Most would agree that there is still much work to be done.

Certainly, we as evangelical Christians may learn from the world, but I have a complaint as well. Why do we so often think that the world has a better answer to the problem of racial prejudice

---

[1] The entire resolution may be found at http://www.sbc.net/resolutions/amResolution.asp?ID=899. Accessed on April 17, 2009.

[2] Ibid.

[3] Ibid.

than we do? Why do we so often follow secular advice "lock, stock, and barrel"? Why do we have the very same multicultural programs with a thin Christian veneer? Why is our diversity training so often virtually indistinguishable from that of the world? I can only conclude that we as evangelical Christians believe that we must look to the world for solutions to racism. I do not have space to argue for this here, but we need to evaluate critically the multicultural and diversity programs that are rife in our culture. In many ways they are contrary to the gospel, and instead of advancing racial reconciliation, they actually foster and encourage racial polarization. We as Christians have a better answer to racial problems—an answer that goes back to Jesus Christ, the apostle Paul, and others who wrote sacred Scripture. In other words, we as Christians believe that the answer to racism is found in the Bible. The answer is found in the gospel of Jesus Christ.

If the answer is found in the gospel, why have Christians so often been on the wrong side of the issue? Too often we do not live by the gospel we proclaim. Cultural norms and sinful patterns crowd out the liberating message that Jesus taught. Even as Christians we easily forget about the good news and live by another norm. But our failure to live consistently by the gospel does not mean that we should abandon the gospel as the answer. Rather, the gospel calls upon us to confess our sins, repent of our evil, and commit ourselves anew to Jesus Christ. Many Christians today are convinced, as they adopt wholesale the multicultural and diversity agenda of our culture, that they represent the vanguard of righteousness. But insofar as they promote a norm other than the gospel, they lead us astray.

How refreshing, then, it is to read a book by an African-American scholar where the New Testament message of reconciliation through Christ is taken seriously as the answer to our racial problems. Jarvis Williams believes that the gospel of Christ speaks to our racial sins and prejudices today, and he shows through careful exegesis what the gospel has to say to our churches and our world. All of us who confess Jesus Christ as Lord and Savior are brothers and sisters. We are all descendants of Adam (Acts 17:26; Rom 5:12–19), and we have all sinned and fall short of what God requires (Rom 3:23). We are all justified in the same way through faith in Jesus Christ (Rom 3:28–30), and we are reconciled to God and one another through Jesus Christ (Eph. 2:14–18). As Jarvis Williams shows, our fundamental task is not to become one, but to live out the oneness that has already been accomplished in Christ. We *are* brothers and sisters because we belong to Jesus Christ. May we live out this glorious gospel! May the world know that we are Christians by our love for one another (John 13:34–35)! Jarvis Williams's book does not pretend to provide the answer to all the questions before us, but it provides a rock-solid foundation and starting point.

Thomas R. Schreiner
James Buchanan Harrison Professor of New Testament
Interpretation
The Southern Baptist Theological Seminary

1

introduction

Racism has produced many of the world's problems. It lies at the root of much violence, discrimination, hatred, murder, and a host of other atrocities in the United States of America and other parts of the world. Racial hostility has reoccurred throughout history, especially in the practice of slavery in medieval Europe and during the colonial period of the United States, the treatment of the Jews during the holocaust, the tactics of the Ku Klux Klan, the execution of Emmett Till, the militant practices of the Black Panthers, the policies and implementation of segregation and integration of blacks in the United States, the teachings on race of the Nation of Islam, the race riots of the civil rights movement, the assassinations of Dr. Martin Luther King Jr. and the Kennedy brothers, the circumstances involving the protest of Rosa Parks, the beating of Rodney King, the violent act of the Jena 6, racist lyrics expressed through music, and the bitter rhetoric articulated by various people throughout the presidential campaign of Barack Obama.

Unfortunately, racism has also impacted the church.[1] To find racism in the church, one does not need to look too long or too

---

[1] For example, see E. S. Morgan, *American Slavery, American Freedom: The Ordeal of Colonial Virginia* (New York: Norton, 1975); M. A. Noll, *A History of Christianity in the United States and Canada* (Grand Rapids: Eerdmans, 1992), 7–8, 37, 68, 77–80, 90, 108–10, 136–41, 184, 234; ibid., *The Old Religion in a New World: The History of North American Christianity* (Grand Rapids: Eerdmans, 2002), 55, 65, 69, 117, 275. For examples of racism in certain African-American ecclesiological contexts, see the various works written by advocates of Black Theology such as J. H. Cone and G. S. Wilmore, eds., *Black Theology: A Documentary History*, vol. 1: 1966–1979, 2nd ed. (New York: Orbis, 1993).

far from one's own congregation, regardless of the denomination, the ethnic groups, and the theological tradition that comprise the congregation. Racial tension can be easily detected on any Sunday morning, at any Christian church, during any worship service, and within any congregation, because racism crosses ethnic, ecclesiological, theological, and denominational lines. The impact of racism on the church is evident by either a lack of ethnic diversity in certain congregations or a lack of sincere, familial, Christ-like love for those from different ethnic groups within the body of Christ. The lack of racial harmony in the church is partly due to the culture's influence on Christians. Consequently, many Christians form racist opinions toward ethnic groups simply because they do not have a biblical worldview of race.[2]

Goal and Thesis of the Book

This book aims to provide Christians with a biblical worldview of race and race relations. By primarily focusing on the Pauline corpus, I address the issue of *racial reconciliation*.[3] That Jesus' death for humanity's sin is foundational to Paul's theology of racial reconciliation is the argument that runs throughout my book. In other words, sin is the fundamental reason that humanity needs to be reconciled first to God and second to one another and that Jesus' sacrificial death for sin is the only provision for and solution to racial hostility in Paul's theology. The logic of the arguments I

[2] The opinions of many Christians in the South during the heyday of slavery in the colonial period of the United States of America vividly illustrate this lack of a biblical worldview of race. For specific examples, see sources in n. 1 above.

[3] Here *racial reconciliation* and *racial harmony* are used synonymously. Nevertheless, S. Burns ("A Practical Theology for Racial Harmony," *Southern Baptist Journal of Theology* 8, no. 2 [2004]: 34–54, esp. 34–37) rejects such a use since he thinks that *racial reconciliation* assumes a pre-existent relationship between whites and blacks in the United States that in reality never existed. Burns prefers the term *racial harmony*. Nevertheless, Burns has created a false dichotomy between the two phrases, because his choice of *racial harmony over racial reconciliation* is predicated on his false assumption that racial reconciliation refers only to the need for blacks and whites to be reconciled. This assumption leads Burns to conclude (1) that racial reconciliation assumes a relationship between blacks and whites that never existed and (2) that racial reconciliation is an inappropriate phrase since (for the most part) blacks and whites did not have a pre-existent relationship in the United States of America, which needs to be restored. The discussion of racial reconciliation in this book is not limited to one or two ethnic groups. Rather, the thesis argues that all races need to be reconciled to one another because of sin. Since Jesus' death purchased salvation for Jews and Gentiles and since reconciliation is part of the salvation his death accomplished for them (see Rom 5:9–10), Jesus' death therefore achieves racial reconciliation for both Jews and Gentiles who place faith in him. To limit the phrase *racial reconciliation* only to blacks and whites undermines the universal impact of sin. The universal impact of sin suggests that all races need to be reconciled to God and one another. Besides, racial reconciliation is a Pauline concept (see Eph 2:18–19).

put forth throughout the book to advance my thesis can be sum-marized as follows: (1) Paul argues that sin has broken humanity's relationship with God and with fellow human beings. (2) Paul ar-gues that Jesus is God's provision for the universal problem of sin and that he offered Jesus to die vicariously as a penal substitute for sin to restore humanity's broken relationships with God and fellow human beings. Therefore, according to Paul, Jesus' vicarious death as payment for humanity's sin is God's only solution to racial hos-tility and his only provision for racial reconciliation.[4]

What Is Racial Reconciliation?

According to Genesis 3, the fall seriously damaged human rela-tionships. Adam's transgression caused the breakage of humanity's relationship with God and with fellow human beings. Conse-quently, humanity and human relationships need to be restored to the original state in which God created them. Furthermore, the fall in Genesis 3 not only severed humanity's relationship with God, but it especially severed humanity's relationship among fellow hu-man beings (see Genesis 1–11). Two examples of sin's impact on humanity in the latter way are the accounts about Cain's murder of Abel (Gen 4:1–11) and the tower of Babel (see Gen 11:1–9). In both cases, sin caused the shattering of relationships.[5] Racial divi-sion, then, results from the sin introduced into God's good cre-ation because of the disobedience of Adam and Eve in Genesis 3.

Therefore, racial reconciliation has the following definition in this book: Humanity's relationship with God and with fellow humans is broken because of the sin introduced into God's good creation through the disobedience of Adam and Eve. As a result of sin, every relationship needs to be restored to the original state in which God intended before sin entered the creation. All races—not just blacks and whites—scattered throughout the entire world need to be reconciled first to God and second to one another be-cause of the universal impact of sin. This restoration is called rec-onciliation. As it relates to the restoration of broken relationships between different races, it refers to racial reconciliation.[6]

---

[4]Implicit in this book's thesis is the belief that sociological, psychological, or cultural methods of extinguishing racism fall short of curing the real problem of racism, that is, sin.

[5]See chap. 2 for a detailed discussion of Genesis 3 and 11.

[6] One reason racial reconciliation is an appropriate phrase (against Burns) is because racial reconciliation does not presume a previous relationship between different races when

Method

An exegetical method is central to the development of my thesis in this book. I incorporate biblical texts from both the Old and New Testaments to argue my viewpoint, but I primarily examine selected texts from the Pauline corpus. The exegetical method I use here should not intimidate readers who are not members of an academic guild of biblical studies or who are not seminary trained. This work aims not to overwhelm the reader with unnecessary technical arguments or with hundreds of gratuitous footnotes in each chapter, which cite all of the relevant secondary literature written in the last century about racism, Jesus' death, or atonement. Instead, I endeavor to present a lucid, scholarly investigation of Paul's understanding of racial reconciliation in light of his conception of Jesus' death, while I also critically engage some of the most important scholars and exegetical issues related to my position.

I discuss several issues throughout the book that are technical at the exegetical and theological levels. Many footnotes document the scholarly discussion on important exegetical and theological issues that relate to my argument. Nevertheless, I seek to discuss these issues with as much simplicity as possible so that scholars, students, and pastors will profit from this book. For example, translation accompanies Greek and Hebrew words and phrases. Certain technical discussions are reserved to footnotes as often as possible. In addition, footnotes point the reader to sources that offer more detailed explanations of particular exegetical, grammatical, and theological points than time or space allow here.

Why Is This Book Necessary?

This book is necessary and should benefit its readers because it endeavors to discuss the issue of racial reconciliation from a biblical and exegetical perspective. New Testament scholarship greatly needs this approach since no biblical scholar has recently written a work on racial reconciliation for the church using biblical ex-

---

a previous relationship did not exist between different races. Rather, the phrase, as it is used here, presumes that a perfect relationship existed between God, Adam, and Eve before the fall, but that this relationship was shattered because of sin and that the shattering of humanity's relationship with God was the impetus behind the shattering of man's relationship with man—hence, the need for racial reconciliation.

egesis as the means of discussing the issue.[7] This book attempts to show the reader that faith unites all Christians in Christ regardless of their race. Consequently, Christians should be willing to reach and extend love to the different ethnic groups that serve in their churches and that live in their respective communities. In addition, this book is necessary since many New Testament scholars have altogether neglected the issue of racism in their writings. Furthermore, it is painfully obvious that African-American New Testament scholars have not discussed the issue of racism and race relations through careful biblical exegesis.[8] Thus, since I am an aspiring New Testament scholar who has a strong multiethnic background, I sensed the need to write this book.

My ethnic background is primarily African-American, but my family has a multiethnic heritage: African-American, Caucasian, German, and Native American. In addition, my wife is Hispanic since her mother is from Nicaragua and her father is from Costa Rica. Our son is a combination of my wife's and my own ethnic heritages. In addition, my mom and my aunts have white skin; my uncles and cousins have dark, brown, or white skin; my wife and son have light skin; and some of my other relatives have blue eyes. Because of these family connections, racial diversity is very important to me. Nevertheless, racial diversity is not enough,

Many Christians and Christian organizations have affirmed—either consciously or subconsciously—a secular model of race relations. Many Christians equate racial diversity with racial reconciliation, so they conclude if racial diversity is present, then racial reconciliation must be present as well.[9] As an African-American with a strong multiethnic background, married to a Hispanic woman, the father of a multiethnic son, and as one who is passionate about multiethnic, urban ministry, I agree that ethnic diversity is a good thing. It more accurately reflects the world today than

---

[7] For example, simply peruse the most recent works on cultural anthropology, ethnic studies, or African-American studies.

[8] For a similar point, see T. M. Anyabwile, *The Decline of African American Theology: From Biblical Faith to Cultural Captivity* (Downers Grove, IL: InterVarsity Press, 2007), 15. That New Testament scholarship has neglected to discuss issues pertaining to race relations and racial reconciliation is evident by observing the various New Testament monographs that are yearly published. Very few New Testament monographs focus on the issue of race and ethnicity unless they discuss Jewish ethnocentrism.

[9] For support of this perspective, see the commitment that many Christian institutions of higher education have made to advance racial diversity and to use affirmative action.

ethnic unanimity. Nevertheless, I also strongly disagree that ethnic diversity is the same as racial reconciliation. The former does not guarantee the latter, and the presence of racial diversity in a particular sociological, ecclesiological, or educational context does not mean that racial reconciliation exists.

This book calls for something much more radical than ethnic diversity. It calls for something much more radical than a strict implementation of affirmative action. Because of Jesus' vicarious death for all ethnic groups, it calls Christians to love, serve, minister to, and embrace their brothers and sisters in Christ regardless of their ethnicity. This book contends that racial diversity is not the same as racial reconciliation. Racial diversity is a phrase that speaks to the visual manifestation of different races in a particular society or context. That is, the phrase acknowledges the presence of different races in a particular society or context, and it often acknowledges the importance of ethnic diversity or multiethnicity for the advancement of a particular society. Still, racial diversity does not "reach the core of what the scriptures call us to pursue" in the area of race relations as Christians and as the Christian church.[10]

As stated above, racial diversity can be a good thing, but racial diversity does not guarantee or duplicate what racial reconciliation does. For example, the Grand Dragon of the Ku Klux Klan could theoretically work in an environment in which his boss is an African-American and in which his coworkers are from ethnic backgrounds other than Caucasian. But he could still vehemently hate his boss and coworkers because of their race, and he could still participate in hate crimes outside his work environment, notwithstanding that his coworkers are from different ethnic backgrounds. Likewise, a parishioner could attend a church in which different races worship, but that parishioner could hate a fellow church member and thus might not show the love of Christ to him or her because of his or her particular race. Therefore, racial diversity is present in both preceding examples, but racial reconciliation is not.

Racial reconciliation, on the other hand, can be present in a particular society or context even if and when racial diversity is not. In some situations ethnic diversity is not possible because a particular community might be populated with those either

---

[10] Burns, "A Practical Theology for Racial Harmony," 34–35, esp. 34.

primarily or exclusively from the same race. For example, I grew up in a very small town in eastern Kentucky, where as a child, I was one of few African-Americans in my town. As a teenager, I became a Christian and joined the First Baptist Church in a small town approximately 15 minutes away from my home. I was the first African-American to join this congregation in its history.

Approximately one year later, my uncle became the second African-American to join this church. The congregation and its leadership loved, embraced, nurtured, and ministered to us the same as they ministered to those who were either white or of Anglo descent. Ethnic diversity was not and is not a reality in this church since very few ethnic minorities reside in the immediate or surrounding community where the church is located. In fact, 12 years later, my uncle is currently both the *only* African-American and the *only* ethnic minority member of this congregation. Nevertheless, racial reconciliation is present in this church since its community of faith works extremely hard to welcome and love all people regardless of race.

Unfortunately, many churches regardless of the race of their members do not share the same passion for racial reconciliation. Instead of the biblical text, many Christians allow cultural prejudices to shape their understanding of race.[11] This book endeavors to help Christians understand what the gospel says about race and race relations by focusing on selected texts from the Pauline corpus. Since many churches have either intentionally or unintentionally limited their ministry to those within their respective race or *homogeneous unit* (i.e., people within the same ethnic, social, cultural, linguistic, or class context),[12] this book could liberate individual Christians and also churches from their bondage to racist ideologies, from a secular model of race relations, and from their disdain toward different races, which arise from both the impact of their respective cultures and the universal impact of sin.

Furthermore, since I have seen God magnify his glory through the reconciling power of the gospel, I think this book is necessary. As a university professor, seminary professor, and preacher, I have had the privilege of teaching and ministering to people from many

---

[11] For a recent critique of this kind of cultural influence in the African-American community, see the book by Anyabwile, *The Decline of African American Theology*.

[12] This controversial church growth principle was developed and favored in D. A. McGavran, *Understanding Church Growth*, rev. ed. (Grand Rapids: Eerdmans, 1980).

different ethnic backgrounds, and of seeing others do the same. Although I am in my early thirties and have been a Christian for only approximately 14 years, I have seen Christians from different ethnic groups live out the reconciling power of the cross by their deep love for and devotion toward one another regardless of race. This book could create a longing within the readers to see the glory of God in Christ's death through the practice of racial reconciliation. The book could help them understand that an important accomplishment and application of the reconciliation that Jesus has achieved by his death for humanity's sin is racial reconciliation.

A Chapter-by-Chapter Summary

Chapters 2, 3, and 4 are crucial to the proposed thesis. Chapter 2, titled "The Reason for Racial Reconciliation," argues that sin is the fundamental reason races need to be reconciled first to God and second to one another. Chapters 3 and 4 discuss the connection between Jesus' death and racial reconciliation. Chapter 3, titled "The Provision for Racial Reconciliation," argues that Jesus' death for humanity's sin was God's provision for reconciliation. Chapter 4, titled "The Accomplishment of Racial Reconciliation," argues that Jesus' death for humanity's sin reconciles Jews and Gentiles to God and to one another. Chapter 5, titled "Conclusion: The Practice of Racial Reconciliation," argues that since God reconciles Jews and Gentiles to himself by their faith on the basis of Jesus' death for humanity's sin, he has also reconciled Jews and Gentiles to one another. As a result, Jews and Gentiles who place faith in Christ should live in unity with one another as the Christian church in the world and should fight to overcome any racist ideologies inherited from their sin and their culture. Chapter 5 also argues that the common bond of faith in Christ and the salvation that Jesus' death for humanity's sin has accomplished for all races are far superior and more important than any differences that Christians from different ethnic groups have with one another because of their races. Finally, I conclude this discussion in chapter 5 with practical applications that relate to Christian fellowship, racial slurs, worship, missions, evangelism, and interracial relationships.

2

the reason for
racial reconciliation

A number of biblical texts claim that sin is the fundamental reason that races need to be reconciled first to God and second to one another. The goal here is not to present an exhaustive biblical investigation, but to provide evidence from key texts to demonstrate that sin shattered humankind's relationship with God and one another.

The Consequences of Sin

Genesis

Sin is the fundamental reason that human beings (regardless of their race) need to be reconciled first to God and second to one another, for sin has shattered the relationship of human beings with God and one another. This assertion is evident from the Bible's presentation of the broken relationship of human beings with God and one another. The entrance of sin into God's good creation resulted from Adam and Eve's disobedience. The sin introduced by them was the fundamental cause of the division between God and human beings.

Genesis 1–2 states that God created the heavens and earth and everything in them. After completing his creation, God announced that everything that he made was "exceedingly good"

(Gen 1:31).[1] God's good creation culminates with male and female human beings (Gen 1:26–31), for they were the "crown of God's handiwork."[2] Genesis 1 makes that point evident since (1) its creation account emphasizes human life as the pinnacle of God's creation;[3] (2) divine deliberation occurs prior to God's creation of humankind;[4] (3) the expression "let us make," which refers to human life in Gen 1:26, replaces the impersonal words "let there be," which refer to the rest of God's creation in Genesis 1;[5] (4) God creates male and female in his "image" and "likeness" (Gen 1:26);[6] (5) the author[7] emphasizes God's creation of humans by using the verb ברא ("to create") on three occasions,[8] and (6) the author gives more written space to the creation of human life than to other aspects of creation (see Genesis 1–2).[9]

After the author discusses the completion of God's good creation, he records the introduction of sin into God's good creation. Sin was introduced into God's creation via Adam and Eve's rebellion in the garden of Eden (Gen 3:6–7).[10] The "fall" was human-

---

[1] Unless otherwise indicated, all translations throughout the book are mine.

[2] K. A. Mathews, *Genesis 1–11:26* (NAC; Nashville: Broadman & Holman, 2002), 160.

[3] Ibid.

[4] Ibid.

[5] Ibid.

[6] Ibid. Genesis 1:26, translated from the Masoretic Text (MT), reads as follows: "And God said: 'Let us make man in our image according to our likeness. And let them rule over the fish of the sea and over the birds of the heavens and over all the earth and over every animal which crawls upon the earth.'" As can be seen from the preceding translation, the phrases "let us make" (נעשה), "in our image" (בְּצַלְמֵנוּ), and "according to our likeness" (כִּדְמוּתֵנוּ) are plural forms, and each plural form refers to God (see Gen 3:22; 11:7; and Isa 6:8). The Septuagint's rendering of these words supports the plurality of these terms conveyed in the MT: καὶ εἶπεν ὁ θεός ποιήσωμεν ἄνθρωπον κατ' εἰκόνα ἡμετέραν καὶ καθ' ὁμοίωσιν ... Since in Gen 1:26 the MT and the Septuagint (LXX) suggest that there is one God with the terms אֱלֹהִים and ο θεός and since in Gen 1:27 the MT and the LXX affirm God's singularity (בְּצַלְמוֹ, "in his image"; κατ' εἰκόνα θεοῦ , "according to the image of God"), the plural terms "let us make," "in our image," and "according to our likeness" in Gen 1:26, the context of Genesis 1–2, and a canonical reading of Gen 1:26 support that the plurals in Gen 1:26 refer to a "divine plurality" and thus provide evidence that God is a Trinity. For a similar view, which provides interaction with the major views and a bibliography, see Mathews (*Genesis 1–11:26*, 160–63).

[7] There is a longstanding debate regarding the authorship of the Pentateuch. The term "author" instead of "authors" is used throughout this chapter to refer to the composer of the Pentateuch, that is, to the singular authorship of the majority of the Pentateuch. For a recent, conservative critique of the documentary hypothesis, for a survey of antecedent discussions regarding Pentateuchal Criticism, and for a bibliography, see T. D. Alexander, *From Paradise to the Promised Land: An Introduction to the Pentateuch* (2nd ed.; Grand Rapids: Baker, 2002).

[8] So Mathews, *Genesis 1–11:26*, 160.

[9] Ibid.

[10] Old Testament scholars debate both the meaning and authenticity of Genesis 3. For example, see L. F. Hartman, "Sin in Paradise," *CBQ* 20 (1958): 26–40; J. M. Higgins, "Myth

kind's most tragic mistake, since all forms of evil flow from it and since a universal curse resulted from Adam's and Eve's disobedience (see Genesis 3; Rom 5:12–21; 1 Cor 15:22). The "fall" severed humankind's relationship with both God and one another (see Genesis 3; Rom 3:9–19; 3:23).

Early in the Genesis narrative, the author mentions that God created a garden in Eden (Gen 2:8) and placed trees in it from which Adam and Eve could eat (Gen 2:9). The author highlights in Gen 2:9 two specific trees that God placed in the midst of the garden of Eden, trees more important than the rest: (1) the tree of life and (2) the tree of the knowledge of good and evil.[11] The narrative of Genesis 2 emphasizes the tree of knowledge. Interpretation of the tree of the knowledge of good and evil receives continued debate because textual clues and textual commentary about it are

---

of Eve: The Temptress," *JAAR* 44 (1976): 639–47; J. T. Walsh, "Genesis 2:4b–3:24: A Synchronic Approach," *JBL* 96 (1977): 161–77; J. G. Williams, "Genesis 3," *Int* 35 (1981): 274–70; D. M. Joy, "Toward a Symbolic Revival: Creation Revisited," *RelEd* 80 (1985): 399–412; T. Stordalen, "Man, Soil, Garden: Basic Plot in Genesis 2–3 Considered," *JSOT* 53 (1992): 3–25; L. M. Bechtel, "Genesis 2:4b–3:24: A Myth about Human Maturation," *JSOT* 67 (1995): 3–26; W. Vogels, "Like One of Us, Knowing Good and Evil (Gen 3:22)," *Semeia* 81 (1998): 144–57; W. P. Townsend, "Eve's Answer to the Serpent: An Alternative Paradigm for Sin and Some Implications in Theology," *CTJ* 33 (1998): 399–420; J. E. McKinlay, "To Eat or Not to Eat: Where Is Wisdom in This Choice?" *Semeia* 86 (1999): 73–84; B. Gosse, "L' écriture de Genesis 3, Le Serpent Dualité de la femme et L' home," *BN* 98 (1999): 19–20; G. A. Yee, "Gender, Class, and the Social-Scientific Study of Genesis 2–3," *Semeia* 87 (1999): 177–92; K. I. Parker, "Mirror, Mirror on the Wall, Must We Leave Eden, Once and for All?: A Lacanian Pleasure Trip through the Garden," *JSOT* 83 (1999): 73–84; C. M. Kenneth, "Misspeaking in Eden or Fielding Questions in the Garden (Genesis 2:16–3:13)," *PRSt* 27 (2000): 235–47; J. C. Collins, "What Happened to Adam and Eve? A Literary-Theological Approach to Genesis 3," *Presb* 27 (2001): 12–44; M. Emmrich, "The Temptation Narrative of Genesis 3:1–6: A Prelude to the Pentateuch and the History of Israel," *EvQ* 73 (2001): 3–20; W. Dumbrell, "Genesis 2:1–3: A Biblical Theology of Creation Covenant," *Evangelical Review of Theology* 25 (2001): 219–30; E. A. Phillips, "Serpent Intertexts: Tantalizing Twists in the Tales," *BBR* 10 (2002): 233–45; H.-P. Müller, "Eva und Das Paradies," in *Ex Mesopotamia et Syria Lux* (Münster: Ugarit-Verlag, 2002), 501–10; J. A. Soggin, "And You Will Be Like God and Know What Is Good and What Is Bad: Genesis 2–3," in *Sefer Moshe* (Winona Lake, IN: Eisenbrauns, 2004), 191–93; A. Wénin and J. Bowden, "The Serpent and the Woman, or the Process of Evil according to Genesis 2–3," in *Original Sin* (London: SCM Press, 2004), 41–48; C. Boureux and C. Theobald, *Original Sin: A Code of Fallibility* (London: SCM Press, 2004); P. B. Yoder, "Will the Real Adam Please Stand Up!" *Perspectives on Science and Christian Faith* 58 (2006): 99–101; J. McIntyre, "The Real Adam and *Original Sin*," *Perspectives on Science and Christian Faith* 58 (2006): 90–98; J. I. Gellman, "Gender and Sexuality in the Garden of Eden," *Theology and Sexuality* 12 (2006): 319–335.

[11] The phrases ועץ הדעת טוב ורע and ועץ החיים בתוך הגן ("and the tree of the living ones in the midst of the garden" and "and the tree of the knowledge of good and of evil") introduced by waw-consecutives suggest that the tree of life and the tree of the knowledge of God and of evil are different trees.

lacking.[12] Nevertheless, Gen 2:16–17 indicates that God prohibited Adam and Eve from partaking of this tree (Gen 2:16–17). Their eating from it enabled them to attain godlike knowledge (Gen 3:5,22).

When God led Adam to the garden to toil and to attend to the ground, he specifically told him that he was permitted to eat from any tree in the garden except the tree of knowledge in the midst of the garden (Gen 2:16–17). God also told Adam that on the day that he ate from the forbidden tree, "he will certainly die" (Gen 2:16–17). A serpent, however, appears in the garden in order to deceive Eve (Gen 3:1). Both a Jewish reading (Wis 2:24; Sir 21:2; 4 Macc 18:8) and a canonical reading (Rom 16:20; Rev 12:9,14–15; 20:2) of the text suggest that the serpent was Satan's instrument and possibly Satan himself in the form of a serpent.[13] The serpent's deceptive purposes are evident in the author's comments that the serpent was "craftier" than any living thing that God had made (Gen 3:1) and in the author's presentation of the serpent as the reason Eve doubted God's initial word about the tree (Gen 3:4–5).[14] Unfortunately, both Adam and Eve disobeyed God's stipulation regarding the forbidden tree (Gen 3:6–7). Their disobedience introduced sin into God's good creation (see Genesis 3), and sin produced many devastating consequences for his creation (e.g., Genesis 4–6).

Broken Relationships: Sin Has Broken Humankind's Relationship with God

The sin of Adam and Eve severed humankind's relationship with God.[15] As a result, humankind's spiritual condition dramatically changed after the fall. Prior to the fall, Adam and Eve enjoyed the presence of God (see Gen 3:8), they enjoyed the garden of Eden (Gen 2:15), and they embraced their nakedness (Gen 2:25).

---

[12] For example, see Mathews, *Genesis*, 203–07; N. Ansell, "The Call of Wisdom/The Voice of the Serpent: A Canonical Approach to the Tree of Knowledge," *CSR* 31 (2001): 31–57.

[13] The OT nowhere states that the serpent is Satan, but the NT appears to equate them (2 Cor 11:3; Rev 12:9). See Mathews, *Genesis*, 233–34, esp. 233.

[14] Although Job 1:9–11 and 2:4–5 do not refer to Satan as a serpent, Satan questions God's word regarding Job similarly as the serpent questions God's word when speaking with Eve in Genesis 2.

[15] Eve sinned and violated God's command first, but Gen 3:9–11 emphasizes the fault of Adam. The dialogue between God and Adam and God's confrontation with Adam before Eve suggest that Adam must bear greater culpability than Eve since God created Adam first (see Rom 5:12–21; 1 Tim 2:13–14).

After their disobedience, their relationship with God significantly differed.[16]

After their disobedience, when Adam and Eve heard the voice of God, who was walking in the garden in the cool of the day,[17] they hid themselves "from the face of the Lord God in the midst of the garden" (Gen 3:8). They did not flee to God, who was their source of life and existence. Rather, they fled from him. This garden, which God provided them as a source of sustenance and enjoyment and over which he placed them to cultivate (Gen 2:8–9,15–16), became a place of refuge for them. It became a fortress where they sought to hide from their Creator (Gen 3:8).[18]

Genesis 3:9 supports the view that sin shattered their relationship with God: "And the Lord God said to the man: 'where?'" Since Gen 3:8 states that Adam and Eve hid themselves in the midst of the garden, the interrogative איכה ("where") could convey the idea of "where are you?" Furthermore, since Genesis 1–2 emphasizes God's comprehensive sovereignty over all things as the Creator and Sustainer of his creation, God's question ("Where are you?") implies neither that his knowledge is deficient nor that he is unaware of the physical location of Adam and Eve.[19] Instead, this question is rhetorical and serves to provoke Adam to consider his transgression.[20] In addition, God's question likely implies a deficiency in Adam's and Eve's spiritual condition since sin entered God's good creation through their rebellion against him.

Genesis 3:10 conveys the spiritual deficiency of Adam and Eve. Adam said, "I heard your sound in the garden, I saw that I am naked, and I hid myself." Adam and Eve hid themselves because of their nakedness (Gen 3:10).[21] Yet, it is equally true that they hid themselves out of fear of God because their sin had broken their relationship with God. That is, their original status before God and their fellowship with him were shattered as soon as they

---

[16] See Mathews, *Genesis*, 239–40.

[17] The language of God "walking" in the garden emphasizes his presence with his people and particularly the fellowship that they enjoyed with him. See Mathews, *Genesis*, 239.

[18] Ibid.

[19] The view popularly known as Open-theism posits a different thesis regarding God's knowledge. For a summary and critique of Open-theism, see B. A. Ware, *God's Lesser Glory* (Wheaton: Crossway, 2000); idem, *God's Greater Glory* (Wheaton: Crossway, 2004).

[20] Mathews, *Genesis*, 239–40.

[21] Public nakedness was disgraceful both in the ancient Near East and in the Bible (see Gen 9:22–25). Genesis 2:25 suggests the shame of nakedness comes from the presence of sin.

disobeyed. In fact, Adam and Eve did not hide themselves from God until after they had rebelled against him (Gen 3:7–8), for their disobedience against God resulted in a broken relationship (see Gen 2:25; 3:7–10).

God's dialogue with Adam and Eve in the subsequent verses after the fall in Genesis 3 affirms that sin shattered the relationship that they once enjoyed with him. God asked Adam, "Who made known to you that you are naked? Have you eaten from the tree from which I commanded you not to eat?" (Gen 3:11).[22] Instead of replying with a repentant "yes," Adam blamed both God and Eve for his sin, saying, "The woman, whom you gave to me, she gave to me from the tree, and I ate" (Gen 3:12).[23]

God subsequently interrogates Eve: "What is this that you have done?" (Gen 3:13a). Like Adam, Eve does not respond with repentance. Instead, she demonstrates that she is spiritually dead. She no longer possesses the spiritual innocence that she once had before sin entered the creation, for she blames the serpent for her transgression, saying, "The serpent deceived me, and I ate" (Gen 3:13b). Initially, Eve's response might seem appropriate since the serpent deceived her (Gen 3:1–5). Her response to God, however, is *only* partially correct since she was also complicit for her disobedience (see Gen 2:17; 3:1–6).[24]

---

[22] The syntax of the MT suggests that the second part of God's question to Adam is emphatic: המן־העץ אשר צויתיך לבלתי אכל־ממנו אכלת (". . . From the tree, which I commanded you not to eat from it, have you eaten?"). The author records this question with a *casus pendens construction*. He places the prepositional phrase המן־העץ of the main verb first in the main clause; he suspends the main verb אכלת from the prepositional phrase until the end of the sentence; he places a relative clause (המן־העץ אשר צויתיך לבלתי אכל־ממנו) within the main verb and the prepositional phrase of the main verb, and he attaches a pronoun, whose antecedent is the tree, to the prepositional phrase that modifies the infinitive in the relative clause (אכל־ממנו). Such a construction emphasizes the tree, for the tree occurs first in the main clause, the action of the main verb is directed toward the tree, and the relative clause describes the tree. For other examples of the *casus pendens construction*, see P. J. T. Muraoka, *A Grammar of Biblical Hebrew: Syntax* (2nd ed.; trans. and rev. T. Muraoka; Roma: Editrice Pontificio Istituto Biblico, 2003), 586–87; esp. 587.

[23] The author uses another *casus pendens construction* for emphasis in Gen 3:12:
ויאמר האדם האשה אשר נתתה עמדי הוא נתנה־לי מן־העץ ואכל: ("and Adam said: 'the woman, whom you gave with me, she gave to me from the tree, and I ate.'"). The latter verse emphasizes the woman's role in Adam's sin. Additionally, that Adam's comments suggest that God is partially to blame for his transgression can be seen at the lexical level by the word נתן ("to give") that appears twice in Gen 2:12. Adam states that God gave (נתתה) the woman to him and that she gave to נתנה־לי מן־העץ fruit from the forbidden tree. The implication is that if God had not given the woman to him, then he (i.e., Adam) would not have eaten from the forbidden tree.

[24] Mathews (*Genesis*, 242) notes that unlike Adam, Eve "can rightly claim to be the victim of the serpent."

Genesis 3:1–6 begins by emphasizing the serpent's craftiness (see Gen 3:1), but the text nowhere suggests that the serpent is solely to blame for Eve's disobedience or that the serpent forced Adam and Eve to disobey God (see 1 Tim 2:13). Rather, the text simply states that the serpent deceived Eve by contesting God's word (Gen 3:1–5). The serpent's contestation caused Eve to question the validity of God's word (Gen 3:1–5), for she believed the serpent's words rather than God's when he asserted that God's motivation for his prohibiting Adam and Eve from eating fruit from the forbidden tree was to withhold godlike knowledge from them (Gen 3:6; see Gen 3:4–5). Consequently, *only* after believing the serpent's lie did Eve "see that the tree was good for eating and that it was desirable to both eyes and that the tree was desirable to give insight, and she took from its fruit and ate. And she even gave to her husband with her, and he ate" (Gen 3:6).

Disobedience Produced Spiritual Death

Adam and Eve. The disobedience of Adam and Eve severed humankind's relationship with God. In other words, as soon as Adam and Even disobeyed God, they introduced death into God's good creation.[25] After they sinned, God first cursed his good creation (see Gen 3:14–21). This curse and the events that followed it demonstrate that the human condition radically changed after the disobedience and fall of Adam and Eve. Prior to sin's entrance into the creation, Adam and Eve enjoyed both the presence of God and his creation (see Genesis 1–2). After they sinned, they fled from God's presence (see Genesis 3). Because of their transgression, God cursed (1) the animals (Gen 3:14), especially the serpent (Gen 3:15), (2) the woman (Gen 3:16), (3) the man (Gen 3:17), and (4) the ground (Gen 3:17–19). This universal curse introduced death into God's good creation (Gen 3:19) and fulfilled God's promise to Adam in Gen 2:17 that if he ate from the forbidden tree, he would certainly die.

The death that sin introduced includes both physical and spiritual death. God's remarks to Adam and Eve after they sinned refer to physical death: "You are dust, and to dust you will return" (Gen 3:19c). That death in Gen 2:17 also refers to spiritual death

---

[25] Similarly, J. Calvin, *Institutes of the Christian Religion* (trans. H. Beveridge; Grand Rapids: Eerdmans, 1997), 2.1.5.

is evident in the narrative of Genesis 3.[26] Genesis 3:8 states that Adam and Eve fled from God after they sinned. Because of their sin, Gen 3:16 states that "enmity" would exist between "his seed" and "her seed" and that the seed of the serpent would crush the heel of the "seed of the woman" while the "seed of the woman" would crush the head of the "seed of the serpent." A canonical reading of Gen 3:15–16 suggests that Jesus is the promised seed who would fulfill the promise in Gen 3:16. The seed of the woman will crush the seed of the serpent since Jesus crushes Satan under his feet (see Rom 16:20; 1 Cor 15:24–27; Rev 12:17) and since the New Testament states that Jesus is the promised "seed of Abraham" (Gal 3:1–29).[27]

Genesis 6:5 further indicates that spiritual death resulted from the sin of Adam and Eve. The wickedness of man only multiplied after the fall in Genesis 3: "And the Lord saw that the evil of man multiplied on the earth and [that] every form of thoughts in his heart was only evil all the day" (see Judg 21:25). Thus, since (1) God's pronouncement of the curse in Gen 3:15–16 results from the entrance of sin into God's good creation through Adam's and Eve's disobedience, (2) God promised in Gen 3:15 that enmity would exist between the woman's seed and the serpent's seed, (3) a canonical reading of Gen 3:15 suggests that the serpent's seed refers to Satan and his offspring and the woman's seed refers to Jesus and his offspring (see John 7; Galatians 3–4), and (4) Gen 6:5 states that sin multiplied after the fall, one can infer that the woman's seed serves as a solution to humankind's spiritual plight, a solution which would have been unnecessary if Adam and Even had not died spiritually.

Cain and Abel. Spiritual death manifests itself through humankind's sinful actions in other parts of Genesis. After Genesis 3, spiritual death first manifests itself through Cain. Eve conceived Cain and Abel after she and Adam transgressed God's command and thus introduced sin into God's good creation (Gen 4:1, see 3:1–24). When Cain and Abel presented offerings to God, he rejected Cain's offering and accepted Abel's (Gen 4:3–5). A canonical reading of the text suggests that God rejected Cain's offering

---

[26] Spiritual death is further supported by a canonical reading of Genesis 3 (see Rom 5:12–21).

[27] See Mathews, *Genesis.*

because he had not presented it to God by faith (see Heb 11:4).[28] Since anything that is not done in faith is sin (Rom 14:23), one can infer from Gen 4:3–5 that God rejected Cain's offering because it was a sinful offering.[29] According to Gen 4:7, sin ruled over Cain, for God informed Cain of the presence of sin in his life and exhorted him to master the power of sin (see Romans 6).[30] Other aspects of the text display the impact of sin on Cain. Cain became angry with God after he rejected his offering (Gen 4:6).[31] He killed his brother (Gen 4:8), and then he lied to God when he questioned him about Abel (Gen 4:9).

The Universal Sinfulness of Humankind. In Genesis 6:1, the human population had vastly increased (see also 5:1–5:32).[32] With humankind's numerical prosperity, sin likewise increased. The zenith of humankind's sin in Genesis 6 is marked by the marital and sexual relationships between the sons of God and the daughters of men (Gen 6:2,4).[33] Commentators do not agree on the identity of the sons of God since the text does not explicitly state their identity.[34] Regardless of their identity, the marriage and sexual relationships between the sons of God and the daughters of men offended God and provoked him to "blot out" humankind. Genesis 6:5–6

---

[28] Similarly, Mathews, *Genesis*, 268.

[29] Ibid.

[30] MT Gen 4:7 is very difficult to translate, which is evidenced by the translation in LXX Gen 4:7. My brief comments above in no way intend to suggest that the grammar of Gen 4:7 is easily understood.

[31] M. I. Gruber ("Was Cain Angry or Depressed?" *BAR* 6 [1980]: 35–36) suggests that the clause חרה אף ("anger of a nose") conveys anger, but the clause חרה לי ("it burns to him"), which is similar to the clause in Gen 4:6, conveys despondency. Thus, one could argue that Cain was despondent, not angry. I reject the supposition that Cain was only despondent since the author uses the verb חרה ("to be angry") in Gen 4:5.

[32] The focus in Gen 5:1–6:8 is Adam's family line. Nevertheless, this unit demonstrates that sin vastly multiplied throughout Adam's line although Seth (Gen 5:6–20) and Enoch (Gen 5:21–24) walked with God.

[33] For discussion of the sons of God, see Mathews, *Genesis*, 322–35.

[34] For example, see F. Delitzsch, *A New Commentary on Genesis* (Edinburgh: T&T Clark, 1888), 226; B. S. Childs, *Myth and Reality in the Old Testament* (London: SCM Press, 1960), 49; L. Eslinger, "A Contextual Identification of the bene ha Elohim and Benoth ha Adam in Genesis 6:1–4," *JSOT* 13 (1979): 65–73; W. A. van Gemeren, "The Sons of God in Genesis 6:1–4 (An Example of Evangelical Demythologization?)," *WTJ* 43 (1981): 320–48; A. Ross, *Creation and Blessing: A Guide to the Study and Exposition of the Book of Genesis* (Grand Rapids: Baker, 1988), 182. Texts from several pseudepigraphal books (1 Enoch 6–11; Jub 4.15–22; T. Reub. 5.6–7; 2 Enoch 18:3–8; 2 Apoc. Bar. 56.11–14), the DSS (e.g., 1QapGen 2:1,16; CD 2:17–19), Philo (*On the Giants* 2.6), and Josephus (*Ant.* 1.73) suggest that the sons of God in Genesis 6 are rebellious angels. Mathews (*Genesis*, 329–30) is on target when he argues that the "sons of God" refer to the Sethites (i.e., the righteous lineage of Seth) and that the "daughters of men" refer to the Cainites (i.e., the lineage of Cain).

states that "the Lord saw that the evil of men increased in the land, and every form of thoughts in his heart was only evil all the day. And the Lord regretted that he made man in the earth, and he grieved in his heart." Two events in Gen 6:5–6 especially demonstrate sin's universal impact upon humankind: (1) human wickedness increased after sin had entered into the creation, and (2) God regretted that he had created human beings.

Rebellion at the Tower of Babel. Humankind's rebellion at the Tower of Babel demonstrates the impact of sin upon humankind and their spiritual decline. God's destruction of most of humankind in Genesis 6 did not remedy their problem of sinning (see Genesis 7–10). To the contrary, sin continued to exist after the flood and to manifest itself through sinful actions. Genesis 11, for example, records that human beings spoke one and the same dialect after the flood (Gen 11:1). Hence, humankind was fully united at the dialectical level.[35] At the linguistic level, nothing seemingly should have hindered humankind's relationship with God and one another. Dialectical unanimity was not enough to sustain humankind's relationship with either God or one another. Humankind's spiritual deadness is evident here since human beings did not use a universal language to worship and serve God, but instead used it to build a city, to erect a tower, and to make a name for themselves rather than for God (Gen 11:4).[36]

Sodom and Gomorrah. The sin of Sodom and Gomorrah and God's destruction of these cities demonstrate the universal impact of sin upon humankind. Sodom and Gomorrah were exceedingly wicked cities (Gen 18:20). While Lot was sitting at the gate of Sodom, two "messengers" or "angels" entered the city (Gen 19:1). Lot saw them entering the city from a distance, so he arose to meet them (Gen 19:1). Since Lot's reaction to these visitors suggests that they were angelic beings, "angels" is the appropriate translation here for the term מלאכים. These angels were likely two of the three angels who appeared to Abraham and Sarah in Genesis 18 since the author uses language to describe Abraham's reaction to the men (Gen 18:1–8), which is similar to what he used to describe Lot's reaction toward them, since these men journeyed toward

---

[35] So Mathews, *Genesis*, 477.
[36] Similarly, Mathews, *Genesis*, 481–82.

Sodom and Gomorrah after they departed from Abraham (Gen 18:16,21–22), and since the narrative in Genesis 19 begins with comments about "two angels" (Gen 19:1).

Lot persuaded the angels to lodge with him (Gen 19:2–3). As they were preparing to retire in Lot's house, the citizens of Sodom attempted to have sexual relations with the angels (Gen 19:4–6). The citizens of Sodom surrounded Lot's house and demanded that Lot surrender the visitors so that they could have sex with them: "Before they lay down, also the men of Sodom, from young to old (all of the people) surrounded against the house from all sides, and they called out to Lot and said to him: where are the men who entered to you tonight? Cause them to come out to us so that we will know them" (Gen 19:5–6).[37] The verb נדעה ("to know") refers to sexual intercourse in Gen 19:5 since Lot offered the Sodomites his virgin daughters instead of the angels (Gen 19:8).[38] Sin's impact is evident at two junctures in the narrative: (1) the men of Sodom endeavored to engage in sexual sin with angels; (2) Lot vicariously offered his virgin daughters to the Sodomites to gratify their sexual desires.

Exodus and Deuteronomy

Pharaoh's Hardened Heart. Sin's universal impact on humankind's relationship with God is evident in Exodus and Deuteronomy. Pharaoh's disobedience against Yahweh in Exodus is a clear example of sin's impact. Moses pleaded with Pharaoh on multiple occasions to release Israel from slavery (Exod 5:1–11:10). On each occasion, however, Pharaoh refused to heed Yahweh's command delivered through Moses and Aaron. Since Yahweh hardened Pharaoh's heart so that he would disobey (Exod 7:13–14,22; 8:19; 9:7,12,35; 10:1,20,27; 11:10; 14:8), Yahweh's divine work in

---

[37] The syntax of MT Gen 19:4 is emphatic: אנשי סדם נסבו על־הבית מנער ועד־זקן כל־העם מקצה טרם ישכבו ואנשי העיר The author positions the subject אנשי ("men") first in the clause. He places an appositional construction אנשי סדם ("men of Sodom") after the subject, and he delays the main verb נסבו ("they surrounded") after the subject and after the appositional phrase. In addition, the author adds three more phrases that further describe the subject ואנשי. The first two phrases form the prepositional phrase מנער ועד־זקן ("from young and to old"). The last prepositional phrase that references the subject is כל־העם ("all people"), which is in apposition to the subject ואנשי. Finally, the prepositional phrase מקצה ("from all sides") adds further emphasis to the sentence since the author delays the preposition until the end of the sentence and since he separates the preposition from the verb that it modifies by several phrases. Thus, in this clause the author accentuates the gross sin of the Sodomites with an emphatic syntactical construction.

[38] See LXX Gen 19:5–8.

Pharaoh's life was the foundation of his disobedience. Nevertheless, Pharaoh's disobedience also demonstrates sin's impact on humankind since Exodus states that Pharaoh hardened his own heart against Yahweh's word (Exod 8:32).

Israel in the Wilderness: Grumblings Against Moses. Israel's constant disobedience in the wilderness demonstrates sin's universal impact on humankind's relationship with God. Yahweh showed Israel his power by inflicting Egypt with various plagues (Exodus 5–11), by delivering the Israelites from slavery (Exodus 12–13), and by destroying Pharaoh and his army in the sea (Exodus 14). Immediately, after Yahweh delivered Israel from slavery and destroyed Pharaoh in the sea (Exod 12:33–14:31), Israel sang a song of praise to Yahweh (Exod 15:1–21). Nevertheless, as the Israelites journeyed in the wilderness without food and shelter, the people grumbled against Moses (Exod 16:2). They accused him of bringing them out of Egypt in order to kill them (Exod 16:3).

Sin and thus spiritual stubbornness caused Israel to grumble against Moses. This point is supported by the Israelites' attack against Moses. Israel's attack against him was an attack against Yahweh himself since Moses led the people out of Egypt as Yahweh instructed him (see Num 11:1; 12:1–9). As Moses and Israel journeyed through the wilderness, the people again grumbled against Moses because they did not have any water (Exod 17:1–2). The people accused Moses of leading them out of Egypt in order to kill them in the wilderness (Exod 17:3).

Israel's spiritual stubbornness is further evident when the spies returned to give a report about the land (Num 13:25–33). The spies informed the people that they could not possess the land because its inhabitants were too many for Israel to overcome (Num 13:32–33). Consequently, Israel cried out to Yahweh and wept (Num 14:1). The sons of Israel subsequently "murmured" against Moses and Aaron (Num 14:1; see 16:11,41): they wished that they were still in Egypt (Num 14:2); they accused Yahweh of wanting to bring them into the promised land to kill them (Num 14:3); and they expressed that they would rather return to Egypt than enter the promised land (Num 14:3).

Israel became bitter. The people desired to stone Moses and Aaron (Num 14:10). Yahweh's response to Moses' prayer reveals that the people's grumblings did not simply involve their questioning of Moses' and Aaron's leadership. Rather, the people were rejecting Yahweh and refusing to trust him: "And the Lord said to Moses: How long will this people reject me? How long will they not trust in me, in all of the signs that I have done in their midst?" (Num 14:11). Israel responded this way on account of their rebellious hearts (see Num 14:9). The people's response can *only* be accredited to their sin (Num 14:18–19), which is a direct corollary of the disobedience of Adam and Eve.

The Golden Calf. The Golden Calf incident also demonstrates sin's impact upon humankind. In Exod 19:3, Moses went up Mount Sinai to converse with God. During most of the time covered in Exod 19:3–32:19, Moses was on Mount Sinai, receiving Yahweh's law for the people. Because of Moses' delay, the people became restless (Exod 32:1).[39] They summoned Aaron to make a god for them who would lead them through the wilderness (Exod 32:1). Aaron appeased the people's request. He created for them a golden calf from the jewelry that they acquired while enslaved in Egypt (Exod 32:2–4). Once Aaron constructed the calf, the people proclaimed: "These are your gods, Israel, who caused you to come up from the land of Egypt" (Exod 32:4).[40] Aaron encouraged the people to worship the calf although they should have directed this worship only to Yahweh (Exod 32:5–6; see Exod 20:3–6). Aaron built an altar before the golden calf (Exod 32:5), held a feast in its honor (Exod 32:5), and allowed the people to bring burnt offerings and peace offerings to it (Exod 32:5).

Israel's worship of the calf was idolatry. The people's idolatry violated the first and second commandments (see Exod 20:1–6). The people broke their covenant with Yahweh, the covenant they had promised to honor without hesitation (see Exodus 24). Exodus 32:7–8 confirms sin's impact on Israel by mentioning that Yahweh tells Moses that Israel "has acted wickedly" and that the people have turned aside from obeying him to worship false gods. In Exod 32:9

---

[39] This delay refers to the time between Exod 24:18, when Moses returned to Yahweh for 40 days and 40 nights, and 32:19, when Moses returned to the camp.

[40] So MT and LXX of Exod 32:4. MT: אלה אלהיך ישראל אשר העלוך מארץ מצרים ("these are your gods, O Israel, which caused you to come up from the land of Egypt"). LXX: οὗτοι οἱ θεοί σου Ισραηλ οἵτινες ἀνεβίβασάν σε ἐκ γῆς Αἰγύπτου ("these are your gods, O Israel, who brought you up from the land of Egypt").

Yahweh further reveals the stubbornness of Israel's spiritual heart when he states that they are a "stiff-necked people."

The Historical Books

Joshua

The Sin of Achan. Achan's sin demonstrates sin's universal impact on humankind. When Israel crossed the Jordan and conquered Jericho (Joshua 1–5), the Israelites burned the city, plundered the treasures of Jericho, and put them in the house of the Lord (Josh 6:24). Jericho was under a ban (Josh 6:17–19). Under Joshua's orders, Israel was expected to burn the city, spare Rahab and her family, and put the treasures of Jericho in the Lord's treasury (Joshua 6). Nevertheless, Achan disobeyed the stipulations of the ban. He sinned against the Lord and thus invoked Yahweh's judgment upon the people: "Achan took [some things] from under the ban" (Josh 7:1; see 7:20–21). Achan himself attested that by his actions, he "sinned against Yahweh" (Josh 7:20). The punishment for Achan's sin was physical death (Josh 7:24–25). His disobedience was sin. His sin resulted from the universal impact of Adam's sin upon humanity.

Judges

Rebellion in the Promised Land. When Israel entered the promised land, Joshua did not lead the people to conquer all of the territories of the land (Judges 1). The angel of the Lord rebuked the Israelites for not keeping themselves separate from the land's inhabitants. He asserted that the people disobeyed Yahweh (Judg 2:1–4; esp. 2:2). After Joshua's generation died, Israel further sinned against Yahweh by serving pagan gods (Judg 2:11). According to Judg 2:12, "They forsook Yahweh, the God of their fathers, who caused them to come out from the land of the Egyptians, and they went forth after other gods, from the gods of the people who surround them, and they worshiped them, and they vexed Yahweh." Judges 2:13 succinctly reiterates 2:12: "They forsook Yahweh, and they served Baal and the Ashtaroth." With the exception of a few faithful followers of Yahweh (e.g., Deborah, Gideon, and Samson), the book of Judges is a story about Israel's rebellion against Yahweh and his judgment of the nation (Judg 3:5–8,12; 4:1; 21:25).

1–2 Samuel

Saul. Sin's impact on humankind's relationship with God is evident from the life of Saul; his relationship to God affected the Israelites. Saul had a great beginning but a tragic end. He was a handsome Benjaminite (1 Sam 9:1–2), he was Israel's first king (1 Sam 9:15–16; 10:17–24; 15:1), and he defeated Israel's enemies (e.g., 1 Samuel 11; 14:47–52). Nevertheless, he often disobeyed Yahweh and Samuel, Yahweh's prophet.

Saul's digression is especially seen toward the end of his life. In 1 Samuel 15, Yahweh commanded Saul through Samuel to destroy Amalek and all of his possessions on account of his dealings with Israel (1 Sam 15:1–3). Saul only partially obeyed this command. He ambushed the Amalekites (1 Sam 15:6), but he spared the Kenites (1 Sam 15:6) and Agag, the king of the Amalekites (1 Sam 15:8–9). Saul's actions might at first appear to be acts of mercy toward those whom he spared. Nevertheless, Samuel's response to Saul suggests that Saul sinned against Yahweh. Yahweh said that he regretted that he had made Saul king: "for he has turned from after me, and he has not caused my word to rise" (1 Sam 15:11). Samuel later states that Saul's actions were evil (1 Sam 15:19). Samuel's other statements imply that Saul was rebellious and insubordinate because he rejected Yahweh's word (1 Sam 15:23). After Samuel rebuked Saul, Saul responded, saying "I have sinned because[41] I have transgressed the mouth of Yahweh and your words, because I feared the people and listened to their voice" (1 Sam 15:24).

Samuel tells Saul that he "has rejected the word of Yahweh" (1 Sam 15:25). Consequently, "Yahweh will reject" him as Israel's king (1 Sam 15:26). On more than one occasion in 1 Samuel, the author states that an "evil spirit of Yahweh" came upon Saul (1 Sam 16:14–15; 18:10; 19:9; see 16:16,23).[42] Saul's constant disobedience of Yahweh throughout his kingship displays the power of evil over him and the impact of sin in his life. Saul failed to protect Israel from Goliath (1 Samuel 17). He spent most of his kingship relentlessly pursuing David's life (1 Sam 18:10–19; 19:2; 24:1–22;

---

[41] I understand the כי-clause, כי־עברתי את־פי־יהוה ואת־דבריך, ("because I have passed over the mouth of Yahweh and your word") in 1 Sam 15:24 in a causal sense. It states the reason that Saul asserts he has sinned. The second כי-clause, כי יראתי את־העם ואשמע בקולם, ("because I have feared the people, and I listened to their voice") states the reason that Saul sinned against Yahweh.

[42] First Samuel 16:14 especially states that "the Spirit of Yahweh turned away from Saul."

26:1–25), and he sought the spiritual aid of the occult rather than the help of Yahweh (1 Sam 28:1–25).

David. Sin's universal impact on humankind's relationship with God is evident from David's life. David's kingship is not as tragic as the kingship of Saul. In fact, a canonical reading of David's life suggests that he was a man of great faith (see Heb 11:32–33). Nevertheless, certain aspects of David's life are devastating and reveal sin's universal reign over human beings (see Romans 6). The chief example of the impact of sin in David's life is his affair with Bathsheba. Unlike Saul, he eventually repented of this sin (2 Samuel 12; Psalm 51). By repenting, he demonstrated that he was genuinely devoted to Yahweh. Still, the narrative indicates sin's impact on David.

First, David committed adultery with and impregnated Bathsheba (2 Sam 11:1–5). Second, David attempted to cover up his sin by summoning Uriah from war (2 Sam 11:6). Third, David sought to persuade Uriah to abandon his military responsibilities and sleep with his wife during the time of war in order to cover up David's sexual sin with Bathsheba (2 Sam 11:8–13). Fourth, David executed Uriah by placing him on the frontlines of war (2 Sam 11:14–17). Fifth, the author concludes the narrative in 2 Sam 11:27 with the following words: "But the thing that David had done was evil in the eyes of Yahweh."

1 and 2 Kings and 1 and 2 Chronicles

Solomon and the Divided Kingdom. Sin's impact on humankind's relationship with God can be seen through the lives of the various kings who succeeded David. When David died, his son Solomon assumed the kingship (1 Kgs 1:38–53). Solomon brought much success to the kingdom (e.g., the construction of the temple [1 Kings 6–8]). Nevertheless, as with David, sin impeded Solomon's reign and brought devastating consequences upon the kingdom.

As he blessed Solomon's father, Yahweh blessed Solomon's reign. He blessed Solomon with wisdom (1 Kgs 3:16–28), royal officials (1 Kgs 4:1–19), wealth (1 Kgs 4:20–34; 2 Chr 1:14–17; 2 Chr 8:13–30), alliances with other kings (1 Kgs 5:1–12), and a successful construction of the temple (1 Kgs 6:1–8:66; 2 Chr 2:1–7:10). The demise, however, of the Solomonic kingdom began when

Solomon married many foreign women (1 Kgs 11:1). Yahweh commanded Solomon to obey his law and to walk faithfully before him (1 Kgs 9:4). Yahweh likewise warned Solomon that if he disobeyed him by breaking the covenant, he would expel Israel from the land (1 Kgs 9:6–7). Yahweh's covenantal stipulations included a prohibition against idolatry (1 Kgs 9:6). Solomon broke the covenant by marrying foreign women who worshipped other gods and turned his heart away from Yahweh to their gods (1 Kgs 11:4–13).

Solomon's sin divided the kingdom between Israel and Judah (e.g., 1 Kgs 12:16–24). Many of the people in both the northern and southern parts of the kingdom rebelled against Yahweh. First Kings–2 Chronicles record the spiritual decline of the kingdom and the apostasy of the kingship. Conflict arose both within and outside Solomon's kingdom on account of Solomon's sin. Yahweh raised up adversaries against Israel (1 Kgs 11:14–25). Those within Solomon's own house rebelled against Israel (1 Kgs 11:26–40). Furthermore, virtually all of the kings who succeeded Solomon were evil and rebelled against Yahweh.[43] They practiced idolatry (1 Kgs 12:1–15:3 [2 Chr 10:1–19],26,34; 22:51–53; 2 Kgs 3:2–3), committed various sorts of evil in the sight of Yahweh (1 Kgs 16:7,30–32; 2 Kgs 13:2; 15:8–9,17–18,23–24,27–28; 16:1–2; 21:1–9,19–22; 23:31–32; 24:8–9; 2 Chr 11:14–17), and led the kingdom away from following Yahweh (2 Kgs 17:7–23).[44]

The Prophets

Isaiah, Jeremiah, and Ezekiel. Sin's universal impact on humankind's relationship with God is evident in the prophets. Isaiah and Jeremiah warned the people of Israel and Judah they would go into exile because of their sin. Isaiah stated that Israel was a sinful nation, whose people were weighed down with iniquity and whose offspring did evil and acted corruptly (Isa 1:4). Isaiah also stated that Israel abandoned Yahweh, despised him, and turned from him (Isa 1:4; 65:1–3). Isaiah even called Israel a harlot on account of the nation's spiritual infidelity (Isa 1:21).

---

[43] Similar to the judges Gideon, Deborah, and Samson, a few kings (e.g., Josiah, Hezekiah, etc.) obeyed Yahweh. For the most part, the kings and the people within the divided kingdom forsook Yahweh. For example, see 1 Kings–2 Chronicles.

[44] For further details regarding Israel's sin, see 2 Chronicles.

Likewise, Jeremiah proclaimed that evil had overtaken the nation (Jer 2:3) and that it did not walk in accordance with Yahweh's stipulations (Jer 2:2–37). Jeremiah called Israel a spiritual harlot and a spiritual adulteress because the people disobeyed Yahweh (Jer 3:6–10).[45] Ezekiel's prophesy came to him when the nation was in exile because of its sin (Ezek 1:1–3). Through Ezekiel, Yahweh informed the nation that he would judge the kingdom because of the nation's sin against him (Ezek 5:1–7:19). Israel defiled the temple (Ezek 7:20) and endorsed evil (Ezek 11:2). Even the nation's religious leaders were corrupt. The prophets were false prophets (Ezek 13:2), the elders were idolaters (Ezek 14:1–11; see 22:1–31), and the religious shepherds were faithless (Ezek 34:1–10).

The Book of the Twelve. Sin's impact on humankind's relationship with God is also evident in The Book of the Twelve. Hosea depicts Israel as a spiritual harlot since the nation had committed spiritual infidelity against Yahweh. Hosea specifically connects the nation's sin to Adam: "And they, as Adam, have transgressed the covenant" (Hos 6:7). Amos states that Yahweh will judge the nation because of its transgression (Amos 2:6). Amos again states that Yahweh will judge the nation for its iniquities (Amos 3:3). Obadiah suggests that Yahweh will judge Edom because of its sin. Jonah and Nahum suggest that Yahweh will judge Nineveh on account of its sin. Micah speaks of those who scheme iniquity (Micah 2:1). Habakkuk laments before Yahweh about the iniquity that surrounds him (see Hab 1:3). Joel and Malachi speak of the day of Yahweh, a day when he will judge sin.

Sin Has Broken Humankind's Relationship with One Another

Genesis

Cain and Abel. The sin of Adam and Eve severed humankind's relationships with one another. Multiple biblical texts support this break. The author of Genesis first demonstrates that sin has broken human relationships by recording the hostility that existed between Cain and Abel, the physical offspring of Adam and Eve, who introduced sin into God's good creation. After God rejected

---

[45] For Jeremiah's lament over Israel's condition because of the nation's sin, see Lamentations.

Cain's offering (Gen 4:1–8), Cain murdered his brother because he was jealous of God's acceptance of Abel's offering. Genesis 4:5–6 confirms Cain's jealousy: "Cain became exceedingly angry, and his countenance fell. And the Lord said to Cain: 'Why have you become angry, and why has your countenance fallen?'"

The words "sin lies at the door" (Gen 4:7, see also MT Gen 4:13) suggest that Cain's actions toward his brother resulted from sin. A canonical reading of Gen 4:7 demonstrates that Cain's actions resulted from sin since Heb 11:4 suggests that God accepted Abel's offering because he offered it in faith. Hebrews 11:4 implies that God rejected Cain's offering because he sinned when he did not offer it in faith, for whatever is not done in faith is sin (see Rom 14:23). Cain's jealousy resulted in murder. Genesis 4:8*b* records this tragic event: "And it happened when they were in the field that Cain arose against Abel, his brother, and killed him."

The Tower of Babel. The tower of Babel in Genesis 11 likewise demonstrates that sin shattered human relationships. In Gen 11:1, human beings spoke a universal language. Nevertheless, human beings conspired to build a city and a tower that would reach the heavens in order to make a name for themselves (Gen 11:4). God confused humankind's language and scattered the people since they used its universal language to rebel against God (Gen 11:1–9; see Rom 1:18–32).[46]

Genesis 11:3–9 confirms that sinful aspirations had motivated the people to construct this city and tower. (1) Human beings said to one another, "*Let us* build *for us* a city and a tower," and "*Let us* make *for us* a name, lest *we* scatter on the face of all the earth" (Gen 11:4; see 11:3). (2) God said that humankind would use this one language to succeed in whatever it desires (Gen 11:6). Since human beings endeavor in Gen 11:3–4 to make a name for *themselves* and since God judges human beings in Gen 11:7–9 by confusing their speech, one can infer from 11:6 that humankind would have used its universal language to accomplish atheistic aspirations.[47] (3) God judges humankind by confusing its speech and scattering the people throughout the earth (Gen 11:6–9). Different dialects resulted from sin, and these dialects brought universal divisions

---

[46] Ironically, the name that the people built for themselves is characterized by confusion. See J. Ellul, *The Meaning of the City* (trans. D. Pardee; Grand Rapids: Eerdmans, 1970), 18.

[47] I use the term *atheistic* as a reference to actions that are against God.

among humankind on account of linguistic confusion. Therefore, sin produced dialectical and cultural divisions among human beings.

Abraham. Genesis 13 demonstrates that sin has broken humankind's relationship with one another. God establishes a covenant with Abraham in Genesis 12. In essence, God told Abraham to leave his country, his relatives, and his father's house (Gen 12:1). God then promised Abraham that he would bless him, make him a great nation, and bless all of the nations of the world through him (Gen 12:2–3).

Abraham left his homeland. He took Sarah, Lot, and their possessions with him. He journeyed first to the land of Canaan and then to Egypt (Gen 12:4–20). When they approached Egypt, Abraham solicited Sarah, his wife, to lie about their marriage to the Egyptians. Since she was beautiful, Abraham feared that the Egyptians would see Sarah's beauty, kill him, and take her to Pharaoh's house (Gen 12:11–16). This story demonstrates that sin has broken human relationships in at least two ways: (1) Abraham *lied* to his fellow man regarding his relationship with Sarah. (2) Abraham believed that the *Egyptians would kill him* unless he lied.

Abraham and Lot. Genesis 13–14 demonstrates that sin has broken humankind's relationship with one another by the separation of Abraham and Lot. Abraham and Lot journeyed from the Negev to Bethel (Gen 13:1,3). Abraham was very rich in livestock, gold, and silver (Gen 13:2). Lot had many flocks, herds, and tents (Gen 13:5). Consequently, "the land could not carry them, because their possessions were much, and they were not able to dwell together" (Gen 13:3–6, esp. 13:6).

Subsequently, Gen 13:7 states a disagreement: "And a dispute came between the shepherds of the possession of Abram and between the shepherds of the possession of Lot." This "dispute" between the two parties was a quarrel of some sort, which the MT's ריב ("quarrel") and the LXX's μάχη ("quarrel") support.[48] Genesis 13:4–6 suggests that the paucity of the land led to Abraham and Lot's separation in Gen 13:7. Nevertheless, sin was the central reason Abraham's and Lot's shepherds disputed with each other.

---

[48] See the uses of these terms in MT Exod 13:1–7, esp. 13:7, and in LXX Gen 13:7; Josh 4:13; and Judg 11:25.

Genesis 14 further demonstrates sin's impact on human relationships. Genesis 14:1–16 records that a war arose between competing kings and nations (Gen 14:1–3).[49] War implies that hostility and enmity existed between these kings who fought against one another in battle. Certain kings joined with Chedorlaomer in battle against other nations, but they eventually rebelled against him (Gen 14:4). Nevertheless, Chedorlaomer and his allies defeated the kings of the other nations (Gen 14:5–9). Chedorlaomer and his allies took all of the possessions and food from Sodom and Gomorrah and departed. They also captured Lot and his possessions (Gen 14:12).

A fugitive of the war reported to Abraham that his nephew Lot had been captured. Abraham mounted up forces for battle to seize the armies who captured his nephew in war (Gen 14:13–14). Abraham and his men successfully conquered these kings and rescued Lot and his possessions (Gen 14:15–16). The recorded events, that is, war, rebellion, and seizure of goods, demonstrate that sin has broken human relationships since war, murder, betrayal, and the plundering of one's goods express that enmity existed between human beings.

Jacob and Esau. Genesis 27 supports that human relationships were broken because of sin. Genesis 27 records that Jacob stole Esau's birthright. Esau was the firstborn son and the rightful heir of his father's blessing (Gen 27:1). Nevertheless, when Isaac, the father of Jacob and Esau, became old, he was unable to see (Gen 27:2). Sensing the day of his death was near,[50] Isaac ordered Esau to prepare a dish for him so that he would in turn receive his father's blessing (Gen 27:3–4). Rebekah, Jacob's mother, was listening at the door to Isaac's discussion with Esau (Gen 27:5). She and Jacob worked together to steal Esau's birthright (Gen 27:6–29). To ac-

---

[49] Genesis 14:1–3 states that Amraphel (king of Shinar), Arioch (king of Ellasar), Chedorlaomer (king of Elam), and Tidal (king of Goiim) made war against Bera (king of Sodom), Birsha (king of Gomorrah), Shinab (king of Admah), Shemeber (king of Zeboiim), and Bela (king of Zoar).

[50] The words "Behold! I have become old; I do not know the day of my death" should be interpreted idiomatically to mean that Isaac did not know exactly when he would die although he sensed that his death was near. This reading makes sense in light of Isaac's reference to old age. In addition, Isaac's reference to his death in Gen 27:4 supports the preceding interpretation: ". . . and make for me tid-bits, just as I have loved, and bring *[them]* to me so that I can eat *[them]*, so that my soul would bless you before *I will die.*" Isaac did not know when he would die, but he sensed that death was near.

complish this feat, Rebekah convinced Jacob to disguise himself as his brother by putting on Esau's best garments (Gen 27:15). Since Esau was hairy and since Isaac could not see (Gen 25:25; 27:1), Rebekah also placed goat skin on Jacob's hands and neck so that Isaac would think that Jacob was Esau (Gen 27:16). She gave Jacob the tidbits that Isaac requested from Esau (Gen 27:17).

Their plan worked (Gen 27:21–27a). Isaac thought that Jacob was Esau when he approached his father with his meal. Thus, Isaac gave Jacob Esau's blessing (Gen 27:27–29). Esau eventually returned with his father's dish to discover that Jacob had stolen his birthright (Gen 27:30–38). Consequently, Gen 27:41 states that Esau "treated Jacob as an enemy" and that he desired to kill his brother Jacob. Jacob's deception of his father, his stealing of Esau's birthright, and Esau's emotional response toward Jacob demonstrate that sin has significantly damaged humankind's relationship with one another.

Joseph. Genesis 37–50 demonstrates that sin has broken human relationships. Jacob was the father of several sons. Jacob "loved Joseph, the youngest, more than any of his sons" (Gen 37:3). Jacob's love for Joseph aroused such hatred in his brothers' hearts that they did not speak peacefully to Joseph (Gen 37:4). The brothers' hatred toward Joseph motivated them to plot to kill him (Gen 37:20).

Convinced by Reuben that they should not kill Joseph (Gen 37:22), his brothers instead sold him into slavery (Gen 37:28). Joseph was taken into Egypt as a slave, where God used him profoundly until his death, especially in the courts of Pharaoh (Gen 37:28–36; 39:1–50:25). Sufficient for my position in Genesis 37–50 is the brothers' response to Jacob's love for Joseph. They hated him and did not speak peacefully to him (Gen 37:4). Some of them wanted to kill him (Gen 37:20; see 4:8). The way that the brothers dealt with Joseph elucidates that sin has broken human relationships.

Exodus and Deuteronomy

Slavery. Genesis 50:26 states that Joseph died in Egypt at the age of 110 years old. When he died, many of his descendants were in Egypt with him (Exod 1:1–5). Although Joseph's entire generation eventually died (Exod 1:6), the sons of Israel were fruitful and increased in number (Exod 1:7). A new king arose in Egypt, who did not know Joseph or his descendants (Exod 1:8–10). He feared that the sons of Israel would multiply to the point that the Israelites' power would surpass that of the Egyptians (Exod 1:8–10). Thus, the king forced the Israelites into slavery and inflicted them with hard labor (Exod 1:11). The Israelites' labor did not impede their fertility, but rather enhanced it (Exod 1:12). Israel's continued growth caused the Egyptians to fear the sons of Israel (Exod 1:12). As a result, Egypt rigorously oppressed Israel with more hard labor (Exod 1:13–14). Egypt also attempted to kill Israel's male children at birth (Exod 1:15–16,22). Slavery and the attempted murder of the Israelite boys demonstrate that sin has broken human relationships.

Murder and Strife. Murder and strife in Exodus 2 further demonstrate that sin has broken human relationships. Moses grew up in Pharaoh's court (Exod 2:1–10). When he became an adult, Moses observed the labors of his Hebrew brothers and saw an Egyptian "striking" (מכה) a Hebrew (Exod 2:11). Without hesitation, Moses "killed" (ין) the Egyptian and buried him in the sand (Exod 2:12; see 2:14).[51] On a subsequent day Moses observed two Hebrews quarreling with each other and one of them striking the other (Exod 2:13). Murder and strife in this text show that sin has damaged human relationships.

Ordinances for the People. The ordinances that God prescribed for his people in the Pentateuch demonstrate that sin has broken humankind's relationship with one another. The Ten Commandments in Exodus 20 and in Deuteronomy 5 support this assertion. Commandments 5 to 10 especially highlight the ways human beings should treat one another. While these commandments are prophylactic in nature, they nevertheless assume dysfunctional human relationships since the commandments were given to prevent Jews from treating one another in ways that would dishonor the God who had delivered them from Egypt.

---

[51] The participle (מכה "striking") in Exod 2:11 and the verb ין ("to kill") in Exod 2:12 are from the same root and lexical form, and both verbal forms are in the Hiphil stem. Thus, the Egyptian could have offered death blows to the Hebrew slave just as Moses offered a death blow to the Egyptian. Nevertheless, the text is not clear that the Egyptian killed the Hebrew slave, while it is clear that Moses murdered the Egyptian (Exod 2:14).

The fifth commandment was given to prevent Israelite children from dishonoring their parents (Exod 20:12; Deut 5:16). The sixth commandment was given to prevent Israelites from murdering their fellow man (Exod 20:13; Deut 5:17; 22:13–30; see Genesis 4). The seventh commandment was given to prevent Israel from committing sexual sin (Exod 20:14; Deut 5:18; see Lev 20:10–14,20–21; Num 5:11–22). The eighth commandment was given to prevent Israel from taking the property and possessions of another (Exod 20:15; Deut 5:18). The ninth commandment was given to prevent Israel from falsely accusing a neighbor (Exod 20:16; Deut 5:20). The tenth commandment was given to prevent the Israelites from pining after their neighbor's possessions, including their wives, homes, and livestock (Exod 20:17; Deut 5:21).

Exodus 21–23 offers more prescriptions the Israelites were expected to use to order their life. Many of these prescriptions assume a broken relationship between fellow men. Exodus 21:1–11 prescribes ordinances for Hebrew slaves. While it is true that Jews did not practice the buying and freeing of Hebrew slaves in the same way, for the same reasons, or for the same purposes as the Egyptians did, the Jewish slave trade still elucidates that sin shattered human beings' relationship with one another since no form of slavery existed until after the sin of Adam and Eve.

In addition, Yahweh's prescriptions for personal injuries and disputes (Exod 21:12–36; Deut 25:1–3; see Lev 24:17–23), property rights (Exod 22:1–15; Deut 22:1–4), virgins (Exod 22:16–17), sorcery (Exod 22:18), bestiality (Exod 22:19; Lev 20:15–16), strangers (Exod 22:21), widows and orphans (Exod 22:22–24), the poor (Exod 22:25; 23:3; Lev 25:35–55), and a neighbor's cloak (Exod 22:26–27) assume that sin has broken humankind's relationship with one another. Also, Yahweh's prescriptions for false testimony (Exod 23:1), injustice (Exod 23:2,6), dispute with the poor (Exod 23:3), a neighbor's property (Exod 23:4–5), false charges and the slaughtering of the innocent (Exod 23:7; Lev 20:2–5), bribes (Exod 23:8), oppression (Exod 23:9), and divorce (Deut 24:1–5) likewise suggest that human beings' relationship with one another has been broken since these laws assume that they could possibly wrongfully treat one another. The Israelites needed the above prophylactic prescriptions to prevent them from sinning against one another since the sin of Adam and Eve had universally marred human-kind's relationship with one another.[52]

The Historical Books

Judges. The historical books demonstrate that sin has damaged humankind's relationship with one another. Nevertheless, because of limited space, summarizing the story of the concubine who was raped and cut into pieces (Judges 19) must suffice. The message of Judges quite simply is "everyone did what was right in his own eyes" when Israel was without a king (Judg 21:25). The nation was recalcitrant toward Yahweh. Israel's recalcitrance is seen most vividly in Judges 19.

A Levite's concubine practiced harlotry and then abandoned him for her father's house for a period of four months (Judg 19:2). The Levite pursued his wife at her father's house (Judg 19:3). Since his concubine's father was glad to see his son-in-law, he welcomed him into his home (Judg 19:4). During a period of three days, the concubine's husband and her father ate and drank together (Judg 19:4). The concubine's husband hastened to depart from the house of his father-in-law (Judg 19:5). After much persuasion from the latter, her husband remained with his father-in-law for a longer period of time (Judg 19:5–9).

The Levite and his concubine finally departed (Judg 19:10). As they traveled, they found a place to stay overnight in an Israelite city with a man who took them in for the night (Judg 19:10–21). As they lodged for the night, "wicked men" surrounded the house and requested to have sexual relations with the Levite man (Judg 19:22; see Genesis 19). The impact of sin on human relationships is evident since these men desired a homosexual relationship with a man, a relationship God did not create man to have (see Genesis 1–2; 19; Rom 1:18–32). That humankind's relationship with one another is broken because of sin is further elucidated when the owner of the house offered his virgin daughters and the Levite's concubine to gratify the sexual proclivities of these men (Judg 19:24). When these evil men did not accept his offer, the man[53]

---

[52] Human sacrifice in Num 25:1–9 and in 31:1–24 also demonstrates that sin has severely damaged humankind's relationship with fellow man.

[53] The text is not clear whether the old man or the Levite set the concubine outside for the men to do with her whatever they pleased.

seized the concubine and set her outside of the door so that these men could do to her whatever they pleased (Judg 19:24–25).

The context (Judg 19:22) provides support for concluding that the verb ידע "to know" (נדענו in 19:22 and ידו in 19:25) means that these evil men satisfied their sexual appetites with the Levite's concubine. Also, the occurrence of the verb עלל ("to vex" or "to practice wantonness") in the Hithpael stem in Judg 19:25 suggests that these evil men did not simply engage in a gentle sexual relationship with the concubine. Instead, each one sexually had his way with her and so possibly gang-raped her. Thus, translations such as the New American Standard Bible correctly use the word "rape" in this verse. The phrase כל־הלילה עד־בקר ("all night until morning") suggests that these evil men perpetually had sex with her and made her a spectacle of ridicule, especially since every occurrence of the MT's use of עלל in the Hithpael stem refers to ridicule and insult: Exod 10:2; Num 22:29; 1 Sam 6:6; 31:4; and 1 Chr 10:4. The LXX's rendering of the Hithpael of עלל as ἐμπαίζω, which means "ridicule," "make fun of," "trick," or "deceive," in the five preceding texts also supports that the evil men subjected the concubine to perpetual ridicule since it translates the Hithpael of עלל as ἐμπαίζω ("ridicule, make fun of, trick, deceive").[54] The Levite's response to the rape of his concubine also indicates that sin has shattered human relationships. The Levite awoke the next morning and took her away without any concern for her well-being (Judg 19:27). When he arrived at his home, he took a knife, cut her into twelve pieces, and distributed the pieces among the twelve territories of Israel (Judg 19:29). The Levite's actions, unprecedented amongst Israelites (Judg 19:30), were the result of sin and prove that sin has shattered humankind's relationship with one another.

The Pauline Corpus: Sin Has Broken Humankind's Relationship with God

Romans

Universal Condemnation. That sin has broken human beings' relationship with God is evident in the Pauline corpus. Paul argues in Rom 1:18–3:20 and in 3:23 that all humankind (both Jews and

---

[54]Some of the above LXX texts have the verb ἐνπαίζω instead of ἐμπαίζω. Both verbs mean "to ridicule." They simply have different prefixes.

Gentiles) have sinned and consequently stand condemned before God.[55] Paul first demonstrates the impact of the disobedience of Adam and Eve on humankind and thus sin's impact in severing humankind's relationship with God in Rom 1:18: "For the wrath of God is revealed from heaven upon all ungodliness and unrighteousness of men who suppress the truth in unrighteousness."[56] "For" (γὰρ) in Rom 1:18a connects Rom 1:18–32 with Rom 1:16–17.[57] Romans 1:16–17 provides the reason that Paul is eager to preach the gospel to those in Rome (Rom 1:15): "for I am not ashamed of the gospel, because it is the power of God resulting in salvation for all who believe (to the Jew first and also to the Greek), for the righteousness of God is revealed in it from faith to faith, just as it has been written: 'But the righteous one will live by faith'" (Rom 1:16–17).[58]

---

[55] Many scholars agree that Rom 1:18–3:20 comprises one unit and that the unit refers to the universal condemnation of Jews and Gentiles because of sin. For example, see C. E. B. Cranfield, *Romans* (ICC; London: T&T Clark), 1:104; J. D. G. Dunn, *Romans 1–8* (WBC 38A; Nashville: Nelson, 1988), 1:51; D. J. Moo, *Epistle Romans* (NICNT; Grand Rapids: Eerdmans, 1996), 91; T. R. Schreiner, *Romans* (BECNT; Grand Rapids: 1998), 77. Dunn (*Romans*, 1:54) especially suggests that Paul deliberately alludes to the Adam narratives of Genesis 2–3 in 1:19–25 to set up his argument: "it was Adam who above all perverted his knowledge of God and sought to escape the status of creature, but who believed a lie and became a fool and thus set the pattern (Adam=man) for a mankind which worshiped the idol rather than the Creator." S. K. Stowers (*A Rereading of Romans* [New Haven: Yale University Press, 1994], 83–85) agrees that 1:18–3:20 comprise one unit. He suggests, however, that Paul refers in 1:18–3:20 to the corruption of the non-Jewish peoples, and he calls for a reappraisal of the traditional readings of the text.

[56] Against Stowers, *A Rereading of Romans*, 86–88. Stowers suggests that the "Adamic fall does not serve as the explanation for the human predicament" in pre-AD 70 Jewish literature. Instead, Stowers (*A Rereading of Romans*, 88) posits that post-AD 70 Jewish literature (e.g., 4 Ezra and 2 Baruch) displays a greater emphasis on the effects of Adam's transgression." Paul and his churches were on the other side of post-AD 70 Judaism. Nevertheless, M. D. Hooker ("Adam in Romans 1," *NTS* 6 [1959–60]: 297–306; idem, "A Further Note on Romans 1," *NTS* 13 [1966–67]: 181–83); and A. J. M. Wedderburn ("Adam in Paul's Letter to the Romans," in *Studia Biblica* 3 [ed. E. A. Livingstone; JSNTSup 3; Sheffield: JSOT Press, 1980], 413–30) rightly suggest that Romans 1:18–32 at least alludes to the fall narrative in Genesis 2–3.

[57] So also Dunn, *Romans*, 1:54.

[58] Scholars do not agree on the meaning of δικαιοσύνη θεοῦ ("righteousness of God") in 1:17 (see also 3:21–26). The phrase in Rom 1:17 and 3:21–22 refers to God's saving acts and to his judgment. For a representation of my view, see Moo, *Romans*, 69–74, esp. 74, and Schreiner, *Romans*, 77–78. I discuss the meaning of δικαιοσύνη θεοῦ in more detail in chapter 3. In addition, Paul's citation of Hab 2:4 in Rom 1:17 is likewise intensely debated in New Testament scholarship. For recent exegesis, see M. A. Seifrid, "Paul's Use of Habakkuk 2:4 in Romans 1:17: Reflections on Israel's Exile in Romans," in *History and Exegesis: New Testament Essays in Honor of Dr. E. Earle Ellis for His 80th Birthday* (ed. Sang-Won [Aaron] Son; New York: T&T Clark, 2006), 133–49; R. K. Jewett, *Romans* (Hermeneia; Minneapolis: Fortress, 2007), 141–47.

Romans 1:18–32 is fundamentally about the revelation of God's wrath against the unrighteousness of all who suppress his truth.[59] The word γὰρ ("for") in Rom 1:18 introduces Paul's discussion of the revelation of God's wrath.[60] Verse 18 works with 1:16b–17 to provide the ground for 1:16a.[61] Then, Rom 1:17–18, along with Rom 1:16b, explains Paul's reason for not being ashamed of the gospel: "for it is the power of God resulting in salvation for all who believe, to the Jew first and to the Greek, for the righteousness of God is revealed in it from faith to faith. . . . For the wrath of God is revealed from heaven."[62] Thus, Paul explains in Rom 1:17–18 that the gospel demonstrates God's power by providing salvation, which includes the impartation of God's saving righteousness by faith (Rom 1:17) and deliverance from his wrath against sin (Rom 1:18; see 3:25–26).[63]

God's wrath is revealed in the present age (Rom 1:18) and will also be revealed in the eschaton (Rom 2:5). The latter refers to the last day when God will pour out personal wrath (e.g., Rom 2:5,8; 3:5; 4:15; 5:9; Eph 2:3; 5:6; Col 3:6; 1 Thess 1:10; 2:16; 5:9).[64] Yet, Paul's reference to God's wrath in 1:18 emphasizes the presence of his personal wrath against sin in the present age.[65] Paul's repetition

---

[59] Stowers (*A Rereading of Romans*, 93) thinks that Paul primarily addresses his Gentile audience with his indictments in 1:18–32.

[60] Cranfield (*Romans*, 1:108) suggests that the γάρ in 1:18 connects 1:18–3:20 to 1:17. In his reading, 1:18–3:20 supports that God's righteousness is from faith, not necessarily that it is being revealed. Moo (*Romans*, 99) suggests that the γάρ in 1:18 "introduces the answer to a question implicit in what Paul has just said: Why has God manifested his righteousness and why can it be appropriated only through faith?" Understood in this light, says Moo, γάρ "introduces the entire argument of 1:18–3:20—which, indeed, is encapsulated in v. 18."

[61] Recently Seifrid ("Habakkuk 2:4," 140) suggests that 1:18 explains 1:17 rather than providing a second explanation of 1:15.

[62] Jewett (*Romans*, 151–52) posits that the γάρ in 1:18 functions as "a marker of cause or reason" that "indicates that the discussion of wrath directly supports the thesis about the gospel in 1:16–17 rather than expressing its antithesis, describing the deplorable state of human affairs evident without the perspective of the gospel, or characterizing the era before the proclamation of grace."

[63] In favor of an eschatological understanding of God's wrath in Rom 1:18, see Dunn, *Romans*, 1:54.

[64] Similarly, Schreiner, *Romans*, 84. C. H. Dodd (*The Bible and the Greeks* [2nd ed.; London: Hodder & Stoughton, 1954], 82–95) argued against the personal aspect of God's wrath and thus against the view that his wrath needed appeasement. Scholars subsequent to Dodd demonstrated the weaknesses and the inaccuracies of Dodd's claims. E.g., R. Nicole, "C. H. Dodd and the Doctrine of Propitiation," *WTJ* 17 (1954–55): 117–57; L. Morris, *The Apostolic Preaching of the Cross* (3rd ed.; Grand Rapids: Eerdmans, 1965), 144–213; idem, "The Meaning of ΗΙΛΑΣΤΗΡΙΟΝ in Romans 3:25," *NTS* 18 (1971–72): 3–43; D. Hill, *Greek Words and Hebrew Meanings* (SNTS 5; Cambridge: Cambridge University Press, 1967), 23–48.

[65] A. T. Hanson (*The Wrath of the Lamb* [London: SPCK, 1957], 84–85) altogether limits God's wrath to the present age; he denies any eschatological aspect of God's wrath.

of the present tense verb[66] ἀποκαλύπτω ("to reveal") in Rom 1:17–18 and the phrase ἀπ' οὐρανοῦ ("from heaven") in 1:18 confirm that interpretation.[67] Further, 1:17–18 supports God's active role of revealing his righteousness and his wrath since the verb "to reveal," (used twice) is a divine passive, since the verb παρέδωκεν ("He gave") in 1:24,26, and 28 is in the active voice, and since God is the grammatical subject of the verbs in each of those verses. Therefore, the righteousness of God is revealed (ἀποκαλύπτεται) from faith to faith (Rom 1:17); the wrath of God is revealed (ἀποκαλύπτεται) from heaven upon all the ungodliness and the unrighteousness of men who suppress the truth in unrighteousness (Rom 1:18). God gave the unrighteous over to commit various sins (1:23,24,28).[68] God is personally doing the action of the verbs in 1:17–18 and in 1:23,24, and 28.[69]

Paul states both God's reason for revealing his wrath and the ones upon whom he reveals it in Rom 1:18b: "upon all ungodliness and unrighteousness of men who suppress the truth by unrighteousness." The terms "ungodliness" (ἀσέβεια) and "unrighteousness" (ἀδικία) specifically grant insight into humankind's spiritual

---

[66]The above statement does not mean that the present tense verb *a priori* suggests that Paul refers in 1:18 to God's present, abiding wrath. Context also aids in interpreting the present tense verbs in this manner.

[67]H.-J. Eckstein ("Denn Gottes Zorn wird Himmel her offenbar warden: Exegetische Erwägungen zu Röm 1:18," *ZNW* 78 [1987]: 82–89) disregards the tense of the verbs. He instead argues for a futuristic understanding of God's wrath in 1:18.

[68]Dunn (*Romans*, 1:54) suggests that γάρ provides a connection between 1:17 and 1:18, which is clear by the parallel structure of the verses: "righteousness of God for faith" (1:17) and "the wrath of God upon unrighteousness" (1:18). Jewett (*Romans*, 151) suggests that the "gospel reveals wrath, not simply by reminding of future punishment or the inevitable process of cause and effect in a moral universe, but by indicating the culpability of the human race at so egregious a level as to make retribution morally necessary and inevitable."

[69]Against C. H. Dodd, *The Epistle of Paul to the Romans* (Moffatt New Testament Commentary; London: Hodder & Stoughton, 1932), 21–24; Hanson, *Wrath*, 69, 85; G .H. C. MacGregor, "The Concept of the Wrath of God in the New Testament," *NTS* 7 (1960–61): 101–09. For a further discussion of God's wrath in Paul, see and compare the differences between T. Gorringe, *God's Just Vengeance* (Cambridge: Cambridge University Press, 1996), 72; A. T. Lincoln, "From Wrath to Justification," in *Pauline Theology: Romans* (ed. D. M. Hay and E. E. Johnson; Atlanta: SBL, 2002), 156; S. J. Gathercole, "Justified by Faith, Justified by His Blood: The Evidence of Romans 3:21–4:25," in *Justification and Variegated Nomism: A Fresh Appraisal of Paul and Second Temple Judaism: The Paradoxes of Paul* (ed. D. A. Carson, P. O'Brien, and M. A. Seifrid; Grand Rapids: Baker, 2004), 2:168. Even in 1, 2, and 4 Maccabees, texts in which God uses Antiochus Epiphanes IV to judge Israel, the authors do not hesitate to attribute the wrath of Antiochus to God's personal judgment of the nation, although Antiochus was the agent through whom God imparted his judgment against Israel's sin (see 1 Maccabees 1 with 2 Macc 6:12–17; 7:2–8:5).

condition,[70] for both terms are attributes of the noun ἀνθρώπων (ungodliness "of men," unrighteousness "of men"), and both refer to evil actions committed by human beings.[71] Paul's use of the plural ἀνθρώπων ("of men," "of mankind") in Rom 1:18 confirms that both the universal sinfulness and the universal condemnation of humankind are in view.[72]

Paul subsequently provides in Rom 1:19–23 the reason that God reveals his wrath against the unrighteousness of human beings: namely, idolatry.[73] Although humankind possesses knowledge of God, human beings do not naturally worship the true God.[74] Humankind's failure to worship and honor God with the knowledge that he has given to it results in idolatry (Rom 1:21–23,25,27; see Jer 2:5; Wis 13:1).[75] Idolatry thus establishes the reason for the revelation of God's wrath in Rom 1:18,24,26, and 28. The particle διό ("therefore") supports the latter since it connects Paul's statements regarding the reasons that God manifests his wrath against unrighteousness (Rom 1:18–23) with the manifestation of God's wrath (Rom 1:24–32). As mentioned above, God's wrath in the Pauline corpus is primarily eschatological (e.g., Rom 5:9). Nevertheless, Paul states here that God reveals his wrath in the present age against the ungodliness of human beings by giving the ungodly ones over to practice the desires of their rebellious hearts (Rom 1:24–32).

Romans 2–3 offers further support that humankind's sin has severed their relationship with God. In Romans 2:1–3:20 Paul

---

[70] For a discussion of the difference between ἀσέβεια and ἀδικία, see Jewett, *Romans*, 152. Schreiner (*Romans*, 88) rightly seems to understand these nouns as a nominal hendiadys.

[71] Similarly, Dunn, *Romans*, 1:55; Jewett, *Romans*, 152. I understand the genitive modifier of the above terms to be a subjective genitive.

[72] See Jewett, *Romans*, 152. Against Stowers, *A Rereading*, 91–92.

[73] Schreiner (*Romans*, 81–82, 85–86, 102–03) argues that 1:18 is the theme verse of 1:18–3:20. Thus, 1:18 refers to all of humankind, but Paul specifically focuses his discussion in 1:19–32 on Gentiles. Romans 2:1–3:8 specifically indicts Jews, and 3:9–20 indicts both Jews and Gentiles, so that the unit of 1:18–3:20 as a whole refers to the universal condemnation of both Jews and Gentiles. Stowers (*A Rereading of Romans*, 92) limits Paul's indictments in 1:18–31 to Gentiles.

[74] T. R. Schreiner (*New Testament Theology: Magnifying God in Christ* [Grand Rapids: Baker, 2008], 523) rightly points out that humankind's failure to honor and glorify God constitutes sin in Pauline theology.

[75] The premise that Paul only indicts Gentiles in 1:19–23 is predicated on several arguments, one of which is that Jews would not have committed many of the sins that Paul mentions in the text. Rather, these vices reflect the sins of Gentiles. See Schreiner, *Romans*, 81–82. Nevertheless, 1 Maccabees demonstrates that at least idolatry was by no means foreign to Jews during the Second Temple period.

develops the argument that God reveals his wrath upon Jews and Gentiles on account of sin and that both groups stand condemned before God in the judgment. From his argument in Romans 1:18–32, he infers in Rom 2:1–3:20 that neither Jew nor Gentile has an adequate defense before God for their sin, one which would exonerate them in God's law court, since God's judgment is "according to the truth" (Rom 2:2; see Rom 1:18).[76] Instead, Jews and Gentiles will be judged because of their "hardened and unrepentant heart" (Rom 2:5) since God will "give to each one accordance to his works" (Rom 2:6) regardless of ethnicity (Rom 2:7–3:8). Paul states elsewhere that Gentiles are "dead in trespasses and sins" (Eph 2:1,5), and they live ungodly and immoral lives as a result (Eph 2:2–3).[77] Thus, the depravity of the human heart leads to radical disobedience to God, which results in the revelation of God's righteous judgment against sin (see Rom 1:18–3:8).[78]

In Rom 3:9–20 Paul infers from Rom 2:1–3:8 that human beings stand condemned before God.[79] He asks whether Jews have an advantage over Gentiles in terms of right standing before God since the latter group is not Jewish (Rom 3:9a). He answers with an emphatic "no" (οὐ πάντως) in Rom 3:9b.[80] Paul gives the reason in Rom 3:9c for his answer in Rom 3:9b: "for we accuse both Jews and Greeks, all, to be under sin."[81] That is, Jews and Gentiles are under

[76] Human beings naturally reject and suppress the truth on account of the spiritual deadness of the human heart (Rom 1:18), but God judges in accordance with the truth (Rom 2:2).

[77] To reject Pauline authorship of Ephesians is commonplace in New Testament scholarship. For a thorough discussion of this rejection and for arguments in favor of Pauline authorship, see H. W. Hoehner, *Ephesians* (Grand Rapids: Baker, 2002), 2–61.

[78] God's wrath is eschatological in Romans 2.

[79] So Dunn, *Romans*, 1:144–45; Moo, *Romans*, 196–210; Schreiner, *Romans*, 161. Against, however, Stowers, *A Rereading of Romans*, 176–93.

[80] Paul states earlier in Rom 3:1–2 that Jews have an advantage over Gentiles. His statement in Rom 3:9 does not contradict Rom 3:1–2. Romans 3:1–2 occurs in a context in which Paul lists the privileges that Jews have over Gentiles (see Rom 2:17–18). Paul contends, however, that such ethnic and national privileges were not sufficient for a right standing before God (see Rom 2:19–29). Yet, Jewish ethnic privileges grant them an advantage over the Gentiles in that "the oracles of God were believed" by the Jews (Rom 3:2). On the other hand, notwithstanding that Jews have certain privileges, they are equally condemned before God because of their sin (see Rom 3:9–18). In this sense, Jews have no advantage over Gentiles (see Rom 3:9).

[81] The construction Ἰουδαίους τε καὶ Ἕλληνας ("both Jews and Greeks") includes everyone in the known world of Paul's time. Πάντας ("all") is in apposition to "Jews" and "Greeks," and it further defines the scope of Paul's indictment. That Paul speaks of the universal condemnation of both Jews and Gentiles in 2:1–3:20 is further evident by his statement in 3:19 that "every mouth be made silent and that the entire world be answerable to God." "Every mouth" (πᾶν στόμα) and "the entire world" (πᾶς κόσμος) includes both Jews

the power of sin.[82] To bolster his statement in Rom 3:9, Paul cites a catena[83] of Old Testament texts in Rom 3:10–18: "There is not a righteous one, not even one. There is not one who understands. There is not one who seeks God. All have turned away; together they were debased. There is not one who practices good; there is not even one. Their throat is an opened tomb. They speak deceit with their tongues. Poison of snakes is under their lips, whose mouth is full of cursing and bitterness. Their feet are swift to shed blood. Destruction and misery are in their paths, and they do not know the way of peace. There is no fear of God before their eyes."

The above texts refer to wicked haters of God in their original Old Testament contexts. Paul selects these verses about the wicked and applies them to humankind to illustrate the universal condemnation of humankind, which results from the universal impact of sin (see Genesis 2–3).[84] Paul's specific allusion to Isa 59:7–8 in Rom 3:15–17 attests that sin has significantly damaged humankind's relationship with God: "Their feet are swift to shed blood. Destruction and misery are in their paths, and they do not know the way of peace." Isaiah 59:7–8 states: "Their feet run to evil, and they hasten to pour out the blood of the innocent. Their thoughts are thoughts of evil. Destruction and shattering are in their streets. They do not know the way of peace, and there is no judgment in their ways. They have perverted their paths. No one who walks on it knows peace."

Isaiah 59:2 provides the reason the wicked in Isa 59:3–8 practice wickedness: "Indeed, your sins have caused a separation between you and between your God, and your sins have caused his face to hide from you, from hearing." In other words, their sins separated them from God. Since Paul argues that sin universally impacts the entire human race in Rom 1:18–3:20 and since he

---

and Gentiles. It is likewise further evident from the phrase "all flesh" (πᾶσα σάρξ) in 3:20 and from the clause "all have sinned and lack the glory of God" in 3:23.

[82] So Schreiner, *Romans*, 164.

[83] Compare MT and LXX of Rom 3:10–12 with Pss 14:1–3; 53:1–3; Eccl 7:20, Rom 3:13 with Pss 5:9; 140:3; Rom 3:14 with Ps 10:7; Rom 3:15–17 with Isa 59:7–8; Prov 1:16, and Rom 3:18 with Ps 36:1.

[84] Dunn (*Romans*, 1:149) states that "it needs to be stressed that the point of the catena is not simply to demonstrate that scripture condemns all humankind, but more precisely to demonstrate that scriptures which had been read from the presupposition of a clear distinction between the righteous and the unrighteous (see Jub 21:21–22) in fact condemned all humankind as soon as that clear distinction was undermined." Cranfield (*Romans*, 1:191), Moo (*Romans*, 202), Schreiner (*Romans*, 164), and Jewett (*Romans*, 259–60) more accurately assert that the purpose of the catena is to support the universal impact of sin and the universal condemnation of Jews and Gentiles because of sin.

alludes to Isa 59:7–9 in a unit where he argues for the universal sinfulness of human beings (1:18–3:20), Paul's statement that "all have sinned and have fallen short of the glory of God" (Rom 3:23) summarizes the argument regarding the universal condemnation of humankind because of sin in Rom 1:18–3:20. Romans 3:23 thus confirms that sin produces separation from God, which results in radical disobedience against God.

Adam, Sin, Death, and Christ. In Pauline theology, Adam and Eve's disobedience is the fundamental reason Jews and Gentiles are separated from God, sin, die, fail to honor God as he deserves, and are condemned. In other words, humankind's "hardened" and "unrepentant heart" (Rom 2:5) results from the spiritual death produced by Adam and Eve's disobedience (see Gen 2:17). Paul's statements in Rom 5:12–21 discuss this understanding.

Romans 5:12–21 is part of a larger unit that begins in 5:1 and ends in 8:39.[85] The primary theme of this larger unit is hope. Romans 5:12–21 discusses the death Adam's sin produces and the life Jesus' obedience brings. The primary point in Rom 5:12–21 is "how Christ's life defined the future destiny of believers just as Adam's life defined the future of his descendants."[86] Paul understood Adam's disobedience would produce physical and spiritual death for everybody. This outcome is clear from the outset of Rom 5:12: "For this reason, as through one man sin entered into the world and death through sin, and so death spread to all men . . ." "Death" (θάνατος) in this context certainly includes physical death, for Paul states in Rom 5:14 that "death reigned from Adam until Moses." Nevertheless, "death" here also refers to spiritual death.

The phrase "for this reason" (διὰ τοῦτο) in Rom 5:12 connects 5:13–21 with 5:1–11.[87] Paul explains in the latter unit that justification by faith guarantees tremendous hope for believers (5:1–5) and that Jesus' death is the ground of this hope (5:6–11). Paul further discusses the hope that believers have as a result of justification

---

[85] For examples, see A. Nygren, *Commentary on Romans* (trans. C. C. Rasmussen; Philadelphia: Fortress, 1949), 187–89; Cranfield, *Romans*, 1:253–54; N. Dahl, *Studies in Paul: Theology for the Early Christian Mission* (Minneapolis: Augsburg, 1977), 82–91; J. C. Beker, *Paul the Apostle: The Triumph of God in Life and Thought* (Philadelphia: Fortress, 1980), 83–86; D. B. Garlington, "The Obedience of Faith in the Letter to the Romans—Part 3: The Obedience of Christ and the Obedience of the Christian," *WTJ* 55 (1993): 87–112; Schreiner, *Romans*, 245–49, et al.

[86] Jewett, *Romans*, 370.

[87] So also Cranfield, *Romans*, 1:271.

by faith on the basis of Jesus' death in Rom 5:12–21.[88] Paul states in Rom 5:12 that all men die since "sin entered the world through one man and death through sin." The "one man" of Rom 5:12 refers to Adam and his disobedience in Gen 3:6 since Paul explicitly refers to Adam and his transgression throughout Rom 5:14–21 with the words "in the likeness of Adam's transgression" (Rom 5:14), "the gift" (Rom 5:15), "the transgression" (Rom 5:15), "the transgression of the one man" (Rom 5:15–18), "judgment because of the one man" (Rom 5:16), and the "disobedience of the one man" (Rom 5:18). The relative clause of Rom 5:12*b* supports that Adam died spiritually when he sinned and that this spiritual deadness extends to the whole of humankind: ἐφ' ᾧ πάντες ἥμαρτον ("on the basis of which all sin").

The latter clause in Rom 5:12*b* on account of its phrase ἐφ' ᾧ ("in which") has been the subject of much debate throughout the history of the church.[89] Translation options are plentiful.[90] The keys to an appropriate translation are studying the context, interpreting the theology of Romans 5, and determining the antecedent of the relative pronoun ᾧ ("which").

Scholars have translated ᾧ as a masculine pronoun, whose antecedent is an implicit νόμος ("law").[91] Some have translated the antecedent as θάνατος ("death").[92] Others have understood Adam, who spread universal death to all of humankind, as the antecedent.[93] The latter reading suggests that because of Adam's sin, all human beings sin. Still others have understood ᾧ as a neuter word, and they have taken the phrase ἐφ' ᾧ as a conjunction. With this reading, the phrase could be translated as "because"[94] or "so that,"[95]

---

[88] B. J. Vickers' (*Jesus' Blood and Righteousness* [Wheaton: Crossway, 2006], 114) assertion is correct when he states "when he comes to the second half of chapter 5, Paul moves beyond this discussion of the sins of humanity and his discussion of faith. Perhaps it is better to say that he gets behind the issues of both sin and faith to things that explain both the reality of sin and the reality of justification by faith."

[89] Ibid., 125–41.

[90] Ibid.

[91] So F. W. Danker, "Rom V.12: Sin under Law," *NTS* 14 (1967–68): 428.

[92] So R. Bultmann, "Adam and Christ according to Romans 5," in *Current Issues in New Testament Interpretation: Essays in Honor of Otto A. Piper* (ed. and trans. W. Klassen and G. F. Snyder; New York: Harper & Brothers, 1962), 143–65, esp. 153.

[93] See J. Cambier, "Péchés des hommes et péches d'Adam en Rom v. 12," *NTS* 11 (1964–65): 246–53.

[94] So Dunn, *Romans*, 1:273.

[95] So J. Fitzmyer, *Romans* (ABC 33; New York: Doubleday, 1993), 416; idem, "The Consecutive Meaning of ἐφ' ᾧ in Romans 5.12," *NTS* (1993): 321–39.

and it would refer to humankind's participation in Adam's sin and to its inheriting his depraved nature.[96] Recently, Paul Jewett posits that ἐφ' ᾧ ("on the basis of which") refers to "the realm in which humans were sinning, that is, the κόσμος ('world') mentioned in vv. 12 and 13."[97] His reading suggests that Adam influences the fate of humankind, and human beings are responsible for their sins (see 2 Bar 54:15,19).[98]

Regardless of the translation of ἐφ' ᾧ and the selection of its antecedent,[99] Paul's statements in Roman 5:15–21 indicate that he has in mind the universal impact of sin on all humankind in Rom 5:12b, at least at the conceptual and theological levels. Paul's argument in Rom 5:15–21 contrasts Jesus' obedience with Adam's disobedience in order to highlight the superiority of the justification achieved through Jesus' obedience over the universal condemnation of sin resulting from Adam's disobedience.[100] Paul first pits Adam's transgression against Jesus' gift in Rom 5:15. God's gift, provided through Jesus' obedience, will supremely abound for many since "all died because of the transgression of the one man." Since the grace and gift of God that come to humankind as a result of the obedience of the "one man" in Rom 5:15 refer to justification and eternal life (Rom 5:17), the death that all died as a result of Adam's sin must include spiritual death in Rom 5:12. Just as physical death spreads to all human beings because of Adam's sin, Adam's spiritual death likewise universally affects all human beings by shattering their relationship with God.

Romans 5:16 affirms the universal impact of sin on humankind's relationship with God. Paul states that judgment and condemnation result from Adam's sin, but God's gift results in justification. Romans 5:17 further contrasts Adam's disobedience with Jesus' obedience. By contrasting Adam's disobedience with the "righteousness" and eternal "life" that Jesus achieved through his obedience, Paul suggests that Adam's sin brought death upon human beings. Continuing Paul's initial thought in Rom 5:12,

---

[96] This appears to be Cranfield's view (*Romans*, 1:274–79). Nevertheless, Cranfield's view is a conflation of the view that understands ἐφ' ᾧ as a conjunction and human beings as sinning in their own person since humankind has inherited Adam's sinful nature.

[97] Jewett, *Romans*, 376.

[98] Ibid.

[99] I affirm Cranfield's position, but I do not follow his explanation at every point.

[100] Similarly, Cranfield, *Romans*, 1:270.

Rom 5:18 infers from Rom 5:15–17 that the gift of Jesus' obedience and the curse of Adam's disobedience are completely antithetical to one another. Paul mentions in 5:18 that "condemnation" comes to all as a result of Adam's sin and that "justification" comes to all as a result of Jesus' obedience. Paul reiterates this contrast in Rom 5:19 by stating that Adam's disobedience made many sinners, and Jesus' obedience made many righteous.[101] Finally, Paul concludes the unit of 5:12–21 by stating in Rom 5:20–21 that the law made sin worse, grace abounded over sin through Jesus, sin abounded in death because of Adam, but grace abounded much more and resulted in eternal life through Jesus' obedience. Thus, since Paul contrasts Adam's disobedience with Jesus' obedience in 5:12–21, using the words "sin," "judgment," "condemnation," "justification," "righteousness," and "eternal life," Adam's disobedience resulted in both his and humankind's death. This death shattered both his and humankind's relationship with God.[102]

Slaves of Sin. Adam's sin had an impact on humankind since in Romans 6 Paul argues that humankind is a slave to sin and that sin reigns over human beings. Romans 6 is fundamentally about the believers' freedom from the tyranny of sin on account of their baptism into Christ's death; furthermore, the chapter is about the "triumph of grace over the power of sin."[103] The inferential particle οὖν ("therefore") reveals a connection between Romans 6 and Rom 5:12–21. The connection becomes clear from the question in 6:1: "Therefore, what will we say: should we continue in sin, so that grace would increase?"

Romans 6:1 introduces an inquiry resulting logically from the argument in Rom 5:12–21. In the latter text, Paul argues that Adam's disobedience had produced death, but Christ's obedience conquered the power of sin resulting from Adam's transgression.

---

[101] Bultmann (*Theology of the New Testament* [Waco: Baylor University Press, 2007], 251), arguably the most important New Testament scholar of the 20th century, wrongly asserted that Paul was influenced by gnostic thinking here. Yet, he states that Paul avoids "slipping into Gnostic thinking" since he did not assign Adam's sin to something lying behind his disobedience (such as matter or Satan).

[102] Stowers (*A Rereading of Romans*, 251–55) asserts that Paul is unconcerned in Rom 5:12–21 in demonstrating "a timeless psychology or anthropology of sin from the story of Adam's fall." Nevertheless, Stowers does not seriously interact with either the text of 5:12–21 or with arguments that counter his reading. Rather, he asserts that the traditional reading is unviable and commences to affirm his view.

[103] See Schreiner, *Romans*, 298–303.

Paul concludes the contrast of Christ to Adam in 5:20–21 by saying that God's grace increased through Christ whereas sin had increased through the law. The question raised in 6:1 is built on the following four premises: (1) Adam's disobedience introduced sin and death into the world; (2) Christ's obedience introduced eternal life; (3) the law intensifies the severity of sin introduced to creation by the disobedience of Adam; and (4) God's grace through Christ overcomes the intensification of sin as a result of the law. Thus, "should human beings continue in sin since God's grace increases through Christ when sin is intensified?"

In Rom 6:2, Paul responds to this question with an emphatic "no" (μὴ γένοιτο) since believers have died to sin by dying with Christ in baptism (Rom 6:3–4). Humankind's connection with Adam is especially seen in Rom 6:5–11 where Paul speaks of "our old man." Romans 6:5 gives a reason believers should not live in sin so that grace will abound: namely, since believers are partakers in the likeness of Jesus' death, they likewise will be partakers in the resurrection. Romans 6:6 provides a second reason believers should not live in sin so that grace will abound: "our old man was crucified so that the body of sin would be abolished, so that we would no longer serve sin."

Since Rom 5:12–21 contrasts the death that came through Adam with the life that came through Christ, the "old man" refers to human beings whose spiritual condition resulted from Adam and Eve's disobedience: that is, believers who are in Adam.[104] The statements in Rom 6:4–5 confirm that this condition was at least spiritual death resulting from Adam's sin. In the latter text, Paul states that the believer's baptism into Christ's death results in the believer's new resurrection-life. The phrase "old man" alludes to spiritual death in Rom 6:6 since "old man" refers to the believer's previous identity in Adam (see Rom 5:12–21; 1 Cor 15:22) for several reasons: Paul connects the phrase "old man" with slavery to sin; he connects death with justification from sin in Rom 6:7; he connects death with life in Rom 6:8–10; he connects death to sin with life in Christ in Rom 6:11; and he connects death to the reign of sin and death in Rom 6:12–14.

---

[104]Dunn, *Romans*, 1:332; Schreiner, *Romans*, 315.

Dead in Sin, Alive in Christ. Sin's impact on humankind's relationship with God is further evident from Rom 6:15–23. As in Rom 6:1, Paul anticipates a question in Rom 6:15: "Therefore, what [will we say]: should we sin because we are not under law but under grace?" This question logically follows 6:14 where Paul says that "sin will not reign over you, for you are not under law but under grace." Thus, believers could wrongly infer that they should pursue libertinism since their dying with Christ means they are not under the law. Anticipating this question in Rom 6:15*a*, Paul responds with an emphatic "may it never be!" (μὴ γένοιτο) in Rom 6:15*b*.

In Rom 6:16–23, Paul explains his objection to the question he anticipates in Rom 6:15. He begins with a question pertaining to spiritual slavery. The question illustrates that one is a slave to whatever he obeys: "either a slave of sin resulting in death or a slave of obedience resulting in righteousness" (Rom 6:16). Paul, then, thanks God that although the Romans were slaves of sin, they yielded to the teaching and became slaves of righteousness (Rom 6:17). Romans 6:18 confirms this exegesis of Rom 6:16–17: "you were made to be slaves of righteousness, because you were freed from sin."[105] In light of Rom 6:16, freedom from sin produces freedom from death, and slavery to righteousness produces slavery to eternal life.

Paul commands the Romans to be slaves of righteousness since they have died with Christ (Rom 6:19), for they were freed from righteousness (i.e., dead to sin) when they were slaves of sin (Rom 6:20). Paul states that death is the end or the goal of a life ruled by sin (Rom 6:21). The latter emphasizes spiritual death, for Paul says "but, because you have now been freed from sin and because you have been made slaves to God, you have your fruit resulting in sanctification, and [you have] the goal—namely, eternal life" (Rom 6:22).[106] Paul's statement in Rom 6:23 also stresses spiritual death:

---

[105] I interpret ἐλευθερωθέντες ("having been freed") as an adverbial, causal participle.

[106] I understand τὸ δὲ τέλος ζωὴν αἰώνιον in Rom 6:22 to be a second independent clause in conjunction with the clause ἔχετε τὸν καρπὸν ὑμῶν εἰς ἁγιασμόν ("you have your fruit resulting in sanctification") because τὸ τέλος ("end/goal") and ζωὴν αἰώνιον ("eternal life") are in the accusative case, and here δὲ ("and") introduces a second independent clause. Paul assumes the main verb ἔχετε ("you have") from Rom 6:22*a* with the words τὸ δὲ τέλος ζωὴν αἰώνιον in Rom 6:22*b*. A similar ellipsis occurs in Rom 3:21–22 with the verb πεφανέρωται (Rom 3:21). Technically, τὸ τέλος is the direct object of its own clause in Rom

"for the wages [i.e., the goal or end] of sin is death, but the gift of God is eternal life in Christ Jesus our Lord."

Law, Sin, and Death. Romans 7 confirms the universal impact of sin on humankind's relationship with God. This chapter is one of the most debated chapters in the letter.[107] The goal here, however, is not to offer a detailed exegesis of every line in the chapter.[108] The details of the text receive treatment only in so far as they relate to the thesis.

The fundamental issue in Romans 7 is the Mosaic law, not anthropology.[109] Paul demonstrates this emphasis by developing two primary arguments. First, using an analogy from marriage, he illustrates the law's binding effect before faith in Christ (Rom 7:1–6). Second, he states that the law holds people in bondage to sin (7:7–25). Furthermore, Romans 7 is a continuation of the argument in Rom 5:12–6:23 regarding eternal death in Adam, eternal life in Christ, and freedom from sin.[110] Paul argues in the latter unit that Adam's disobedience produced slaves to sin, which results in death, but Christ's obedience produces slaves of righteousness, which results in eternal life. Romans 7 thus focuses on the condemnation that comes to everyone in Adam who is under the law and outside of Christ.

Especially relevant to examining sin's universal impact on humankind's relationship with God is Paul's discussion about sin in Rom 7:7–25.[111] After discussing that the presence of the law increased the power of sin (Rom 7:7–9), Paul states that "I died" and

---

6:22b, but its clause does not have an expressed verb since there is an ellipsis in Rom 6:22b, and ζωήν αἰώνιον are in apposition to τὸ τέλος.

[107] Similarly, Moo, *Romans*, 409. Also, Schreiner (*Romans*, 343) asserts that Romans 7 is "one of the most disputed and complex chapters in the entire letter . . ."

[108] For a detailed exegesis of Romans 7, see the critical commentaries on Romans. Most chiefly in English scholarship, see Cranfield, *Romans*, 1:331–70; Dunn, *Romans*, 1:269–300; Moo, *Romans*, 409–67; Schreiner, *Romans*, 345–94; and (recently) Jewett, *Romans*, 428–73.

[109] So Moo, *Romans*, 409; F. Thielman, *Theology of the New Testament: A Canonical and Synthetic Approach* (Grand Rapids: Baker, 2005), 364. Schreiner (*Romans*, 343) especially states that "it is generally agreed that the main issue informing the chapter is the relationship between the law and sin." Dunn (*Romans*, 1:377) asserts that 7:7–23 is an apology for the law.

[110] Schreiner (*Romans*, 343) thinks Romans 7 harkens back to 5:20 and explains why the Mosaic law's presence stimulates sin.

[111] Romans 7:7–25 develops the motif of 7:5 (Schreiner, *Romans*, 344). Moo (*Romans*, 424), however, suggests that the main line of development flows from 7:6b to chapter 8. He labels Romans 7 a parenthesis.

that the commandment resulting in life produced "death in me" (7:10). The identity of the "I" (ἐγώ) and "in me" (ἐν ἐμοί) statements in Rom 7:7–25 are the subject of intense debate.[112] At least three views exist. First, "I" refers to Adam and his experience with God's commandment in the garden of Eden.[113] Second, "I" refers to Israel's experience with Yahweh's commandment on Sinai.[114] Third, "I" is an autobiographical reference to Paul's pre-Christian[115] or Christian experience.[116] The third option at first glance best represents the context of Rom 7:7–25 since Paul conveys an agonizing, personal tone in the text. Even so, all three positions accurately reflect the context since Paul's discussion of the law in Romans 7 flows from his discussions about the Jewish inability to keep the law (Rom 2:1–3:20) and the universal impact of Adam's transgressions (Rom 5:12–21).[117] Nevertheless, the fundamental focus of the text is not to convey Paul's personal experience, but to emphasize that sin uses the law to produce death.[118]

The "commandment" (ἐντολή) in Rom 7:8–9 likely refers to a specific stipulation within the Mosaic law since Paul uses the broader term νόμος ("law") in Rom 7:1–10 to refer to the Mosaic covenant and mentions a specific ἐντολή ("you shall not lust") in Rom 7:8. Since Paul was not dead physically when he wrote this statement, death in Rom 7:10 must refer to the spiritual death that the law (i.e., the Mosaic covenant) intensified when it was ratified in a person's life and when a specific commandment in the Mosaic law was broken. Romans 7:11 supports this exegesis: "for sin deceived me, and through [the commandment][119] it killed [me] after it took an occasion through the commandment."

---

[112] See Jewett, *Romans*, 440–73.

[113] E. Käsemann, *Commentary on Romans* (trans. G. W. Bromiley; Grand Rapids: Eerdmans, 1980), 196; Dunn, *Romans*, 1:381.

[114] Moo, *Romans*, 427. Moo thinks that a combination of both an autobiographical reference and a reference to Israel best explains Paul's use of ἐγώ in Rom 7:7–25.

[115] Recently, Jewett (*Romans*, 443) affirms a pre-Christian view of "I."

[116] So Schreiner, *Romans*, 359. Schreiner (*Romans*, 364–65) admits that views one and two have viability and thus appears to agree that all three positions could accurately capture Paul's intent in Romans 7.

[117] Similarly, Thielman, *Theology*, 363–64.

[118] Ibid., 390. For a detailed discussion of the pre-Christian versus Christian experience, see Schreiner, *Romans*, 379–90.

[119] The word "commandment" is not in the Greek text of Rom 7:11. Commandment is a correct interpretation of the pronoun αὐτῆς ("it") in Rom 7:11 since ἐντολῆς ("commandment") is its antecedent.

Paul continues his discussion of the law in Rom 7:13. Based on the preceding statement in Rom 7:12 that the "law is holy, and the commandment is holy, righteous, and good," Paul argues that the good law and the holy commandment were not the fundamental sources of death (Rom 7:13). Rather, sin was the fundamental source of death, for sin "worked death through the good, so that sin would produce a sinner according to surpassing greatness through the commandment" (Rom 7:13). The "good" that sin used to produce death includes the law and the commandment, for Paul states in Rom 7:12 that "the law is holy, and the commandment is holy and righteous and good." Romans 7:13, therefore, affirms one of the major points in this chapter: sin has universally shattered humankind's relationship with God. Sin used God's law to increase the power of death and sin. Since Adam's sin produced death for everyone and since only Christ provides spiritual life for everyone and makes all slaves to righteousness (Rom 5:12–6:23), the good law and holy commandment can only intensify sin and bring about more sin and more death (Rom 7:1–13). Romans 7:14–25 provides confirmation for the preceding exegesis.

Romans 7:14a grounds Paul's initial question and answer in 7:13: "Therefore, did the good in me become death? May it never be. . . For we know that the law is spiritual, but I am fleshly, and I have been sold under sin."[120] Romans 7:15a should be interpreted parallel to 7:14. Romans 7:15a provides the second and third grounds to the initial question and answer in 7:13: "Therefore, did the good produce death in me? May it never be (7:13a). . . For we know that the law is spiritual, but I am fleshly, and I have been sold under sin (7:14), for I do not know what I am doing" (Rom 7:15a).

The word γάρ ("for") in Rom 7:15b further explicates the preceding clause in Rom 7:15a, also introduced by γάρ. In addition, Rom 7:15b grounds the initial question and answer in 7:13a. Romans 7:16–20 further develops the argument regarding the condemnation that comes through sin's use of the law. Paul states that sin uses the law to provoke one to do the opposite of what he wants to do (Rom 7:16–20). Interpreters have often argued that Paul's

---

[120]This statement counters that Paul only refers to a Christian experience since Paul would never assert that a Christian is sold under the power of sin. Rather, he arduously argues elsewhere that believers are free from sin's tyranny by the power of the Spirit (see Rom 6:1–7:17; Galatians 3–5).

words in 7:16–20 mean that he experiences an internal struggle with sin to the point that although he does not want to commit sin, he does not have a choice in the matter since "the old man" still influences him.[121] Nevertheless, the preceding interpretation is a case of the right doctrine from the wrong text.[122] Also, this interpretation is nonsensical in light of Paul's argument in Romans 6 that believers have died to sin and that the power of sin no longer reigns over them.

In Rom 7:16–20, therefore, Paul emphasizes that when the law took root in his conscience (and in the conscience of all Jews), it proved that he (and all under the law) was a transgressor of the law (i.e., a violator of a specific command) since sin used the law to stimulate sin, to confirm death, and to increase the power of sin (see Rom 5:20–6:23; 2 Cor 3:6). This point explains Paul's earlier statement in Rom 7:8 that he "was formerly living apart from the law, but that sin came to life after the commandment came." Paul's statements in Rom 5:12–21 regarding the transgression of Adam that produced death prior to the giving of the Mosaic Law provide support for this interpretation of Rom 7:16–20. Romans 7:10–11 provides further support since sin used the law to produce death through the commandment. This interpretation of Rom 7:16–20 is also trustworthy since Paul states in Rom 7:21 that "evil is present in me." In addition, Paul states that he "delights in the law of God in his inner man," (Rom 7:22), "the law of sin" wages war in his body (Rom 7:23), and Christ will deliver him from his body of sin (Rom 7:24–25).

Jesus delivers from death. The unit of Rom 8:1–30 affirms sin's universal impact on humankind's relationship with God. Romans 8:1–11 summarizes the argument regarding the law's condemnation in Romans 7. Paul infers in Rom 8:1–11 from 7:1–25 that Jesus delivers those condemned by the law. His logic can be summarized as follows: Paul is in Christ Jesus. Since Jesus will deliver him from the law's condemnation (Rom 7:24), "no condemnation exists for those in Christ Jesus" (Rom 8:1). The condemnation from which Jesus delivers would include the condemnation that

---

[121] This interpretation is a common one frequently heard from laypersons and pulpits.

[122] I get the phrase "right doctrine from the wrong text" from G. K. Beale, *The Right Doctrine from the Wrong Texts: Essays on the Use of the Old Testament in the New* (Grand Rapids: Baker, 1994).

comes to everyone as a result of Adam's sin and thereby as a result of sin's universal impact on humankind's relationship with God (Rom 5:12–21). Paul especially refers in Rom 8:1 to deliverance from the condemnation that Adam's sin introduces to everyone and that the law makes more severe for everyone. This deliverance from condemnation is supported by Rom 8:2: "For the law of the Spirit of life in Christ Jesus freed you from the law of sin and of death."

Νόμος ("law") in Rom 8:2 is possibly metaphorical, which would warrant its translation as "rule," or "principle," since the noun that the genitives τοῦ πνεύματος τῆς ζωῆς ("of the Spirit of life")[123] modify is νόμος, since the genitives refer to the Holy Spirit and eternal life, and since the Mosaic covenant was not characterized by eternal life through the Spirit, but by obedience (see Lev 18:5).[124] Nevertheless, the phrase ἀπὸ τοῦ νόμου τῆς ἁμαρτίας καὶ τοῦ θανάτου ("from the law of sin and of death")[125] in 8:2 refers to the Mosaic law since Paul has already stated that sin used the law to produce death (Rom 7:8–13) and since Paul's discussion in 2:1–7:25 includes a discussion about the law, sin, and death. References to life through the Spirit and death in the flesh in Rom 8:5–17 further support sin's active role in producing death. Life[126] in the flesh, life apart from the Spirit, and life apart from Christ equal life under the law (see Romans 5–8). Thus, the law that is characterized by the Spirit and eternal life frees those condemned by the law by means of Jesus since God condemned sin in Jesus' death for sin (Rom 8:3).[127]

Romans 8:12–25 further demonstrates the universal impact of sin on humankind's relationship with God. The inferential particles ἄρα ("therefore") and οὖν ("then") in Rom 8:12 together suggest that 8:12–17 comprises an inference to the preceding unit in 8:1–11. Paul's argument in Rom 8:1–17 can be outlined as follows: (1) No condemnation exists for those in Christ Jesus since God provided a solution for those whom the law condemned by

---

[123] I understand the genitives as descriptive genitives: "the law *[characterized by]* the Spirit and life."

[124] Against a metaphorical use, see Schreiner, *Romans*, 400. Rightly, Moo, *Romans*, 473–75, esp. 475.

[125] I understand the genitives as objective genitives: "the life that produces sin and death."

[126] I use "life" in the above sentence to refer to the human condition, not to "eternal life."

[127] The sacrificial nature of Jesus' death in Romans 8 will be discussed in chapter 3.

offering Jesus as a sin offering, so that Jesus would fulfill the righteous requirement of the law for those who rely upon the Spirit, not upon the law (Rom 8:1–4). (2) That is, God provided this solution because those who are in the flesh cannot please God, whereas those who have the Spirit will experience resurrection and eternal life (Rom 8:5–11). (3) Therefore, believers are not in the flesh, but in the Spirit, for those who are in the flesh will die and those who are in the Spirit are children of God (Rom 8:12–17). Especially pertinent are the words "to live" (Rom 8:12–13) and "to die" (Rom 8:13). Since "to live" occurs in the context of life through the Spirit and "to die," in the context of death through the flesh, Paul's language here references spiritual life and death. Death comes through humankind's bondage to the law because of sin; sin entered through the disobedience of Adam and Eve. Sin uses the law to increase the severity of sin and thereby to bring about death (see Rom 5:12–21; 7:10–13).

Sin's universal impact on humankind's relationship with God is further seen in Rom 8:18–25. The latter unit connects with Rom 8:1–17. The connection is evident by γάρ ("for") in 8:18. Romans 8:18–25 restates the thesis of 8:1–17 by further discussing the hope that all—Jews and Gentiles—have in Christ since Jesus freed them from the law's condemnation (see Rom 8:1–2). Paul suggests that the current sufferings cannot compare to the glory that will be revealed in believers (Rom 8:18).[128]

Paul grounds this proposition in 8:19–21. He suggests that the present sufferings cannot be compared to the future glory, "for the longing of creation awaits the revelation of the sons of God" (Rom 8:19) and "for the creation was submitted in futility—not willingly but because of the one who submitted it—because the creation itself will be freed from the slavery of corruption resulting in the freedom of the glory of the children of God" (Rom 8:20–21). Paul explicates Rom 8:18–21 in Rom 8:22. The unit of Rom 8:22–25 resumes discussion of the hope of the future redemption of the entire creation. Here, sin has a universal impact on humankind's relationship with God since Paul describes creation as "groaning" (Rom 8:22) and "suffering birth pangs" (Rom 8:22) and since he states that believers currently await the redemption of their bodies (Rom 8:23).

---

[128] Scholars debate the meaning of the phrase εἰς ἡμᾶς ("in us"). Translation options are "in us," "for us," "toward us," or "with respect to us."

2 Corinthians. Second Corinthians 3:6–18 demonstrates sin's universal impact on humankind's relationship with God.[129] Second Corinthians 3 is part of a broader unit that consists of 2 Cor 1:12–7:16.[130] Paul defends his apostolic ministry in this unit. Second Corinthians 3:6–18 discusses the authenticity of Paul's apostleship: he is a minister of the new covenant. Paul argues in 3:1–18 that his apostolic ministry is authentic since he is a minister of the new covenant and since the glory of the new covenant surpasses the glory of Moses' ministry in the old covenant. Thus, Paul argues that he does not need letters of commendation either from or to the Corinthians to validate his apostolic ministry since the Corinthians' initial conversion attests to the authenticity of his ministry of the new covenant (2 Cor 3:1–3).

Paul provides pertinent statements pertaining to the Mosaic law in 2 Cor 3:3 and 3:6–18. Paul states in 2 Cor 3:2 that the Corinthians' individual conversions serve as letters of commendation for Paul's apostolic ministry, letters read and evaluated by all men. In 3:3, Paul develops 3:2 by stating that the Corinthians manifest that they are an "epistle of Christ" because he ministered to them. He subsequently states that the Corinthians were not an epistle written with ink, but were written "by the Spirit of the living God" and "not on stone tablets, but on fleshly heart tablets" (3:3*b*). Paul assures the Corinthians in 3:4–6 that he and his companions do not have confidence in themselves as the source of the Corinthians' conversions, but have such confidence through Christ. He also assures them that they themselves were not sufficient for this new covenant ministry, but that their sufficiency came from God since God "made us to be ministers of the new covenant, not [a covenant] of the letter but [a covenant] of the Spirit, for the letter kills and the Spirit gives life" (2 Cor 3:6). The words "to be written" (γράφω), "ink" (μέλαν), "stone tablets" (πλαξὶν λιθίναις), "tablets of human hearts" (πλαξὶν καρδίαις σαρκίναις), "new covenant" (καινῆς διαθήκης), "letter" (γράμμα), "Israel," "Moses," and "glory" (δόξα) throughout 3:3–18 suggest that Paul has the Mosaic covenant in mind in 3:6 and that he is specifically alluding to the Sinai

---

[129] For a detailed exegesis of 2 Corinthians 3, see S. J. Hafemann, *Paul, Moses, and the History of Israel: The Letter/Spirit Contrast and the Argument from Scripture in 2 Corinthians 3* (Nottingham: Paternoster, 2005).

[130] So M. J. Harris, *The Second Epistle to the Corinthians* (NIGTC; Grand Rapids: Eerdmans, 2005), 127.

covenant. It follows, then, that when Paul suggests that the "letter kills," he means the old covenant does not bring spiritual life since an integral part of Paul's teaching and preaching was that the law does not justify. Instead, one is justified by faith and thereby receives the gift of the Spirit (see Gal 3:1–14). The verb "to kill" here alludes to the death that comes to human beings on account of Adam's sin since the text contrasts the death that the Mosaic covenant brings with the life that the new covenant brings through the Spirit (2 Cor 3:6).

Galatians. The universal impact of sin on humankind's relationship with God is evident in Gal 2:18–21. This unit forms part of Paul's argument in Gal 2:11–21.[131] The gospel is at stake in Galatians, for many of the Galatians were beginning to turn, or at least they were contemplating a turn, away from Paul's gospel (Gal 1:6). In Gal 1:11–2:10, Paul endeavors to establish the authenticity of his apostolic ministry of preaching the gospel (Gal 1:6–2:10). Thus he demonstrates that his gospel did not originate with man, but with God (Galatians 1–2). Central to this premise is Paul's delay of his journey to Jerusalem to see the apostles until years after his conversion and his ministry of preaching the gospel (Gal 1:13–2:10). In Gal 2:11–21, Paul demonstrates not only that his gospel was consistent with the other apostles' gospel before he journeyed to Jerusalem, but also that he remained faithful to the gospel even when Peter wavered.

Paul mentions that sin severed humankind's relationship with God in 2:18–21 in order to argue that a sinner's seeking justification in Christ does not make Christ a minister of sin (see Gal 2:15–17): "for, if I rebuild again what I destroyed, I make myself to be a transgressor" (Gal 2:18). Paul follows this statement in Gal 2:19 with an explanation of 2:18: "for I died to the law through the law, so that I would live to God; I have been crucified with Christ." With the verb "to live," Paul indirectly refers to spiritual death during his life under the law. He was dead to eternal life before faith in Christ, but his death to the law and his faith in Christ secured eternal life (see Gal 2:19–21).

---

[131] For a detailed exegesis of Gal 2:11–21, see the critical commentaries of the Greek text. E.g., F. F. Bruce, *Galatians* (NIGTC; Grand Rapids: Eerdmans, 1982), 128–47; R. N. Longenecker, *Galatians* (WBC 41; Nashville: Nelson, 1990), 62–96.

Ephesians. Sin's universal impact on humankind's relationship with God is evident in Ephesians. The classic text in support of this premise is Ephesians 2. Paul begins the body of his letter to the Ephesians with a long doxology pertaining to the spiritual blessings in Christ (Eph 1:3–14).[132] These spiritual blessings in Christ are the basis upon which Paul prays for the Ephesians (1:14–15). Paul essentially prays that the Ephesians will understand more clearly the great work of salvation that God has performed in their lives through Christ (Eph 1:16–22). Ephesians 2 elaborates on God's great work of salvation by highlighting the spiritual state of the Ephesians before their conversion.

In Eph 2:1, Paul states that the Ephesians "were dead in trespasses and sins." He follows this indictment with reminding the Ephesians that they walked in their sins "in accordance to the age of this world" (Eph 2:2*a*). Paul develops the preceding statement with a series of explicative phrases that define more precisely the way the Ephesians "walked" (i.e., how they lived their lives) before their conversion: "in accordance with the ruler over the authority of the air, i.e., [in accordance with] the spirit of the one who works in the sons of disobedience" (Eph 2:2).

In short, Paul asserts that the Ephesians were dead to the point that they lived their lives in a satanic fashion. As a result, they fulfilled the desires of their sinful nature (Eph 2:3). In Eph 2:4–8, Paul explains how the Ephesians passed from death to life: "God made [you] alive by means of Christ Jesus while you were dead in trespasses and sin" (Eph 2:4–5). God's supernatural work in the dead hearts of sinners rejecting Christ is the only way their hearts can be resurrected. Several statements in this text affirm that death here is fundamentally spiritual: "you were dead in trespasses and in sins" (Eph 2:1); "you walked in sin" (Eph 2:2); "we lived in the lusts of our flesh" (Eph 2:3); "we practiced the desires of the flesh" (Eph 2:3); "God made [you] alive while you were dead in trespasses" (Eph 2:5); "God raised [you] and sat [you] in the heavenly places in Christ" (Eph 2:6); and "by grace you have been saved through faith" [i.e., saved from spiritual death] (Eph 2:8).

---

[132] Scholars duly note that Eph 1:3–14 is one Greek sentence. For this, see recently H. W. Hoehner, *Ephesians* (Grand Rapids: Baker, 2002), 153.

Sin Has Broken Humankind's
Relationship with Fellow Man

Romans 14–15. Paul teaches that sin has broken humankind's relationship with their fellow man. Romans 14–15 is the first place canonically in the Pauline corpus where such brokenness is evident. The tone of the letter suggests that Paul wrote Romans to a church consisting of Jews and Gentiles.[133] Conflict between Jews and Gentiles within the Roman church is evident from Romans 14–15 because of Paul's discussion of the weak and the strong brothers. In Rom 14:1, Paul urges the Romans to receive "the one who is weak in the faith." That Paul gives this command to a mixed group of Jews and Gentiles is evident in Rom 14:2 because of its discussion of table fellowship: "On the one hand, someone believes [that it is okay] to eat all things, but, on the other hand, the one who is weak eats vegetables."[134]

Romans 15:1–13 continues the discussion of the weak and the strong brothers. Romans 15:1 suggests that the strong brother ought to bear the burdens of the weak one. Romans 15:7–9 appeals to the Romans to "receive one another" as Christ received them since Christ "became a minister of the circumcision for the truth of God, so that he would confirm the promises of the fathers and so that the Gentiles would glorify God for the sake of mercy." Paul specifically mentions Jews with the term περιτομῆς ("circumcision") in 15:8, and Gentiles with the term ἔθνη ("Gentiles") in 15:9. Paul highlights the Gentiles in Rom 15:9–12. Since Paul refers to the strong and weak brothers in Romans 14, since the language of the strong and weak brothers in 1 Corinthians 8 refers to relationships between Jews and Gentiles, and since Paul mentions Jews and Gentiles in Romans 15, the fundamental issue in Romans 14–15 is likely relationships between Jews and Gentiles.

---

[133] The above statement does not suggest that the Roman congregation had an equal number of Jews and Gentiles, but that Jews and Gentiles possibly comprised the ethnic composition of the church. A. A. Das (*Solving the Romans Debate* [Minneapolis: Fortress, 2007]) recently challenged this thesis. Das argues that Romans was written to an exclusively Gentile audience. Das's thesis did not originate with him. N. Elliott (*The Rhetoric of Romans: Argumentative Constraint and Strategy and Paul's Dialogue with Judaism* [JSNTSup 45; Sheffield: Sheffield Academic Press, 1990; Fortress edition, 2006]) and Stowers (*A Rereading of Romans*) advocated the same thesis years earlier.

[134] Against Das, *The Romans Debate*, 53–114.

Furthermore, Paul's command "to receive one another" in Rom 15:7 is a call to Jews and Gentiles to accept one another since Paul gives this command in a context in which he speaks of Jesus becoming a servant for Jews and Gentiles. Thus, there appears to be a tension between two groups of people among the Roman Christians. One group (believing Jews) consists of people whose weak conscience prevents them from partaking of certain types of food. The other group (believing Gentiles) consists of people whose strong conscience enables them to eat anything without harming their conscience. The command to receive one another in Rom 15:7 assumes that potential for division could exist among the two groups since one group (Jews) would abstain from eating certain foods but the other group (Gentiles) would eat anything (see 1 Corinthians 8–10).[135]

1 Corinthians. Perhaps the most obvious Pauline example of human relationships broken because of sin is found in 1 Corinthians. The church at Corinth was a divisive church (1 Cor 1:11). The Corinthians were full of jealousy and selfish ambition. Some of the Corinthians yielded their allegiance to certain apostles. They were divided over the apostles and Christ: "I am of Apollos; I am of Cephas; but I am of Christ" (1 Cor 1:12).[136] Such divisions provoked Paul to argue in 1 Cor 1:12–4:13 that the Corinthians should not be divided over men, because the apostles were simply servants of Christ. Further, Paul demonstrates that the Corinthians were hostile toward one another in that they took one another to court (1 Cor 6:1–11).

As stated above, Paul demonstrates that the Corinthians were divided over issues pertaining to food, specifically over "meat

---

[135] The language of Romans 14–15 reflects a situation similar to that in 1 Corinthians 8 where Paul discusses issues pertaining to meat sacrificed to idols (see 1 Cor 8:1). Paul primarily writes 1 Corinthians to a Gentile congregation (see Acts 18). Nevertheless, since Claudius expelled all Jews from Rome and since at least some Jews emigrated from Rome to Corinth, by the time that Paul preached the gospel there and established the church (see Acts 18:1–4; esp. 18:4), some Jewish converts were likely within the Corinthian congregation (see Acts 18:4). Therefore, Paul's instructions in Romans 14–15 regarding the weak and strong brothers should most likely be understood as instructions regarding Jewish-Gentile decorum in the church as it pertains to food laws since this issue had become a source of division for Jewish and Gentile Christians (see Acts 15; 1 Corinthians 8).

[136] D. E. Garland (*1 Corinthians* [BECNT; Grand Rapids: Baker, 2003], 47–48) argues that Paul uses his name and the names of Christ, Peter, and Apollos to illustrate that the Corinthians were divided over allegiances, not that they were necessarily divided over Paul, Christ, Peter, and Apollos.

offered to idols" (1 Cor 8:1). They were also divided over the way they should celebrate the Lord's Supper (1 Cor 11:17–21). Paul states in 1 Cor 11:20 that the Corinthians did not come together to eat the Lord's Supper when they gathered together as a church. Instead, "each one takes ahead of time his own dinner when he eats" (1 Cor 11:21). The well-to-do Corinthians, who provided the food and drink for the Lord's Supper, were consuming the food and drink before the have-nots arrived. First Corinthians 11:21*b* supports this interpretation: "And, on the one hand, someone is hungry, but, on the other hand, someone is drinking freely."[137]

Paul develops the latter statement in 1 Cor 11:22: "For do you not have houses so that you would eat and drink, or are you despising the church of God, and are you humiliating those who do not have?" That verse clarifies that those who were eating and drinking in 11:21 were doing so to the exclusion of those less fortunate in the body (i.e., the have-nots). This division was gross in Paul's eyes since the Lord's Supper is a meal that should be a source of unity instead of division within the body of Christ. Also, 1 Corinthians 12–15 further suggests that the Corinthians were divided because of their use and views of spiritual gifts (1 Corinthians 12–14) and their understanding of the resurrection of the dead (1 Corinthians 15).

2 Corinthians. Second Corinthians 10–11 suggests that humankind's relationship with fellow man is broken because of sin. Second Corinthians is largely about the sufficiency of God's grace in suffering (see 2 Cor 1:3–2:17; 12:9). In these two chapters, Paul discusses at length the suffering that he experienced by his opponents on account of the gospel. His opponents challenged his apostolic authority (2 Cor 10:3,7–8) and attacked his personal appearance (2 Cor 10:10). Paul asserts that he was imprisoned (2 Cor 11:23), beaten numerously (2 Cor 11:23), in danger of death (2 Cor 11:23), flogged (2 Cor 11:24), and beaten with rods (2 Cor 11:25). In Damascus, he was even lowered in a basket from a window in order to escape the authorities (2 Cor 11:33). Such opposition resulted from sin's universal impact on humankind and particularly on human relationships.

---

[137] The verb προλαμβάνω ("to consume") in 1 Cor 11:21 and the verb ἐκδέχεσθε ("to wait") in 11:33 also support that some within the Corinthian congregation consumed their food and drink without leaving any for "the have-nots."

Galatians. Evidence in Galatians likewise suggests that sin severed human beings' relationship with one another. It is the source
of hostility and division among human beings. In Gal 5:16–26,
Paul contrasts the fruit of the Spirit and the works of the flesh.
He exhorts the Galatians in 5:16 to walk by the Spirit and not to
fulfill the "lust of the flesh." The term "flesh" (σάρξ) is an important Pauline term.[138] Paul uses this term differently throughout his
letters,[139] but σάρξ ("flesh") in the phrase "lust of the flesh" (Gal
5:16) and in the corresponding phrase "works of the flesh" (Gal
5:19) refers to sinful desires that manifest themselves by sinful actions.[140] Σάρξ ("flesh") in Gal 5:16 would certainly include a reference to circumcision (see Gal 3:3; 5:13) and life under the law (see
Gal 5:18; Rom 6:14), but here it primarily refers to sin and to one's
sinful nature.[141]

The preceding interpretation makes sense in light of Gal 5:17
and 5:19. In Gal 5:17, Paul provides a reason the Galatians should
walk in the Spirit and should not fulfill the lust of the flesh: "For
the flesh desires contrary to the Spirit, and the Spirit [desires] contrary to the flesh, for these [i.e., flesh and Spirit] are opposed to
one another." In 5:19, Paul discusses the "works of the flesh," which
mean the works that flow from the flesh.[142] Paul's comment in Gal
5:24 further supports that flesh in Gal 5:16–17 and 5:19 refers to
humankind's sinful nature. In Gal 5:24, Paul states that those in
Christ should "crucify the flesh with passions and desires." "Passions" and "desires" refer to sinful passions and desires since Paul
has already contrasted walking in the Spirit with not fulfilling the

---

[138] According to Gramcord's grammatical search engine, "flesh" (σάρξ) occurs at least 77
times in the Pauline corpus. See also Dunn (*Theology*, 62–70) for Pauline uses of "flesh."

[139] Romans 1:3; 2:28; 3:20; 4:1; 6:19; 7:5,18,25; 8:3–9,12,13; 9:3,5,8; 11:14; 13:14; 1 Cor
1:26,29; 5:5; 6:16; 7:28; 10:18; 15:39,50; 2 Cor 1:17; 4:11; 5:16; 7:1,5; 10:2–3; 11:18; 12:7; Gal
1:16; 2:16,20; 3:3; 4:13,14,23,29; 5:13,16–17,19,24; 6:8,12–13; Eph 2:3,11,14; 5:29,31; 6:5,12;
Phil 1:22,24; 3:3–4; Col 1:22,24; 2:1,5,13,18,23; 3:22; 1 Tim 3:16; Phlm 1:16.

[140] As Bruce (*Galatians*, 240) states in his comments on Gal 5:13, "flesh (σάρξ) is used here
not simply of weak human nature nor yet of the life under bondage to the στοιχεία *['fundamental elements']* as opposed to life in the Spirit; it denotes (as in vv 16,19,24; 6:8) that
self-regarding element in human nature which has been corrupted at the source, with its
appetites and propensities, and which if unchecked produces the 'works of the flesh' listed
in vv. 19f" (brackets mine).

[141] I think this is what E. De Witt Burton (*Galatians* [ICC; 2nd ed.; Edinburgh: T&T Clark,
1975], 292) meant when he asserted that σάρξ ("flesh") has an ethical meaning throughout
Galatians 5. Burton stated that σάρξ refers to "that element of man's nature which is opposed
to goodness, and makes for evil."

[142] The above sense would understand the genitive τῆς σαρκός ("of the flesh") in the phrase
τὰ ἔργα τῆς σαρκός ("the works of the flesh) as a subjective genitive/genitive of origin.

lust of the flesh (5:16) and since he asserts that flesh and Spirit are opposed to each other (5:17) and produce different types of works (5:19–26). Galatians 5:26 supports this interpretation since it mentions some symptoms flowing from fleshly desires and passions: arrogance, irritation, and envy. In other words, sin flows from the flesh.

Paul follows his statement in Gal 5:24 with a statement pertaining to living by the Spirit in 5:25. Then, he states in 5:26 that Christians should not be known as "arrogant ones who irritate one another [and] who are jealous of one another." Thus, in 5:24–26 Paul connects crucifying the flesh with sinful passions and desires, with a reassertion of the importance of living by the Spirit, and with an exhortation not to treat fellow Christians with hostility. The latter connections suggest that flesh refers to one's sinful nature. The above interpretation of flesh is consistent with Paul's statement in Eph 2:3 that Jews and Gentiles prior to their faith in Christ lived by the lusts of their flesh "by doing the will of the flesh and of the mind" (see Eph 2:1–3; 4:17–24). Therefore, flesh refers to one's sinful nature in Gal 5:16–21 and the sinful works that flow from one's sinful nature. More to the point, Paul states in Gal 5:19 works that come from one's flesh. Some of these works that Paul mentions directly impede human relationships: "enmities" (Gal 5:19), "selfishness" (Gal 5:20), "jealousy" (Gal 5:20), "angers" (Gal 5:20), "rivalry" (Gal 5:20), "divisions" (Gal 5:20), "factions" (Gal 5:20), and "envies" (Gal 5:21).

Philippians. Broken human relationships because of sin are evident in Philippians. The preceding is first apparent in Philippians by Paul's imprisonment. He was imprisoned on account of the gospel (Phil 1:13). Imprisonment suggests that humankind's relationship with fellow man is broken since human beings imprison one another. In addition, while Paul was in prison, some were preaching the gospel with false motives "because of envy and selfish-ambition" (Phil 1:15,17). They did this with the expectation that they would "arouse affliction" in Paul's chains (Phil 1:17).

According to Philippians 2, the Philippian congregation itself was also experiencing broken human relationships. This problem is evident not only because Paul exhorts the Philippians to be humble toward one another and serve one another by imitating

Christ's example (Phil 2:1–11), but also because Paul specifically singles out two women, Euodia and Syntyche, in Phil 4:2 who were evidently divided over a particular issue.[143] In light of Paul's exhortations before Phil 4:2 regarding unity within the church, the division between these two women possibly infected the entire Philippian congregation. Thus, again Paul demonstrates that sin severed humankind's relationship with his fellow man.

Conclusion

This chapter has presented evidence that sin is the fundamental reason human beings need to be reconciled to one another. Sin's universal impact upon humankind has first severed humankind's relationship with God, and has second severed human beings' relationships with one another. Along with a discussion of selected Old Testament and Pauline texts, two primary arguments are developed throughout the chapter: (1) because of Adam and Eve's disobedience, humankind's relationship with God has been broken so that human beings die spiritually; (2) because of Adam and Eve's disobedience, human beings' relationships with one another have been broken, and hostility exists between one another. Thus, human beings need to be reconciled first to God and second to one another because of sin. Chapter 3 considers God's provision for these broken relationships.

---

[143] W. Schmithals' (*Paul and the Gnostics* [Nashville, 1972], 112–14) assertion, that these women disagreed on account of gnostic agitation and threatened the unity of the church by opening their homes—which hosted house churches—to the Gnostics, is at worst mere speculation and at best provocative conjecture. P. T. O'Brien (*Philippians* [NIGTC; Grand Rapids: Eerdmans, 1991], 478) is right to suggest that we only know that these two women were apparently active members of the church and that their discord (whatever the exact nature) was a threat to the unity of the Philippian congregation.

3

the provision for racial
reconciliation[1]

C hapter 2 considered the reason for racial reconciliation. I argued that sin's universal impact on humanity is the fundamental reason races need to be reconciled first to God and second to one another. Since sin is the root cause of the hostility between God and humankind and between fellow human beings, here I argue that Jesus' sacrificial death for sin is God's provision for racial reconciliation and that Paul grounds God's work of salvation in Jesus' sacrificial death for sin.[2] In this chapter I defend this thesis

---

[1] Portions of this chapter were presented at the 2008 annual meeting of the Evangelical Theological Society in Providence, RI, during a Pauline Studies group.

[2] The nature and significance of Jesus' death have been and continue to be strongly debated in both scholarly and popular literature. For example, see A. Deissmann, "ἱλαστήριος und ἱλαστήριον: Eine lexicalische Studie," ZNW 4 (1903): 193–212; C. H. Dodd, *The Bible and The Greeks* (2nd ed.; London: Hodder & Stoughton, 1954); R. Nicole, "C. H. Dodd and the Doctrine of Propitiation," WTJ 17 (1954–1955): 227–33; L. Morris, *The Apostolic Preaching of the Cross* (3rd ed.; Grand Rapids: Zondervan, 1965); idem, *The Cross in the New Testament* (Grand Rapids: Baker, 1965); S. Lyonnet and L. Sabourin, *Sin, Redemption, and Sacrifice: A Biblical and Patristic Study* (Rome: Biblical Institute Press, 1970); E. Käsemann, "The Saving Significance of the Death of Jesus in Paul," in *Perspectives on Paul* (trans. M. Kohl; Philadelphia: Fortress, 1971), 32–59; J. D. G. Dunn, "Paul's Understanding of Jesus' Death," in *Reconciliation and Hope* (ed. R. Banks; Grand Rapids: Eerdmans, 1974), 76–89; S. K. Williams, *Jesus' Death as Saving Event: The Background and Origin of a Concept* (HDR 2; Missoula: Scholars Press, 1975); G. Friedrich, *Die Verkündigung des Todes Jesu im Neuen Testament* (BThSt; Neukirchener-Vluyn: Neukirchener Verlag, 1982); J. B. Green, *The Death of Jesus: Tradition and Interpretation in the Passion Narrative* (WUNT 2; Tübingen: Mohr, 1988); C. Breytenbach, *Versöhnung: Eine Studie zur paulinischen Soteriologie* (WMANT 60; Neukirchener-Vluyn: Neukirchener Verlag, 1989); idem, "Versöhnung, Stellvertretung und Sühne: Semantische und traditionsgeschichtliche Bemerkungen am Beispiel der paulinischen Briefe," NTS 39 (1993): 59–79; C. B. Cousar, *A Theology of the Cross: The Death of Jesus in*

by an examination of Rom 3:24–26; 5:6–11; 8:1–4; 1 Cor 11:23–26; 2 Cor 5:14–21; Gal 1:4; 3:10–14; and selected texts from Ephesians 1–2 and Colossians 1–2.

Sacrificial Atonement in Romans

Romans 3:24–26 in Context

Rom 3:21–26 is the central section of the letter.[3] Scholars have debated virtually every component of this text.[4] Thus, there is no

---

the Pauline Letters (Minneapolis: Augsburg Fortress, 1990); M. D. Hooker, *Not Ashamed of the Gospel: New Testament Interpretations of the Death of Christ* (Grand Rapids: Eerdmans, 1994); S. K. Stowers, *A Rereading of Romans: Justice, Jews, and Gentiles* (New Haven: Yale University Press, 1994), 206–226; J. B. Green and M. Baker, *Rediscovering the Scandal of the Cross: Atonement in New Testament and Contemporary Contexts* (Downers Grove, IL: InterVarsity Press, 2000); D. Tidball, *The Message of the Cross* (Downers Grove, IL: InterVarsity Press, 2001); T. Knöppler, *Sühne im Neuen Testament* (WMANT 88; Neukirchen-Vluyn: Neukirchener Verlag, 2001); R. H. Bell, "Sacrifice and Christology in Paul," *JTS* 53 (2002): 1–27; S. Chalke, *The Lost Message of Jesus* (Grand Rapids: Zondervan, 2003); C. E. Hill and F. A. James III, eds., *The Glory of the Atonement* (Downers Grove, IL: InterVarsity Press, 2004), 127–36; S. Finlan, *The Background and Content of Paul's Cultic Atonement Metaphors* (Atlanta: SBL, 2004); idem, *Problems with Atonement* (Minnesota: Liturgical Press, 2005); H. Boersma, *Violence, Hospitality, and the Cross: Reappropriating the Atonement Tradition* (Grand Rapids: Baker, 2004); S. McKnight, *Jesus and His Death: Historiography, the Historical Jesus, and Atonement Theory* (Waco, TX: Baylor University Press, 2005); J. Beilby and P. R. Eddy, eds., *The Nature of the Atonement* (Downers Grove, IL: InterVarsity Press, 2006); J. Dennis, "Jesus' Death in John's Gospel: A Survey of Research from Bultmann to the Present with Special Reference to the Johannine Hyper-Texts," *CBR* 4.3 (2006): 331–63; D. A. Brondos, *Paul on the Cross: Reconstructing the Apostle's Story of Redemption* (Minnesota: Fortress, 2006); B. Jersak and M. Hardin, eds., *Stricken by God?: Nonviolent Identification and the Victory of Christ* (Grand Rapids: Eerdmans, 2007); F. S. Thielman, "The Atonement," in *Central Themes in Biblical Theology: Mapping Unity in Diversity* (ed. S. J. Hafemann and P. R. House; Grand Rapids: Baker, 2007), 102–27; J. J. Williams, "Penal Substitution in Romans 3:25–26?" *PTR* 13 (2007): 73–81; S. McKnight, *A Community Called Atonement* (Nashville: Abingdon, 2007); P. Lampe, "Human Sacrifice and Pauline Christology," in *Human Sacrifice in Jewish and Christian Tradition* (ed. K. Finterbusch, A. Lange, and K. F. Diethard; Leiden: Brill, 2007), 191–209; J. I. Packer and M. Dever, *In My Place Condemned He Stood* (Wheaton: Crossway, 2008); I. H. Marshall, *Aspects of the Atonement: Cross and Resurrection in the Reconciling of God and Humanity* (London: Paternoster, 2008); D. Tidball, D. Hilborn, and J. Thacker, eds., *The Atonement Debate: Papers from the London Symposium on the Theology of Atonement* (Grand Rapids: Zondervan, 2008).

[3] For example, see C. E. B. Cranfield, *Romans* (ICC; Edinburgh: T&T Clark, 1975), 1:199.

[4] For example, see E. Käsemann, "Zum Verstädnis von Römer 3:24–26," *ZNW* 43 (1950–1951): 150–54; S. Lyonnet, "Le sens de πάρεσις en Rom 3:25," *Bib* 38 (1957): 40–61; U. Wilckens, "Zu Römer 3:21–25," *EvT* 24 (1964): 584–610; G. Klein, "Exegetisch Probleme in Röm 3:21–25," *EvT* 24 (1964): 678–83; C. H. Talbert, "A Non-Pauline Fragment at Romans 3:24–26?" *JBL* 85 (1966): 287–96; Cranfield, *Romans*, 1:199–218; B. F. Meyer, "The Pre-Pauline Formula in Rom 3:25–26a," *NTS* 29 (1983): 198–208; J. D. G. Dunn, *Romans*, WBC 38 (Nashville: Nelson, 1988), 1:161–83; W. Kraus, *Der Tod Jesu als Heiligtumsweihe: Eine Untersuchung zum Umfeld der Sühnevorstellung in Römer 3:25–26a* (WMANT 66; Gfttingen: Vandenhoeck & Ruprecht, 1991); D. A. Campbell, *The Rhetoric of Righteousness in Romans 3:21–26* (JSNTSup 65; Sheffield: JSOT Press, 1992); Douglas J. Moo, *The Epistle to the Romans*, (NICNT; Grand Rapids: Eerdmans, 1996), 218–43; Thomas R. Schreiner, *Romans*

consensus regarding the text's meaning, the meaning of the syntax, the origin of the text, the background of the text, or the composer of the text.[5] Nevertheless, Paul appears to offer in 3:21–26 an antithesis to his thesis in 1:18–3:20: namely, Jews and Gentiles can be justified by faith because of Jesus' death for sin.[6] Paul's argument in the latter unit suggests that both Jews and Gentiles are guilty before God since neither group is capable of meeting the law's demands.[7] With the words "but now" in 3:21, Paul offers in the unit of 3:21–26 a solution to the problems of universal sin and the law's universal condemnation of Jews and Gentiles on account of sin (see 3:9–20). Paul's solution to the problems is justification by faith in Jesus on the basis of his death (3:21–26).[8]

(BECNT; Grand Rapids: Baker, 1998), 179–99; P. Jewett, *Romans* (Hermeneia; Minneapolis: Fortress, 2007), 268–93; M. Seifrid, "Romans," in *Commentary on the New Testament Use of the Old Testament* (ed. G. K. Beale and D. A. Carson; Grand Rapids: Baker, 2007), 618–22.

[5] See Käsemann, "Zum Verständis von Römer 3:24–26," 150–54; Lyonnet, "Le sens de πάρεσις en Rom 3:25," 40–61; Wilckens, "Zu Römer 3:21–25," 678–83; Meyer, "The Pre-Pauline Formula," 198–208.

[6] So most scholars. For bibliography, see Campbell, *Rhetoric*, 22–23.

[7] For decades, Pauline scholars have vigorously debated Paul's view of the law. The view presented above assumes that certain strands of Second Temple Judaism were legalistic and that Paul believed that the law demanded perfect obedience. In current scholarship, see T. R. Schreiner, *The Law and Its Fulfillment* (Grand Rapids: Baker, 1993); F. S. Thielman, *From Plight to Solution: A Jewish Framework for Understanding Paul's View of the Law in Romans and Galatians* (Leiden: Brill, 1989); idem, *Paul and the Law: A Contextual Approach* (Downers Grove, IL: InterVarsity Press, 2000); D. A. Carson, P. O'Brien, and M. A. Seifrid, eds., *Justification and Variegated Nomism: The Complexities of Second Temple Judaism* (2 vols.; Grand Rapids: Baker, 2001); and S. J. Gathercole, *Where Is Boasting? Early Jewish Soteriology and Paul's Response in Romans 1–5* (Grand Rapids: Eerdmans, 2002). Nevertheless, with the publication of E. P. Sanders' revolutionary work on Paul in 1977 (*Paul and Palestinian Judaism* [Minneapolis: Fortress, 1977]), many New Testament scholars began to reject the above understanding as Paul's view of the law. Sanders' work introduced (what has been known as) the *New Perspective*. He basically argued that Judaism was not a legalistic religion and that the law did not require perfect obedience. Instead, argued Sanders, Judaism was a religion of grace that taught *covenantal nomism*: God graciously entered into a covenant with his people, and he did not require perfect obedience to his law before he entered into this covenant. Election makes one part of the covenant, but obedience keeps one in the covenant. Paul's problem with the law, said Sanders, was simply that it did not provide universal salvation (i.e., salvation for both Jews and Gentiles). In addition to Sanders, the most popular representatives of this *New Perspective* on the law in Paul are J. D. G. Dunn (*Jesus, Paul, and the Law* [London: SPK, 1990]; idem, *The New Perspective on Paul* [WUNT 185; Tübingen: Mohr-Siebeck, 2005]) and N. T. Wright (*The Climax of the Covenant* [Minneapolis: Fortress, 1991]). Although Sanders, Dunn, and Wright would not unanimously agree on every aspect of Pauline theology, they all agree that Paul was not reacting against a legalistic view of Judaism in texts in which he speaks of the law's inability to justify. For a good summary of the scholars in the debate, see S. Westerholm, *Perspectives Old and New on Paul: The Lutheran Paul and His Critics* (Grand Rapids: Eerdmans, 2004). For a general summary of the key scholars in the debate, see G. Prentiss Waters, *Justification and the New Perspectives on Paul: A Review and Response* (Phillipsburg, NJ: P&R, 2004).

[8] Whether justification by faith is an accurate interpretation of δικαιοσύνη θεοῦ ("righteousness of God") is debated in New Testament scholarship. In addition, whether "faith in Christ" accurately represents the Greek phrase πίστεως Ἰησοῦ Χριστοῦ in Rom 3:22 is

Jesus' Death and Salvation

God's Righteousness and Justification. Paul's first reference to
the sacrificial nature of Jesus' death in Romans appears in 3:24–26.[9]
Paul states that Jesus' "redemption" (ἀπολυτρώσεως) is the foundation of justification by faith (3:21–22,24) for those who have sinned
(see 1:18–3:20; 3:23).[10] Paul states that all have sinned (3:23) and
that no one can be justified by the works of the law (3:20). God
must, therefore, take the initiative and act on behalf of Jews and
Gentiles in order to deliver them from sin (3:20,23–24), whose
power increased when the law entered into salvation-history (see
4:15; 5:13,20).[11] The "all" who have sinned in 3:23 refers to Jews
and Gentiles since Paul arduously argues in 1:18–3:20 that Jews
and Gentiles are guilty and stand condemned before God on account of their sin and the law's condemnation of both groups (see
2:1–3:20).

---

likewise debated in New Testament scholarship. Wright (*Saint Paul*, 119, 122, 124–26, 129)
has fervently argued that the phrase δικαιοσύνη θεοῦ in Rom 1:17 and 3:21–22 does not
refer to justification by faith, but to God's "covenantal faithfulness." According to Wright,
the phrase refers to "a quality in God" and to an "active power, which goes out, in expression of that faithfulness, to do what the covenant always promised: to deal with evil, to save
his people, and to do so with impartiality." One reason that Wright argues this view is he
believes that evidence in Jewish literature supports it (e.g., 4QMMT). For a discussion of
the various translation options and interpretations of δικαιοσύνη θεοῦ, see Moo, *Romans*,
70–90. For an important work that argues against the translation "faith in Christ" for the
phrase πίστεως Ἰησοῦ Χριστοῦ, see R. B. Hays, *The Faith of Jesus Christ: An Investigation of
the Narrative Substructure of Gal. 3:1–4:11* (3rd ed.; Grand Rapids: Eerdmans, 2002). Hays
specifically discusses the translation "faith in Christ" as it relates to Galatians. See in opposition to Hays, K. P. Yong's unpublished dissertation, "The Faith of Jesus Christ: An Analysis
of Paul's Use of Pistis Christou" (Ph.D. diss., The Southern Baptist Theological Seminary,
2003). Yong interacts with the major arguments and scholars throughout New Testament
scholarship prior to 2003 who have argued in favor of the subjective genitive.

[9]Stowers (*A Rereading of Romans*, 206–30) offered a notable rejection of a sacrificial
understanding of 3:24–26. He states that "Rom 3:24–25 has been the most important New
Testament text for interpreting the meaning of Jesus' death. Even today scholars and readers suppose that these verses describe a doctrine of sacrificial and vicarious substitutionary
atonement for human sinfulness. But this reading is like a house of cards, which collapses
when one card is removed. . . ." Stowers continues: "These considerations indicate that even
if there is some sacrificial language or allusion in 3:21–26—and that is far from certain—
one cannot move easily from such language to a conception of Jesus' death as a sacrifice of
vicarious atonement analogous to the sacrifice of animals in the Jewish cultus" (*A Rereading
of Romans*, 206).

[10]Several New Testament scholars have argued that Paul introduces a pre-Pauline, traditional formula in 3:24–26. For example; Käsemann, "Zum Verständis von Römer 3:24–26,"
150–54; Talbert, "A Non-Pauline Fragment," 287–96.

[11]For sin as a power, see T. R. Schreiner, *Paul: Apostle of God's Glory in Christ* (Downers
Grove, IL: InterVarsity Press, 2001), 127–50.

Romans 3:23 parallels Paul's previous statement in 3:22*b* in which he explained why the "righteousness of God" has been revealed apart from the law through faith in Jesus (see 3:21–22*a*): "for there is not a distinction." The distinction to which Paul refers must be the distinction between Jews and Gentiles since he has argued in 1:18–3:20 that both the Jews who received the law and instruct others by it (2:17–21) and the Gentiles who have the law written on their hearts (2:14–15) will perish if they do not obey the law (2:12–16). Neither Jews nor Gentiles merit justification before God apart from faith irrespective of their religious heritage (see 3:20); both groups are guilty and stand condemned before God because of their sin (2:1–3:20,23). Romans 3:22*b*–23, then, provides the reason the "righteousness of God," mentioned in 3:21–22*a* (see 1:17), has been revealed "through faith in Jesus to all who believe" (3:22): namely, Jews and Gentiles are guilty before God (see 1:18–3:20), and neither group is capable of meriting God's righteousness by works (3:20; see 9:30–10:21).

The meaning of δικαιοσύνη θεοῦ ("righteousness of God") in Rom 3:21–22 (see 1:17) has been intensely debated throughout the history of New Testament scholarship.[12] One reading of the phrase suggests that it refers to "the embodiment of the saving action of God in Christ, which recreates new life for believers as they face judgment."[13] A second reading concludes that the phrase refers to God's covenantal faithfulness.[14] A third reading influenced

---

[12] The debate has in part focused on whether the phrase refers to justification by faith or to God's covenantal faithfulness. If the phrase "righteousness of God" is interpreted to mean justification, two questions arise: is justification forensic (i.e., a legal declaration imparted by God, the righteous judge) or ethical (moral transformation accomplished through obedience to God)? My above interpretation ("justification by faith") of the Greek phrase δικαιοσύνη θεοῦ ("righteousness of God") in Rom 3:21–22 represents one of many views. For recent discussions of the phrase "righteousness of God" in Paul and for interaction with key voices in the debate, see B. J. Vickers, *Jesus' Blood and Righteousness* (Wheaton: Crossway, 2006); J. Piper, *Counted Righteous in Christ: Should We Abandon the Imputation of Christ's Righteousness?* (Wheaton: Crossway, 2002); idem, *The Future of Justification: A Response to N. T. Wright* (Wheaton: Crossway, 2007). For a recent work that challenges both old and new perspectives on the law and justification in Paul, see C. VanLandingham, *Judgment & Justification in Early Judaism and the Apostle Paul* (Peabody, MA: Hendrickson, 2006), 242–332.

[13] So P. Stuhlmacher, *Reconciliation, Law, and Righteousness: Essays in Biblical Theology* (Philadelphia: Fortress, 1986), 78. Similarly J. H. Roberts, "Righteousness in Romans with Special Reference to Romans 3:19–31," *Neot* 15 (1981): 18.

[14] So J. A. Ziesler, *The Meaning of Righteousness in Paul: A Linguistic and Theological Enquiry* (SNTSMS; Cambridge: Cambridge University Press, 1972), 160; Dunn, *Romans*, 1:40–42; Wright, *Saint Paul*, 104–05. D. Peterson ("Atonement in the New Testament," in *Where Wrath and Mercy Meet: Proclaiming the Atonement Today* [ed. D. Peterson; Carlisle,

by Martin Luther has argued that the phrase refers to a status before God and essentially means the same as the verb "to justify" (δικαιόω) in 3:24.[15] Fourth, recent exegesis suggests that Paul uses the phrase (and all δικ-words) "to embrace both the notions of (1) forgiveness, cleansing, and purification of past sins and (2) an emancipation from sin as a ruler over humanity."[16]

With the exception of the fourth position, some overlap is present in the preceding views. Nevertheless, the third view is preferred here for four reasons. First, in 3:24 Paul mentions the concept of justification with the participle δικαιούμενοι ("being justified"), a verbal form of δικαιοσύνη ("righteousness"). He connects this verbal form in 3:24 with the sinfulness of human beings in 3:23 and with the phrase "redemption in Christ Jesus" in 3:24.

Second, the phrase δικαιοσύνη θεοῦ ("righteousness of God") in 3:21–22 (see 1:17) and the word δικαιούμενοι ("being justified") in 3:24 refer to a change of status before God (i.e., "justification") since Paul connects the preceding δικ-words in Romans with the salvation that comes through the gospel by faith (1:16–17; 3:21–5:1; 9:30–10:21) and since he connects the phrase "righteousness of God" with the presence of God (3:20).

Third, the phrase "righteousness of God" occurs in a text in which Paul emphasizes that faith is the means through which one receives salvation through the gospel (see 1:16–17; 3:21–5:1; 9:30–10:21). Although scholars continue to debate vigorously whether the phrase πίστεως 'Ιησοῦ Χριστοῦ should be translated as "faith in Christ" or "faithfulness of Christ,"[17] its context in 3:22 best supports the translation "faith in Christ" since Paul's argument focuses on how the individual personally receives and participates in God's saving righteousness.[18] The emphasis on "faith

UK: Paternoster, 2001], 40) asserts that "righteousness of God" in Rom 3:21 refers to God's covenantal faithfulness. Nevertheless, he quickly clarifies that he affirms a judicial element in the phrase.

[15]So Cranfield, *Romans*, 1:98; Moo, *Romans*, 74–75. See also R. Bultmann, *The Theology of the New Testament* (trans. K. Grobel; Waco, TX: Baylor University Press, 2007), 270–85, esp. 279–80. Bultmann emphasizes the forensic eschatological element of justification and appears to interpret the phrase "righteousness of God" in Rom 1:17 and in 3:21–31 to convey the same idea as the verb "to justify" in 2:13 and 3:24.

[16]Van Landingham, *Judgment and Justification*, 242–332.

[17]Hays, *The Faith of Jesus Christ*, 119–62. See especially 156–60 where Hays specifically discusses Rom 3:21–26. He suggests that "Romans has always been more hospitable territory than Galatians for advocates of the faith of Jesus interpretation" (156).

[18]Seifrid ("Romans," 618) argues that πίστεως 'Ιησοῦ Χριστοῦ ("faith in/of Jesus Christ") is a genitive of source. Seifrid presupposes the "objective sense" since "it is in any case in

in Christ" as the means to receive God's saving righteousness also highlights the forensic element of this righteousness since Paul has argued in 1:18–3:20 that Jews and Gentiles stand condemned in God's presence on account of sin (2:1–16) and can be "justified" by faith on the basis of Jesus' blood (3:20–26; see LXX 1 Kgs 12:7)[19] and since Paul uses Abraham as the example par excellence that God's righteousness comes to the believer by faith (4:1–25; see Gal 2:16–3:9).[20]

Fourth, the word translated as "will be justified" in 3:20*b* is δικαιωθήσεται. The verb is a cognate of the same δικ-word that Paul uses in 3:24 as a participle in connection with the redemption provided through Jesus' death (3:24–26; see 3:27–5:1). Since this verb is connected to the phrase "in his [i.e., God's] presence" in 3:20, since the verb concludes the argument that both Jews and Gentiles are guilty before God (1:18–3:20), since Paul uses this verb in 5:9 to argue that justification in the present age guarantees

---

Paul's larger usage of faith." But Seifrid says that Paul's idea is larger than faith in Christ. Instead, "the faith of Jesus Christ (3:22) is the faith given through Jesus Christ." Paul does not, however, describe "a pattern of obedience in which we participate, but rather the source of faith: God gives us faith as a gift through the crucified and risen Christ and [through] the gospel that proclaims him" (brackets mine).

[19]Δικαιοσύνη ("righteousness") and δικαιόω ("to justify") are not always forensic in either biblical literature (e.g., δικαιοσύνη: LXX Gen 18:19; 19:19; 20:5; 20:13; 21:23; 24:27,49; Exod 15:13; 34:7; Lev 19:15; Deut 9:4–6; 33:19,21; Josh 24:14; Judg 5:11; 1 Kgs 2:10; 12:7; 26:23; 2 Kgs 8:15; 22:21,25; 1 Chr 18:14; 29:17; 2 Chr 6:23; 9:8; Pss 4:2,6; 5:9; 7:9,18; 9:5,9; 10:7; 14:2; 16:1,15; 17:21,25; Matt 3:15; Acts 10:35; 17:31; 24:25; Rom 6:16; 8:10; 2 Cor 6:7; 9:9–10; 11:15; Eph 4:24; 5:9; 6:14; Phil 1:11; 3:6; 1 Tim 6:11; 2 Tim 2:22; 3:16; 4:8; Titus 3:5; Heb 1:9; 5:13; ; 7:2; 11:7,33; 12:11; James 3:18; 1 Pet 2:24; 3:14; 2 Pet 1:1; 2:5,21; 3:13; 1 John 2:29; 3:7,10; Rev 19:11; 22:1; δικαιόω: Gen 38:26) or in extrabiblical literature (e.g., Tob 1:3; 2:14; 4:5–7; 12:8–9; 13:6; 14:6,11; 1 Macc 14:35; 4 Macc 1:4,6,18; 2:6; 5:24; Wis 1:1,15; 2:11; 5:6,18; 8:7; 9:3; 12:16; 14:7; Sir 16:22; 26:28; 44:10; 45:26; Pss Sol 1:2; 2:15; 8:6,24,25,26; 9:2–5; 14:2; 17:23,37; 1 Bar 1:15; 2:6,18; 4:13; 5:2,4,9). The verb δικαιόω ("to justify") primarily has a forensic meaning in the Old Testament (e.g., LXX Gen 44:16; Exod 23:7; Deut 25:1; 1 Kgs 8:32; Isa 1:7; 5:23; 43:9) and in extrabiblical literature (e.g., Sir 1:22; 7:3; 9:12; 10:29; 13:22; 23:11; 26:29; 31:5; 42:2; Pss Sol 8:26). When salvation, faith, and judgment are in view in the New Testament, the verb always carries a forensic meaning (Matt 12:37; Acts 13:38–39), especially in Paul (Rom 2:13; 3:4,20,24,26,28,30; 4:2,5; 5:1,9; 8:30,33; 1 Cor 4:4; 6:11; Gal 2:16–17; 3:8,11,24; 5:4; Titus 3:7; see James 2:21,25).

[20]With the exception of Paul's usage of δέ ("and") instead of καί ("and"), Paul's citation of Gen 15:6 in Rom 4:3 exactly follows the LXX: LXX Gen 15:6: καὶ ἐπίστευσεν Αβραμ τῷ θεῷ καὶ ἐλογίσθη αὐτῷ εἰς δικαιοσύνην ("and Abraham believed God and it was reckoned to him as righteousness."). Paul's citation: ἐπίστευσεν δὲ Ἀβρὰμ τῷ θεῷ καὶ ἐλογίσθη αὐτῷ εἰς δικαιοσύνην ("and Abraham believed God and it was reckoned to him as righteousness"). With the clause ἐλογίσθη αὐτῷ εἰς δικαιοσύνην ("and Abraham believed God and it was reckoned to him as righteousness"), the translators of LXX Gen 15:6 depart from the wording in the MT to emphasize that God counted Abraham's faith in him as the basis for his right standing before him. The MT of Gen 15:6 reads as follows: ויחשבה לו צדקה: ביהוה והאמן ("and he believed God and he reckoned it to him, i.e., righteousness.").

eschatological deliverance from God's wrath in the judgment, and since reconciliation through Jesus' death in 5:10 is closely connected to justification by Jesus' blood in 5:9, δικαιωθήσεται ("he will be justified") in 3:20 refers to a change of status before God. Hence, the phrase "righteousness of God" in 3:21–22 refers to God's saving righteousness,[21] and this saving righteousness includes a change of status before God.[22]

Redemption. Paul connects justification by faith in 3:21–22 and in 3:24 with one social term (ἀπολύτρωσις ["redemption," 3:24]) and with two sacrificial terms (ἱλαστήριον ["sacrifice of atonement," 3:25] and αἷμα ["blood," 3:25]). "Redemption" (ἀπολύτρωσις) is an economic term.[23] The term appears here for the first time in Romans.[24] Its occurrence at this juncture in Paul's argument suggests that in addition to faith in Christ, Jesus' redemption is the means through which God justifies all who have sinned (3:21–24, esp. 3:23–24). Since Paul uses "redemption" (ἀπολύτρωσις) in 3:24 in the context of blood (3:25) and since the redemption that Jesus has accomplished for Jews and Gentiles by his blood was the means through which God provided justification for them (see 3:21–22,24), "redemption" likely suggests in 3:24 that Jesus' death was some sort of sacrificial payment that was offered to purchase justification for all who have sinned (3:23–24).[25] As such, Jesus' death

---

[21] I understand the phrase "righteousness of God" to include both God's saving and judging righteousness, but the emphasis in 3:21–22 is his saving righteousness.

[22] Throughout his book, Vickers (*Jesus' Blood*, esp. 23–70) discusses the key trajectories in the discussion of Paul's theology of justification. Vickers specifically argues that imputation is a significant component to Paul's theology of justification.

[23] So Finlan, *Atonement Metaphors*, 164–69.

[24] The term occurs elsewhere in the New Testament in Luke 21:28; Rom 8:23; 1 Cor 1:30; Eph 1:7,14; 4:30; Col 1:14; Heb 9:15, and 11:35. Paul only connects ἀπολύτρωσις ("redemption") with blood in Rom 3:24 and Eph 1:7. Paul also, however, suggests elsewhere that Jesus' death was a ransom with the words ἀγοράζω ("to buy," 1 Cor 6:20; 7:23), ἐξαγοράζω ("to redeem," Gal 3:13; see 4:5; 5:16; Col 4:5), and λυτρόω ("to redeem," Titus 2:14).

[25] A. Deissmann (*Light from the Ancient East* [New York: Harper, 1927], 319–30) argued that Paul's background for redemption language was Greco-Roman and that slaves in the Greco-Roman world could be liberated by the paying or depositing of money in the sanctuary of Apollos's shrine. By such a transaction, the slaves would become the property of Apollos. Scholars subsequent to Deissman questioned his thesis. They argued instead that Paul's background was primarily, even if not exclusively, Jewish. See L. Morris, *The Apostolic Preaching of the Cross* (3rd ed.; Grand Rapids: Eerdmans, 1965), 11–64, esp. 9–26; idem, "Redemption," in *Dictionary of Paul and His Letters* (ed. G. F. Hawthorne, R. P. Martin, and D. G. Reid; Downers Grove, IL: InterVarsity Press, 1993), 784–86. I have recently argued that Paul's background is martyrological (see Williams, *Maccabean Martyr Traditions*, 60). Paul's assertion that Jesus' death accomplished ἀπολύτρωσις ("redemption") for Jews and Gentiles closely resembles the author's descriptions of the deaths of the Jewish martyrs in

was a ransom since it liberated those who were otherwise guilty before God (see 1:18–3:24).[26]

Some scholars have rejected the notion that Jesus' death was a ransom because they reject the ransom theory of the atonement.[27] Nevertheless, notwithstanding the error of the ransom theory, "redemption" (ἀπολύτρωσις) in 3:24 suggests that Jesus' death was a ransom since it paid the necessary price for justification (3:24–25).[28] Paul does not state to whom the ransom was paid in 3:24, but he expressly states in 3:25 that God is the author of the redemption and that the price by which both redemption and justification were accomplished for Jews and Gentiles was Jesus' blood (see 3:24–25).[29]

The participle "being justified" (δικαιούμενοι) in Rom 3:24 grammatically modifies either one or both of the clauses ("all have sinned," "all have fallen short of God's glory") in Rom 3:23. It likely modifies both clauses since the conjunction καί ("and") links the two clauses and since πάντες ("all") is the subject of both clauses in 3:23. Paul highlights, then, in Rom 3:23–24 "the total religious impotence of humanity": both Jews and Gentiles have sinned and stand condemned before God (1:18–3:20, 3:23), and neither group can be justified by keeping the law (3:20).[30]

---

4 Macc 6:29*b* and 17:21. In both texts, the author places the term ἀντίψυχον ("ransom"), a synonym for Paul's ἀπολύτρωσις ("redemption"), on the lips of Eleazar (a Jewish martyr) as he prayed that God would receive his death as a sufficient payment for Israel's sin (see 4 Macc 6:28–29; 17:21–22).

[26] Seifrid ("Romans," 619) does not discount the idea of ransom in Rom 3:24, but he places the accent on liberation.

[27] For example, see D. Hill, *Greek Words and Hebrew Meanings: Studies in the Semantics of Soteriological Terms* (SNTS 5; Cambridge: Cambridge University Press, 1967), 49–81. Hill primarily rejects the idea of ransom in Rom 3:24 on lexical grounds. For an explanation of the ransom theory, see M. J. Erickson, *Christian Theology* (2nd ed.; Grand Rapids: Baker, 1998), 810–13.

[28] See B. B. Warfield, "The New Testament Terminology of Redemption," in *Bible Doctrines: The Works of Benjamin B. Warfield* (Grand Rapids: Baker 2003), 2:327–98; Morris, *Apostolic Preaching*, 11–64, esp. 9–26; Moo, *Romans*, 229; Finlan, *Atonement Metaphors*, 164–69. Against the idea of ransom, see F. R. Swallow, "Redemption in St. Paul," *Sacrament* 10 (1958): 21–27; Hill, *Greek Words*, 49–81.

[29] See Peterson, "Atonement," 41. Hill (*Greek Words*, 73), however, contests that the presence of blood supports a ransom idea even when the term occurs in a context with sacrificial ideas since the preposition διά ("through") + the genitive in Classical, Koine, or LXX Greek never expresses cost.

[30] For the above quotation, see Moo, *Romans*, 227. Moo agrees with Cranfield's analysis (that the participial clause in 3:24 is dependent on πάντες ["all"] in 3:23 and that it indicates the other side of what Paul has indicated in 3:23 [namely, the universal sinfulness of Jews and Gentiles]). See Cranfield, *Romans*, 1:205. Nevertheless, Moo emphasizes that "Paul's stress on the gift character of justification in v. 24 illuminates from the positive side the 'lack of distinction' in God's dealings (vv. 22–23b) even as it continues and explains the theme

Once more, Rom 3:24 provides further evidence that Jesus' death was a ransom, for Paul states that justification was accomplished "through the redemption which is in Christ Jesus."[31] The theme of Jesus' death underlies 3:24 since Paul states that God offered Jesus as a ἱλαστήριον ("sacrifice of atonement") by his blood in 3:25. Paul uses blood in 5:9 as a metonymy for Jesus' death in 5:8 (see 1 Cor 10:16; 11:25,27; Eph 1:7; 2:13; Col 1:2; LXX Leviticus 1–17). By combining the δικ-words (3:21–22,24) with "redemption" (3:24) and Jesus' death (3:25), Paul indicates the priceless foundation upon which the verdict of justification is pronounced and the basis upon which the status of Jews and Gentiles changes before God.[32]

Hilastērion. The sacrificial nature of Jesus' death is further evident in 3:25–26.[33] The terms ἱλαστήριον ("sacrifice of atonement"), "blood," "righteousness," and "sin" are especially important for the above premise. One of the difficulties of interpreting 3:25–26 is determining the exact meaning of ἱλαστήριον in 3:25.[34] Since Rom

---

of 'righteousness by faith' from v. 22a" and that the "all" who are justified do not refer to everybody (i.e., universality), but refers to anybody (particularity).

[31] The Greek phrase in 3:24 διά τῆς ἀπολυτρώσεως τῆς ἐν Χριστῷ Ἰησοῦ ("through the redemption in/by Christ") accentuates that Jesus is the one in whom and the means by which humanity's redemption is possible.

[32] So Moo, *Romans*, 229.

[33] The goal here is not to offer an exhaustive exegesis of the text, but rather to discuss the various issues in this text that relate to my thesis for this chapter. For detailed discussions, see Cranfield, *Romans*, 1:209–18; Moo, *Romans*, 230–43; Schreiner, *Romans*, 191–99; Lyonnet, "Le sens de πάρεσις en Rom 3:25," 40–61; Meyer, "The Pre-Pauline Formula in Rom 3:25–26a," 198–208; B. M. Metzger, *A Textual Commentary on the Greek New Testament* (2nd ed.; Stuttgart: Deutsche Bibelgesellschaft, 1994), 449; Finlan, *Atonement Metaphors*, 123–62.

[34] The meaning of ἱλαστήριον has been fiercely debated in New Testament scholarship. For example, see A. Deissmann, *Bible Studies* (trans. A. Greive; Edinburgh: T&T Clark, 1895), 124–35; H. Rashdall, *The Idea of Atonement in Christian Theology* (London: Macmillan,) 130–32; T. W. Hanson, "ἱλαστήριον," *JTS* 46 (1945), 1–10; Dodd, *The Bible and the Greeks*, 82–95; Nicole, "C. H. Dodd and the Doctrine of Propitiation," 117–57; L. Morris, "The Meaning of ΗΙΛΑΣΤΗΡΙΟΝ in Romans 3:25," *NTS* 18 (1971–1972): 3–43; idem, *The Apostolic Preaching*, 144–213; Hill, *Greek Words*, 23–48; K. Wengst, *Christologische Formeln und Lieder des Urchristentums* (SNT 7; Gütersloh: Mohn, 1972); P. Stuhlmacher, "Zur neueren Exegese von Römer 3:24–26," in *Versöhnung, Gesetz, und Gerechtigkeit* (ed. E. Ellis and E. Grässer; Göttingen: Vandenhoeck & Ruprecht, 1981), 117–35; idem, *Paul's Letter to the Romans: A Commentary* (trans. S. J. Hafemann; Louisville: Westminster/John Knox, 1994), 58–61; W. Sanday and A. C. Headlam, *The Epistle to the Romans* (ICC; 5th ed.; London: T&T Clark, 1980), 87–88, 91–94; N. S. L. Fryer, "The Meaning and Translation of Hilastērion in Romans 3:25," *EvQ* 59 (1987), 99–116; Campbell, *Rhetoric*, 107–13; W. Kraus, *Der Tod Jesu als Heiligtumsweihe: Eine Untersuchung zum Umfelt der Sühnevorstellung in Römer 3:25–26a* (WMANT 66; Neukirchener-Vluyn: Neukirchener Verlag, 1991); J. W. Van Henten, "The Tradition-Historical Background of Romans 3:25: A Search for Pagan and Jewish Parallels," in *From Jesus to John: Essays on Jesus and New Testament Christology in Honour of Marinus De Jonge* (JSNTSup 84; ed. M. C. de Boer; Sheffield: JSOT Press, 1993), 101–28; S. K. Stowers, *A Rereading of Romans: Justice, Jews, and Gentiles* (New Haven: Yale

3:25–26 is one complex relative clause in the Greek text, the prepositional phrases "through faith,"[35] "in his blood,"[36] "for the demonstration of his righteousness,"[37] "because of the passing over of the previously committed sins,"[38] "in the forbearance of God,"[39] and "in the present time,"[40] add to the complexity of the verses.

While there is no scholarly consensus as to how one should translate ἱλαστήριον in 3:25 and while there are nuanced categories within the general translation options,[41] suggested meanings are mercy seat,[42] propitiation,[43] and expiation.[44] Recent exegesis

University Press, 1994), 206–13; Moo, *Romans*, 230–40; Schreiner, *Romans*, 164–66; K. Haacker, *Der Brief des Paulus an die Römer* (THKNT 7; Leipzig: Evangelische Verlagsanstalt, 1999), 90–92; Williams, *Jesus' Death*, 39–41, 165–202, 233–54; C. H. Talbert, *Romans* (Macon: Smyth & Helwys, 2002), 110–15; D. S. Ben Ezra, *The Impact of Yom Kippur on Early Christianity* (WUNT 163; Tübingen: Mohr Siebeck, 2003), 198–202; D. P. Bailey, "Jesus as the Mercy Seat: The Semantics and Theology of Paul's Use of Hilastērion in Romans 3:25" (Ph.D. diss., Cambridge University Press, 1999); T. Knöppler, *Sühne im Neuen Testament* (WMANT 88; Neukirchener-Vluyn: Neukirchener Verlag, 2001), 112–17; N. T. Wright, *The Letter to the Romans* (NIBC; Nashville: Abingdon, 2002), 272–79; T. Holland, *Contours of Pauline Theology: A Radical New Survey of the Influences on Paul's Biblical Writings* (Scotland, UK: Mentor, 2004), 157–82; Finlan, *Atonement Metaphors*, 123–62; Brondos, *Paul on the Cross*, 126–32; Seifrid, "Romans," 618–21.

[35] διὰ τῆς πίστεως (3:25).

[36] ἐν τῷ αὐτοῦ αἵματι (3:25).

[37] εἰς ἔνδειξιν τῆς δικαιοσύνης αὐτοῦ (3:25) and πρὸς τὴν ἔνδειξιν τῆς δικαιοσύνης αὐτοῦ (3:26).

[38] διὰ τὴν πάρεσιν τῶν προγεγονότων ἁμαρτημάτων (3:25).

[39] ἐν τῇ ἀνοχῇ τοῦ θεοῦ (3:26).

[40] ἐν τῷ νῦν καιρῷ (3:26).

[41] See Finlan, *Atonement Metaphors*, 141–42.

[42] Origen, *Commentary on the Epistle to the Romans: Books 1–5* (trans. Thomas P. Scheck; Washington, DC: The Catholic University of America Press, 2001), 216–25; J. Calvin, *The Epistles of Paul the Apostle to the Romans and to the Thessalonians* (ed. D. W. Torrance and T. F. Torrance; trans. R. MacKenzie; Grand Rapids: Eerdmans, 1960), 75; K. Barth, *The Epistle to the Romans* (trans. E. C. Hoskyns; London: Oxford University Press, 1933), 104–5; Manson, "ἱλαστριον," 1–10; A. Nygren, *Commentary on Romans* (trans. C. C. Rasmussen; Philadelphia: Muhlenberg Press, 1949), 156–62; S. Lyonnet, "De notione expiationis," *VD* 37 (1959) 336–52; F. F. Bruce, *The Epistle of Paul to the Romans* (TNTC; Grand Rapids: Eerdmans, 1963), 104–7; W. Swain, "For Our Sins: The Image of Sacrifice in the Thought of the Apostle Paul," *Interpretation* 17 (1963): 131–39; Lyonnet and Sabourin, *Sin*, 157–66; U. Wilckens, *Der Brief an die Römer*, Teilband 1: Römer 1–5 (EKKNT 6/1; Zürich: Benziger/Neukirchener-Vluyn: Neukirchener Verlag, 1980), 191–92; E. Käsemann, *Commentary on Romans* (trans. G. Bromiley; Grand Rapids: Eerdmans, 1980), 97, 350–54; Meyer, "The Pre-Pauline Formula," 198–208; A. J. Hultgren, *Paul's Gospel and Mission: The Outlook from His Letter to the Romans* (Philadelphia: Fortress, 1985), 59–60; A. Schlatter, *Romans: The Righteousness of God* (trans. S. S. Schatzmann; Peabody, MA: Hendrickson, 1995), 99; B. Byrne, *Romans* (SP 6; Collegeville, MN: Liturgical Press, 1996), 132–33; D. J. Williams, *Paul's Metaphors: Their Context and Character* (Peabody, MA: Hendrickson, 1999), 247, 253 n. 19; B. Janowski, *Sühne als Heilsgeschehen* (2nd ed.; WMANT 55; Neukirchener-Vluyn: Neukirchener Verlag, 2000); Seifrid, "Romans," 618–19.

[43] Morris, "The Meaning of ΗΙΛΑΣΤΗΡΙΟΝ" 3–43; Nicole, "C. H. Dodd," 117–57; H Ridderbos, *Paul: An Outline of His Theology* (trans. J. R. De Witt; paperback edition; Grand Rapids: Eerdmans, 1997), 186.

[44] Dodd, *The Bible and the Greeks*, 82–95; idem, *Romans* (MNTC; New York: Harper and Brothers, 1932), 20–24, 77.

has argued that Paul's use of the term in 3:25 has nothing to do with expiation or propitiation, but rather it speaks of reconciliation.[45] Paul simply states that Jesus' death provided access to God.[46] Another recent exegesis proposes that Paul uses ἱλαστήριον to state that Jesus was a "revelatory means of atonement."[47] Once more, other scholars have interpreted ἱλαστήριον in 3:25 as either alluding to the Yom Kippur ritual (but does not refer to the mercy seat)[48] or showing that Maccabean martyr traditions (see 4 Macc 17:21–22) influenced Paul.[49]

That ἱλαστήριον only occurs twice in the New Testament (see Rom 3:25 and Heb 9:5) increases the interpretive complexity of the term.[50] The term does, however, occur in several places in the LXX in cultic contexts (see Exod 25:17–22; Lev 16:12–19).[51] In such contexts, ἱλαστήριον is often translated from the Hebrew root כפר ("to atone"), which typically conveys the idea of atoning sacrifice in the Old Testament (see MT Lev 1:4; 4:19–20,26,31,35; 5:6,10,13,18).[52] The term ἱλαστήριον often refers to the mercy seat or the lid of the ark in the LXX (see Exod 25:17–22; Lev 16:12–19). Yahweh

[45] Jewett, *Romans*, 286.

[46] Ibid.

[47] J. D. K. Ekem, "A Dialogical Exegesis of Romans 3:25a," *JSNT* 30 (2007): 75–93. Ekem ("Dialogical Exegesis," 80) asserts, though, that expiation is the more likely reading of ἱλαστήριον in Rom 3:25.

[48] Ben Ezra, *Yom Kippur*, 198–202.

[49] Van Henten, "The Tradition-Historical Background," 101–28; (most recently) J. J. Williams, *Maccabean Martyr Traditions in Paul's Theology of Atonement: Did Martyr Theology Shape Paul's Conception of Jesus' Death?* (Eugene, OR: Wipf & Stock, 2010).

[50] A similar word (ἱλασμός "propitiation") appears in the LXX (see Lev 25:9; Num 5:8; Ps 129:4; Ezek 44; 27; 2 Macc 3:33) and in the New Testament (see 1 John 2:2; 4:10).

[51] Dunn, *Romans*, 1:180.

[52] J. H. Kurtz (*Offerings, Sacrifices, and Worship in the Old Testament* [trans. James Martin; 2nd ed.; Peabody, MA: Hendrickson, 2000], 68–75, esp. 67–68; first published in 1863 by T&T Clark) argued that כפר refers only to expiation even when the verb takes a human as its object since the verb is connected to a human's guilt and iniquity. In support of expiation, I must say that after a brief investigation of both the Hebrew root כפר and the LXX's translation of this root, I discovered that only one clear occurrence exists in the LXX in which ἐξιλάσκομαι ("I atone") without question means to propitiate (see Gen 32:21). Nevertheless, this occurrence is not cultic, and God is not the object of the verb. The Hebrew root in the MT and its Greek translation in the LXX refer to some sort of cleansing in every occasion, either to the cleansing of sin or to the cleansing of something else (see MT and LXX Exod 30:10,15–16; 32:30; Lev 1:4; 4:20,26,31,35; 5:6,10,13,16,18,26; 6:23; 7:7; 8:15,36; 9:7; 10:17; 12:7–8; 14:18–21,29,31,53; 15:15,30; 16:6,10–11,16–17,20,24,27,30,32–34; 17:11; 19:22; Num 5:8; 6:11; 8:12,19,21; 15:25,28; 17:12; 28:22,30). Nevertheless, that the above terms emphasize expiation does not extinguish propitiatory ideas from them since the narratives within which and around which כפר ("to atone") and its Greek translation occur often imply propitiation since God would judge those who disobeyed the stipulations of the covenant (see Lev 9:1–16:29). For a brief discussion of the preceding point, especially as it pertains to Lev 9:1–16:29, see Seifrid, "Romans," 620.

commanded Israel to put the ἱλαστήριον above the ark of the covenant in the holy of holies, the place where only the high priest could enter (Exod 25:17–20; 37:6). The high priest would sprinkle blood over the ἱλαστήριον to provide cleansing for the sin and impurities of the people (Exod 25:18–22; 31:7; 35:12; 37:68; Lev 16:14–15), and Yahweh appeared over the ἱλαστήριον to show his acceptance of the offering of blood (Exod 25:22; Lev 16:2; Num 7:89).

Unlike Paul, the author of Hebrews refers to the mercy seat with ἱλαστήριον in Heb 9:5, for he contrasts the earthly tabernacle that the priest entered in the Mosaic covenant with the heavenly tabernacle that Christ entered in the new covenant (see Heb 9:1–10:18). The apocryphal book of 4 Maccabees is the only other place in any extant literature in which ἱλαστήριον refers to the death of a human in a context in which that human is said to deal with sin.[53] Fourth Maccabees 17:22 suggests that the Jewish martyrs of the Maccabean revolt voluntarily died as sacrifices of atonement for Israel in order to provide salvation for the nation and that the martyrs died a propitiatory death (ἱλαστηρίου τοῦ θανάτου) to atone the nation's sins (see 6:28–29; 17:21–22).[54]

Since ἱλαστήριον never refers to a human's death outside of 4 Macc 17:22 and Rom 3:25 and since ἱλαστήριον occurs in Old Testament cultic contexts, interpreters can plausibly affirm at least three things about the term: (1) it alludes to the Yom Kippur ritual (see LXX Lev 16:14–16); (2) its presence suggests that Jesus' death was an atoning sacrifice, and (3) it suggests that Paul could have fused both the Old Testament's cultic ideas and the ideas of martyr theology to present Jesus' death as an atoning sacrifice for sin in Rom 3:25.[55] The preceding suggestions have the advantage of acknowledging that Paul could have borrowed from two different streams of tradition (i.e., Old Testament and martyrological) to present Jesus' death as a sacrifice of atonement for sin since both traditions speak of sacrificial atonement for sin and since martyr traditions provide the precedent of humans dying as atoning sacrifices for Israel's sin.[56] Paul, thus, conjoins the soteriological

---

[53] So also van Henten, "Tradition-Historical Background," 101–28.

[54] Scholars debate the above reading of the martyrs' deaths in 4 Maccabees. For a discussion of the positions, see chaps. 1 and 2 in Williams, *Maccabean Martyr Traditions*.

[55] See van Henten, "Tradition-Historical Background," 101–28; Williams, *Maccabean Martyr Traditions*.

[56] Against Stowers, *A Rereading of Romans*, 206–30.

vocabulary in Rom 3:21–22 and in 3:24 with cultic and martyrological vocabulary in 3:25 to present Jesus' death as God's sacrifice of atonement that justifies by faith all who have sinned.[57]

Jesus' Death and God's Wrath. As an atoning sacrifice, Jesus' death was penal.[58] The penal nature of Jesus' death is supported by Rom 3:25–26, where Paul's statements indicate that Jesus' death provided both an expiation (provided cleansing) and a propitiation (satisfied God's wrath). James D. G. Dunn has argued that Paul presents Jesus' death as an atoning sacrifice in 3:25, but that Paul does not suggest that Jesus' death was a propitiatory substitute.[59] Instead, Dunn suggests that "substitution shares the defects of propitiation as a description of Jesus' death."[60] According to Dunn, propitiation "still tends to conjure up pagan ideas of Jesus' standing in man's place and pleading with an angry God."[61] Nevertheless, in his critique of propitiation, Dunn has not adequately

---

[57] Against Stowers, *A Rereading of Romans*, 202–26, esp. 210–11; C. H. Talbert, *Romans* (Macon: Smyth & Helwys, 2002), 110–15. Talbert argued that ἱλαστήριον in Rom 3:25 does not refer to Jesus' death as an atoning sacrifice for sin, for Paul does not present Jesus' death as such in his other letters. Even if Talbert were correct (but I do not think that he is [see Gal 1:4; 3:10–13]), to say that since Paul did not present Jesus' death as a sacrifice of atonement for sin in his other letters, he therefore did not believe that Jesus' death was an atoning sacrifice for sin in Rom 3:25 ignores the situational and contextual purposes of Paul's letters. Talbert's view also assumes that the absence of atonement language in Paul is equivalent to unimportance. An absence of atonement language in Paul's other letters would not preclude Paul from presenting Jesus' death as a sacrifice of atonement for sin in Rom 3:25 since Paul addressed different situations in his letter, not all of which required a sacrificial presentation of Jesus' death. That Paul presents Jesus' death as an atoning sacrifice for sin in 3:25 is likely since he refers to Jesus' death as the basis of salvation and as the basis of a right relationship with God (3:21–24), since he states that God offered Jesus as a ἱλαστήριον through blood (3:25), since ἱλαστήριον occurs *only* in two cultic contexts in which the author applies it to the death of a human for the soteriological benefits of others (4 Macc 17:21–22 and Rom 3:25; see 4 Macc 6:28–29), and since ἱλαστήριον occurs often in the LXX in cultic contexts in reference to atonement and/or purification from sin (see Lev 16).

[58] Penal substitution is vigorously contested in current scholarship as proponents for and against penal substitution respond to one another. For example, Hooker, "Interchange in Christ," 349–61; idem, "Interchange and Atonement," *BJRL* 60 (1978): 462–81; Packer, "What Did the Cross Achieve? The Logic of Penal Substitution," 3–45; Travis, *Christ and the Judgment of God*; Stott, *The Cross of Christ*; Green and Baker, *Rediscovering the Scandal of the Cross*; Tidball, *The Message of the Cross*, 188–99; Hill and James, eds., *The Glory of the Atonement*; Beilby and Eddy, eds., *The Nature of the Atonement*; G. J. Williams, "Penal Substitution: A Response to Recent Criticisms," *JETS* 50 (2007): 71–86; Jeffery, Ovey, and Sach, *Pierced for Our Transgressions*; Jersak and Hardin, eds., *Stricken by God?*; Marshall, *Aspects of the Atonement*; Tidball et al., *Atonement*; Williams, "Penal Substitution," 73–81.

[59] See J. D. G. Dunn, "Paul's Understanding of the Death of Jesus as Sacrifice," in *Sacrifice and Redemption: Durham Essays in Theology* (ed. S. W. Sykes; Cambridge: Cambridge University Press, 1991), 35–56; idem, *Romans*, 1:171.

[60] Ibid., "Paul's Understanding," 35–56.

[61] Ibid.

demonstrated why Paul would present Jesus as a sacrifice of atonement for sin, but not as a propitiatory substitute for sin in 3:24–26 when, in fact, Paul states that God set forth Jesus as a ἱλαστήριον "for the demonstration of his righteousness" and "because of the previously committed sins" (Rom 3:25–26).[62]

C. H. Dodd rejected the idea that Jesus' death propitiated God's wrath because he dismissed the belief that God's wrath is personal.[63] Instead, he argued for the *immanentist* view of God's punishment: the effects of sin are simply the outworking of sin.[64] Similarly, in a recent essay, Brad Jersak asserts that Jesus' death did not satisfy God's wrath, but simply manifested God's love and Jesus' victory over violence.[65] If, however, Paul does not present Jesus' death as propitiating God's wrath in 3:25–26, then penal substitutionary atonement should also be rejected here since this text suggests that God dealt with sin by judging it in Jesus' death.[66]

Certainly, Rom 3:25–26 and other verses in the Pauline corpus emphasize the expiatory nature of Jesus' death since Paul states that Jesus' blood provides forgiveness and cleansing of sin (see Rom 4:7–8; 11:27; 1 Cor 15:3; 2 Cor 5:21; Gal 1:4; Eph 1:7; 2:13; 5:26; Col 1:14; Titus 2:14). The propitiatory nature of Jesus' death is likewise evident in 3:25–26 (see Rom 1:18–3:20; 5:8–9) and appears to be the emphasis in these verses.[67] Both the immediate context of 3:25–26 and the larger context of Romans 1–5 support the propitiatory nature of Jesus' death.

---

[62] In his Romans commentary (*Romans*, 1:171–72), Dunn affirms some sort of propitiatory function of Jesus' death. Dunn wrote his commentary before his above essay about Jesus' death.

[63] C. H. Dodd, *The Epistle of Paul to the Romans* (MNTC; New York: Harper and Brothers, 1932), 48, 50; idem, *Bible and the Greeks*, 82–95. Dodd also rejected propitiation on both lexical and theological grounds. Regarding God's wrath in Romans, compare the discussions and note the differences between Dodd and T. Gorringe, *God's Just Vengeance* (Cambridge: Cambridge University Press, 1996), 72; A. T. Lincoln, "From Wrath to Justification," in *Pauline Theology: Romans* (ed. D. M. Hay and E. E. Johnson; Atlanta: SBL, 2002), 3:156; S. J. Gathercole, "Justified by Faith, Justified by His Blood: The Evidence of Romans 3:21–4:25," in *Justification and Variegated Nomism: A Fresh Appraisal of Paul and Second Temple Judaism—The Paradoxes of Paul* (ed. D. A. Carson, P. T. O'Brien, and M. A. Seifrid; Tübingen: Mohr, 2004), 2:168; Williams, "Penal Substitution," 73–81.

[64] Dodd, *Romans*, 48, 50.

[65] Jersak, "Nonviolent Identification," 18–53.

[66] Recently Marshall (*Aspects of the Atonement*, 52–67) speaks negatively of recent presentations of propitiation although he affirmed penal substitution. He suggests that some recent explanations of propitiation do not always accurately represent the biblical presentation of propitiation.

[67] So Williams, "Penal Substitution," 73–81.

First, "righteousness" in 3:25b–26b suggests that Jesus' death was a propitiatory death, for Paul states that God set forth Jesus as a ἱλαστήριον ("sacrifice of atonement") "for the demonstration of his [i.e., *God's*] righteousness because of the previously committed sins" (emphasis mine).[68] The righteousness to which Paul refers here pertains at least to God's judging righteousness since he connects Jesus' death and God's righteousness with the passing over of "previously committed sins" in 3:25–26. Debate continues regarding the meaning of the "previously committed sins" in 3:25.[69] In context, these sins refer at least to the sins committed during the Mosaic covenant since Paul has argued in 1:18–3:20 that the law condemns its transgressors (see Rom 4:15; 5:20). Thus, when Paul states that God set forth Jesus as a ἱλαστήριον "for the demonstration of his righteousness because of the passing over of the previously committed sins" (Rom 3:25; see 3:26), he means that God set forth Jesus to demonstrate his righteous judgment against the previously committed sins that were left unpunished during the Mosaic covenant. This judgment suggests that Jesus' death paid the penalty for the unpunished sins.

Second, although Paul first states in 1:18 that the "wrath of God" currently abides upon all who reject the gospel in that God has given unbelievers over to commit various sins (see Rom 1:18–32), he likewise states in 2:5 that Jews and Gentiles will store up wrath for themselves because of their disobedience to God. The wrath to which Paul refers in 2:5 is eschatological and personal since he states that God *will* judge all who reject the truth of the gospel, since Paul refers to God's "kindness" in 2:4, and since he contrasts God's "kindness" with God's "righteous revelation" and "judgment" in 2:5.

Third, Paul refers to God's future judgment of Jews and Gentiles in accordance to their works in 2:6–11. He states that those who obey the truth *will* receive "eternal life" (Rom 2:7), but those who disobey the truth *will* receive "wrath," "anger," "affliction," and "distress" (Rom 2:7–8). The context suggests that God *will* personally render this distress upon the disobedient.[70]

---

[68] For an alternative translation, see W. G. Kümmel, "Paresis and Endeixis: A Contribution to the Understanding of the Pauline Doctrine of Justification," *JTC* 3 (1967): 1–13.

[69] E.g., Kraus, *Der Tod Jesu*, 95–112; Jewett, *Romans*, 289–90.

[70] Against A. T. Hanson, *The Wrath of the Lamb* (London: SPCK, 1957).

Fourth, Paul states in 3:5 that the "unrighteousness" of men demonstrates the "righteousness" of God in that God will unleash wrath upon those who reject him and suppress his truth. Paul's question in 3:5 supports this interpretation: "God, who brings wrath, is not unrighteous—is he?" Paul answers this question in 3:6a with an emphatic "No!"[71] The wrath to which Paul refers is not the present, abiding wrath that currently resides upon all who suppress the truth (1:18–32) (contra Dodd), but it is God's eschatological wrath that he will unleash on the last day upon all who suppress the truth, for Paul follows his statements in 3:5 about God's wrath with a question pertaining to God's future judgment of the world in 3:6b.

Fifth, Paul again refers in 5:9–10 to God's eschatological wrath that he will personally bestow upon those who suppress the truth and reject the gospel. Here he explicitly states that Jesus' blood and resurrection serve as the means through which God will save Jews and Gentiles from his wrath and reconcile them to himself. That Jesus' death will deliver Jews and Gentiles from God's wrath suggests that they would be the objects of his personal judgment apart from Jesus' blood and resurrection, for Paul states that Jews and Gentiles will be saved from God's wrath through Jesus' blood and life in vv. 9–10. Romans 3:21–26 is the nexus of 1:18–3:20 and 4:1–5:11.

Sixth, the verb "set forth" (προεθετό) in 3:25 supports the propitiatory nature of Jesus' death in 3:24–26 since Paul connects this verb in 3:25 with God's demonstrating of his righteousness in 3:25–26 and since he uses this verb to state that God set forth Jesus as a ἱλαστήριον by means of his blood.[72] The verb means "to set forth" or "to present" in 3:25, because the verb occurs in this context in which God manifests his righteousness against sin through Jesus' death (see 1:17; 3:21–22).[73] Paul's repetition of "demonstration" in 3:25–26 and his reference to God's "righteousness," "glory," "sin," "blood," ἱλαστήριον, and God's "justice" in 3:23–26 suggest that

---

[71] Μὴ γένοιτο ("May it never be!").

[72] Fryer ("The Meaning and Translation of Hilastērion," 98–116, esp. 106) suggests that Paul does not emphasize the means of atonement in Rom 3:25, but the place.

[73] Cranfield (*Romans*, 1:208–09) argued that προτίθεμαι (προέθετο in 3:25) means "to purpose" or "to plan" in 3:25 (see 1:13; 8:28; 9:11) since Paul uses the term to refer to his "intention" or "plan" to visit Rome in 1:13 and since he uses the noun πρόθεσις ("purpose") in 8:28 and 9:11.

the public spectacle of Jesus' death revealed that God "set forth" Jesus as a propitiatory offering for sin.

The public nature of Jesus' death also supports the sacrificial nature of his death in 3:25 since the verb "to set forth" alludes by contrast to the Yom Kippur ritual when the priest sprinkled/presented/set forth blood on the mercy seat in the holy of holies (see Leviticus 16) when Yahweh instructed Aaron to atone for Aaron's sins and for the sins of the people by sprinkling the blood of the slaughtered animals on the mercy seat (see Lev 16:14–16).[74] The verb "to set forth" further supports the sacrificial nature of Jesus' death in that it possibly alludes to Exod 24:5–8 in which Moses publicly presents/sets forth the blood of an animal by publicly sprinkling it on Israel to institute the Mosaic covenant.[75] Since the animals' blood was sprinkled on the mercy seat, on the altar as atonement for sin, and on the people (see Leviticus 16; Exodus 24), "blood" in Rom 3:25 adds another OT sacrificial element to Rom 3:25, and it likewise affirms the sacrificial nature of Jesus' death since it refers to Jesus' blood released in death for sin (see Exod 24:4–8; Lev 16:14–15; Rom 5:9).[76] Paul suggests, therefore, in 3:25–26 that Jesus' death was a penal sacrifice for sin and that his death is the foundation of deliverance from God's wrath for Jews and Gentiles.[77] As the ἱλαστήριον, God set forth Jesus to resolve the problem of humanity's sin since sin requires and produces death (see Lev 1–17; Deut 21:23; Rom 5:12–21; 6:23).[78]

Romans 5:6–11

Jesus' death is the foundation of future hope. Paul speaks of Jesus' death as a sacrifice of atonement for sin in Rom 5:6–11. Here Paul presents Jesus' blood as the foundation of justification by faith and reconciliation. Justification on the basis of Jesus' death is also

---

[74] F. S. Thielman, *Paul and the Law: A Contextual Approach* (Downers Grove, IL: Inter-Varsity Press, 1994), 181.

[75] Ibid.

[76] See L. Morris, "The Biblical Use of the Term Blood," *JTS* 3 (1952): 216–27.

[77] For responses to recent criticisms of penal substitution, see T. R. Schreiner, "The Penal Substitution View," in *The Nature of the Atonement* (ed. J. Beilby and P. R. Eddy; Downers Grove, IL: InterVarsity Press, 2006), 67–98; Williams, "Penal Substitution," 71–86; Jeffery, Overy, and Sach, *Pierced for Our Transgressions*, 204–33.

[78] "Blood" in 3:25 refers to Jesus' death (see 3:15; 5:9; 1 Cor 10:16; 11:25,27; Eph 1:7; 2:13; Col 1:20). See Morris, *Apostolic Preaching*, 112–28, esp. 121–28.

the foundation of the hope that Paul mentions in Rom 5:1–5 (see Rom 5:1–8:39).[79]

In 5:6–11, Paul teaches that Jesus' death was penal, just as he does in Rom 3:24–26. In 5:6–7, he states that Jesus died for the weak. Then he explains 5:6–7 in 5:8: "but God demonstrated his own love toward us; namely, while we were sinners, Christ died for us"[80] In 5:6–8, Paul uses the ὑπέρ-language to speak of Jesus' death for sinners. In 5:6, Paul states that Christ died "for the weak" (ὑπέρ ἀσεβῶν).

In 5:7, he states that someone would scarcely die "for a righteous person" (ὑπέρ δικαίου) and that someone would perhaps die "for a good person" (ὑπέρ ἀγαθοῦ). Then, in 5:8, Paul clarifies how he uses the ὑπέρ-language in 5:6–7 by stating that Christ died "for us" (ὑπέρ ἡμῶν). Christ's death "for us" is a death for sinners since Paul states in 5:8 that Christ's death "for us" occurred "while we were sinners." The ὑπέρ-language in 5:6–8 does not *ipso facto* prove the sacrificial nature of Jesus' death or the importance of his sacrificial death for Paul's soteriology (Rom 1:5; 8:34; 15:30; see Matt 5:44; 10:24). Nevertheless, since Paul states in 5:9–10 that Jesus' blood accomplished justification and reconciliation for those for

---

[79] Many scholars agree that the major theme of Rom 5:1–8:39 is hope. For example, see Nygren, *Romans*, 187–89; Cranfield, *Romans*, 1:253–54; N. A. Dahl, *Studies in Paul: Theology for the Early Christian Mission* (Minneapolis: Augsburg, 1977), 82–91; J. C. Beker, *Paul, the Apostle: The Triumph of God in Life and Thought* (Philadelphia: Fortress, 1980), 83–86; Schreiner, *Romans*, 245–49. Romans 5:2 refers to "the hope of the glory of God." Romans 5:4 states that character produces "hope." Romans 5:5 states that "hope does not disappoint." Romans 8:20 states that the creation was "submitted in hope." Romans 8:24 states that "we were saved in hope" and that the fulfillment of this hope is yet to come. Romans 8:25 states that we await by means of hope what we do not see. Paul states that believers have hope in suffering (Rom 5:1–5). Believers have the hope that Jesus' obedience has triumphed over Adam's disobedience (Rom 5:12–21), so that eternal life has triumphed over eternal death for those in Christ. Believers have the hope that they are slaves to righteousness and dead to sin since they have been baptized into Christ (Rom 6:1–23). Believers have the hope of freedom from the judgment of the law (Rom 7:1–8:11). Believers have the hope that they are not debtors to the flesh, but led by the Spirit and consequently are children/heirs of God (Rom 8:12–17). Believers have the hope that all of creation will be redeemed from the curse of sin (Rom 8:18–25). Believers have the hope that the Spirit helps them in their weakness, and he prays for them according to God's will (Rom 8:26–27). Believers have the hope that God works all things together for the good for his people as the Spirit prays for them (Rom 8:28–30). Believers have the hope that nothing will separate them from God's love in Christ since God delivered Christ over to death on their behalf (Rom 8:31–39).

[80] For a discussion of the Χριστὸς ἀπέθανεν ὑπέρ-formula ("Christ died for"-formula), see M. Hengel, *The Atonement: A Study of the Origins of the Doctrine in the New Testament* (trans. John Bowden; London: SCM, 1981), 47–55; C. Breytenbach, "Christus starb für uns: Zur Tradition und paulinischen Rezeption der sogennanten Sterbeformeln," *NTS* 49 (2003): 447–75.

whom Jesus died and since Jesus' blood was the foundation of the hope mentioned in 5:1–5, the ὑπέρ-language in vv. 6–8 should be understood to mean that Jesus' death was a penal sacrifice of atonement for sin.[81]

Moreover, with his inference from 5:8 in 5:9, Paul connects Jesus' death mentioned in 5:8 with salvation: "Therefore, how much more we will be saved through him from wrath, because we were justified by his blood." Jesus' death for sinners is the basis of this salvation in Rom 5:8–10. Paul states that Jesus died for sin in Rom 5:8 and in 5:9–10 that Jesus' blood *justifies* and *reconciles* the ungodly (see 4:25).[82] In addition, Rom 5:10 states that Jesus' death will save those who were once enemies with God, because they were reconciled to God through Jesus' death and resurrection: "for, if although we were enemies we were reconciled to God through the death of his son, how much more we will be saved by his life, because we were reconciled."[83] Therefore, that Paul presents Jesus' death as a penal sacrifice for sin and that his penal death for sin is foundational to his soteriology are evident in 5:8–10 since Paul states that Jesus' blood justifies the ungodly before God, reconciles the ungodly to God, and saves the ungodly from his wrath.[84]

---

[81] O. Hofius ("The Fourth Servant Song in the New Testament Letters," in *The Suffering Servant: Isaiah 53 in Jewish and Christian Sources* [ed. B. Janowski and P. Stuhlmacher; trans. D. P. Bailey; Grand Rapids: Eerdmans, 2004], 172–83) argues that Paul understood Jesus' death as "inclusive place taking" rather than as substitution. That is, Jesus "takes the place of sinners in such a way that he does not displace them (as in the substitutionary model) but rather he encompasses them as persons and affects them in their very being." For further explanation of Hofius' view, see D. P. Bailey, "Concepts of Stellvertretung in the Interpretation of Isaiah 53," in *Jesus and the Suffering-Servant: Isaiah 53 and Christian Origins* (ed. W. H. Bellinger and W. R. Farmer; Harrisburg, PA: Trinity Press International, 1998), 223–50.

[82] Because of Paul's argument in Romans 1–8 regarding sin and the condemnation of the law and since he suggests in Romans 1–8 that Jesus' blood/death is the solution to humanity's spiritual plight, Jesus' death for humanity's sin in Rom 5:8 should be understood as a sacrifice of atonement for humanity's sin that accomplishes salvation for those condemned by the law. The latter interpretation is likely, for Paul says Jesus died for humanity's sin since humanity could not keep the law and since humanity stands condemned before God on account of its sin apart from Jesus' death (see Rom 1:18–5:11; 8:1–4, esp. 3:21–26; 4:25; 5:8–9; 8:3). The preceding analysis explains why Paul states in Rom 5:9 that Jesus will save the ungodly from God's wrath: namely, he has justified the ungodly by his blood (see Rom 3:21–26; Leviticus 16).

[83] For a discussion of reconciliation in Paul, see chapter 4.

[84] See R. Martin, *Reconciliation: A Study of Paul's Theology* (Atlanta: John Knox, 1981), 147. Against D. Seeley, *The Noble-Death: Greco-Roman Martyrology and Paul's Concept of Salvation* (JSNTSup 28; Sheffield: JSOT Press, 1990), 99–102. Seeley argued that Jesus died as an example. Against also C. Breytenbach, "Salvation of the Reconciled: With a Note on the Background of Paul's Metaphor of Reconciliation," in *Salvation in the New Testament: Perspectives on Soteriology* (ed. J. G. der Watt; Leiden: Brill, 2005), 284–85. Breytenbach

Romans 8:1–4

Jesus' death for others delivers them from condemnation. Romans 8:1–4 teaches that Jesus died as a sacrifice of atonement for sin. Romans 8:1 states that condemnation no longer exists for those who are in Christ. Then Rom 8:2 provides the reason condemnation no longer exists: "For the law of the Spirit of life by means of Christ freed you from the law of sin and of death." Romans 8:3 explains 8:2 by stating how those in Christ receive such freedom: "For God [did] what the law was incapable [of doing] because it was weak through sinful flesh, and he condemned sin in [Jesus'] flesh" in that he sent his own son concerning sin in the likeness of sinful flesh.[85]

Paul first introduces sacrificial language in Rom 8:1–4 with the phrase περὶ ἁμαρτίας (lit., "concerning sin") in Rom 8:3. The latter phrase is cultic and alludes to the Old Testament's sin offering since the LXX uses this phrase on numerous occasions to refer to the sin offering in cultic contexts (see LXX Lev 5:6–11; 7:37; 9:2–3; 12:6,8; 14:13,22,31; 15:15,30; 16:3,5,9; 23:19) and since he uses it to refer to Jesus' death for humanity's sin.[86] The language of sin offering suggests that Jesus' death was a penal sacrifice, for Lev 4:1–35 and Lev 5:9 state that the sin offering should be slaughtered and its blood should be presented before Yahweh in order to provide atonement for sin (see Lev 4:26,35). In 8:3, Paul further confirms the penal nature of Jesus' death by stating that God

---

argued against sacrificial atonement in Rom 5:8–10 on the basis that neither blood nor death signifies anything sacrificial or cultic.

[85] For a detailed discussion of 8:3–10, see Cranfield, *Romans*, 1:378–90.

[86] Cranfield (*Romans*, 1:382) rejects the reading of sin offering for περὶ ἁμαρτίας in 8:3 despite that the LXX often uses this phrase in cultic contexts to refer to a sin offering. In addition to above texts from Leviticus, see LXX Num 6:11,16; 7:16,22,28,34; Ps 39:7. Cranfield argues that a sacrificial reading is forced in 8:3 since the context of Paul's argument does not support a sacrificial interpretation. He suggests that περὶ ἁμαρτίας in 8:3 should be connected to the participial clause πέμψας ἐν ὁμοιώματι σαρκὸς ἁμαρτίας ("having sent in the likeness of sinful flesh") and not to the verbal clause κατέκρινεν τὴν ἁμαρτίαν ἐν τῇ σαρκί ("he judged sin in the flesh"). According to Cranfield, 8:3 simply refers to Jesus' mission, not his *[violent]* death for sin (emphasis mine). Schreiner (*Romans*, 401–03) agrees with Cranfield that περὶ ἁμαρτίας in 8:3 modifies the participle and not the verb, but Schreiner more accurately argues that περὶ ἁμαρτίας refers to Jesus as a sin offering since the phrase refers to a sin offering forty-four of fifty-four occurrences in the LXX (see Heb 10:6,8; 13:11). For sin offering in 8:3, see also Dunn, *Romans*, 1:422; P. Stuhlmacher, *Der Brief an die Römer* (NTD 6; Göttingen: Vandenhoeck & Ruprecht, 1989), 107; N. T. Wright, *The New Testament and the People of God* (Minneapolis: Fortress, 1992), 1:220–25; Bell, "Sacrifice and Christology in Paul," 1–27, esp. 5–8.

"judged/condemned" (κατακρίνω) sin in the flesh. The majority of appearances of this verb in the LXX suggests that God's judgment of sin in the flesh was penal (see LXX Est 2:1; Wis 4:16; Pss Sol 4:2; Sus 1:41,48,53). Contrary to the NIV, the phrase "in the flesh" in the clause "God condemned sin in the flesh" refers to Jesus' flesh (not humanity's flesh) since the entire context of Paul's argument in 8:1–11 explains the reason that condemnation no longer exists for those united with Christ. The reason is that God condemned the sin of those who are united with Christ in Jesus' death (see Rom 7:7–8:11).

Furthermore, the phrase "in the likeness of sinful flesh" in 8:3 supports the sacrificial nature of Jesus' death. In the latter text, Paul connects the death of Jesus with sinful humanity. Although he possibly refers to both Jesus' incarnation and death in 8:3 with the words "in the likeness of sinful flesh (see Phil 2:7),[87] the cross event appears to be the emphasis,[88] because the phrase suggests that Jesus fully identified with sinful humanity by taking upon himself God's condemnation/judgment for humanity's sin and by being judged/condemned as a sinner (see Gal 4:5–6; Phil 2:5–9).[89] Jesus identified with sinful humanity by becoming human, by submitting to the sinful realm of existence, and by going to the cross to take upon himself God's death penalty for humanity's sin (see Rom 5:12–21; 1 Cor 15:26).[90] Unlike Adam and the rest of humanity, Jesus remained free from the act of committing sin (see Rom 5:12–21). His sinlessness explains why his death on the cross could

---

[87] So Bell, "Sacrifice and Christology in Paul," 7–8. For a detailed analysis of ὁμοίωμα, see Schreiner, *Romans*, 313–14; F. A. Morgan, "Romans 6:5a: United to a Death like Christ's," *ETL* 59 (1983):267–302. The term ὁμοίωμα ("likeness") in Romans 8:3 is used elsewhere to mean similar in copy (LXX Deut 4:15–18,23,25; 5:8; Josh 22:28; 1 Kgs 6:5; Ps 105:20; Sir 34:3; Rom 1:23; 5:13; 6:5).

[88] Against Bell, "Sacrifice and Christology in Paul," 8. Bell does not emphasize the importance of the cross event in 8:3, but he thinks that Paul refers both to the incarnation and to the cross event. Nevertheless, rightly, J. A. Fitzmyer, *Romans* (AB 33; New York: Doubleday, 1993), 486–87; Schreiner, *Romans*, 404. Bell ("Sacrifice and Christology in Paul," 8 n. 40) does not think that Paul refers to "a satisfaction theory of the atonement" (i.e. penal substitution) when he states that God condemned sin in Jesus' flesh. Rather, states Bell, Paul's theory of atonement in 8:3 more closely reflects the priestly source: Jesus' death dealt with the essence of sin in a human, not the doing of sin (Bell, "Sacrifice and Christology in Paul," 6–7). Rightly, Morris, *Apostolic Preaching*, 279–80.

[89] See Jewett, *Romans*, 483–84.

[90] Other occurrences of the verb "to condemn" (κατακρίνω) in the New Testament suggest that those to whom this verb is applied will either receive the penalty of judgment (Rom 2:1; 8:34; 14:23; see Matt 12:41; 20:18; 27:3; Mark 10:33; 14:64; Luke 11:31; Heb 11:7; 2 Pet 2:6) or will be delivered from the penalty of judgment (Rom 8:1; 1 Cor 11:32).

deliver from the law those who were condemned by it (see Rom 7:1–8:10).[91]

Romans 8:4 states that God's purpose of condemning sin in Jesus' death was to fulfill the righteous requirement of the law: "so that the righteous requirement of the law would be fulfilled in us who are not walking according to the flesh, but according to the Spirit."[92] Since the law was the agent of humanity's condemnation because sin used the law to make sin more defiant (Rom 1:18–7:25; esp. 3:20; 4:15; 5:13; 7:7–25; Gal 3:19), God sent Jesus to overcome the power of sin and death and to fulfill the law's demands through perfect obedience for those who live according to the Spirit (see Rom 5:12–21). With Paul's use of "righteous requirement" (τὸ δικαίωμα), Jesus' obedience is likely in view in Rom 8:4 because of the words "to be fulfilled" and "for/in us" in Rom 8:4 and "righteousness" in 8:10. "Righteousness" in the latter text refers to Jesus' perfect obedience since Rom 8:1–11 as a whole discusses Jesus as the means by which God dealt with humanity's problem of sin and with the law's condemnation (see Rom 7:7–25). In 8:1–11, Paul contrasts the death of the body produced by sin with the life achieved through Jesus' perfect obedience to the law and through his death for sin. Jesus' death for sin delivers from the law's condemnation those who are condemned by it since he died their death for them (see Rom 7:1–8:11).

Sacrificial Atonement in 1–2 Corinthians

1 Corinthians 11:23–26

1 Corinthians 11:23–26 in Context. Paul's discussion of the Lord's Supper in 1 Cor 11:23–26 supports that Jesus' death was a

---

[91] Bell ("Sacrifice and Christology in Paul," 6–7) has argued that the phrase "in the likeness of sinful flesh" refers to Jesus' "full identity and resemblance" with sinful humanity, for he thinks that Paul is concerned with "the sending of Christ into the area of human existence" and that part of such an existence is sin. Nevertheless, Bell incorrectly identifies sinfulness (whether ontological or functional) to Jesus, for Jesus' participation in the sphere of sin does not necessitate that he functions as a sinner. The rest of Rom 8:3 supports the latter: "he judged sin in the flesh." The phrase "in the flesh" in the clause "he judged sin in the flesh" in Rom 8:3 refers to Jesus' flesh, not to the sinful flesh of humans (hence, my above translation). Rom 8:3 does not suggest that Jesus himself was sinful, but affirms that God condemned sin through Jesus' death by sending him in the likeness of sinful humanity and by judging him as the guilty sinner in his death on the cross. To his defense, Bell ("Sacrifice and Christology in Paul," 6–7) states that Jesus did not commit sin. See in comparison with Bell, V. P. Branick ("The Sinful Flesh of the Son of God [Rom 8:3]: A Key Image in Pauline Theology," *CBQ* 47 [1985]: 246–62; esp. 251).

[92] See Cranfield, *Romans*, 1:383–84.

sacrifice of atonement for sin. Paul's discussion in 11:23–26 is connected to 11:17. In the latter, he states that the Corinthians did not celebrate the Lord's Supper in the appropriate manner since there were divisions among them at the supper (11:17–20). Divisions in the church had resulted from the well-to-do believers' consuming of the elements at the meal and leaving nothing for the have-nots (11:21–22), so that one group was hungry and another was drunk (11:21).[93] Such actions were shameful and dishonored the Lord's Supper since they provided the impetus for the divisions at the supper and so had excluded part of the body (11:21–22). In 1 Cor 11:23–34, Paul explains to the Corinthians the appropriate manner for partaking in the meal. The word "for" (γάρ) in 11:23 signals the beginning of Paul's explanation. Here Paul states that he imparts to the Corinthians the tradition that he received from the Lord:

> . . . The Lord, Jesus, took bread on the night he was betrayed, and broke it after he gave thanks, and he said: 'This is my body, which is for you. Do this in my remembrance.' Likewise, he also took the cup after he ate and said: 'This cup is the new covenant in my blood. Do this, as often as you should drink, in my remembrance.' Therefore, as often as you should eat this bread and drink, you proclaim the Lord's death until he comes (11:23–26).

The Bread, Cup, Blood, and Covenant. Paul's comments in the above text suggest that the bread and the cup represent Jesus' death for others and that his death ratifies a new covenant. The sacrificial nature of Jesus' death is evident in Paul's comments that Jesus broke the bread (11:23–24), that the bread represents his body (11:24), and that his body was offered for others (11:24).[94] Furthermore, Jesus' death is sacrificial since Paul states that the cup represents the new covenant ratified by his blood (11:25; see Rom 3:25; 5:9; Col

---

[93] For a detailed exegesis of the text and for a defense of the above interpretation, see O. Hofius, "The Lord's Supper and the Lord's Supper Tradition: Reflections on 1 Corinthians 11:23b–25," in *One Loaf, One Cup: Ecumenical Studies of 1 Cor 11 and Other Eucharistic Texts* (ed. B. F. Meyer. New Gospel Studies 6; Macon, GA: Mercer University Press, 1993), 75–115; D. E. Garland, *1 Corinthians* (BECNT; Grand Rapids: Baker, 2003), 539–42.

[94] Contrary to Roman Catholic exegesis, the statements τοῦτό μού ἐστιν τὸ σῶμα ("this is my body . . .") should be interpreted metaphorically or, even better, as metonymy.

1:20; Matt 26:26–29; Mark 14:22–25; Luke 22:14–20).[95] Paul, thus, connects Jesus' broken body for others (ὑπὲρ ὑμῶν, "for you") in 11:24 with his blood and the ratification of a new covenant in 11:25. The ὑπέρ-formula especially elucidates the sacrificial nature of Jesus' death for humanity's sin in vv. 24–26 since Paul states that Jesus died for the benefit of others (11:24,26; see Luke 22:19–20), since his bloody death results in the ratification of a new covenant,[96] and since Paul states in 15:3 that Christ died "for our sins" (ὑπὲρ τῶν ἁμαρτιῶν ἡμῶν).[97]

The phrase "new covenant" (καινὴ διαθήκη or νέα διαθήκη)[98] occurs six times in the New Testament (see Luke 22:20; 1 Cor 11:25; 2 Cor 3:6; Heb 8:8; 9:15; 12:24), two of which are in Paul (1 Cor 11:25; 2 Cor 3:6). The noun διαθήκη ("covenant") occurs at least 30 times in the New Testament.[99] Διαθήκη ("covenant") likewise appears several times in the LXX.[100] The translators of the LXX often render it from the MT's ברית ("covenant/treaty").[101] Both ברית and διαθήκη can mean "will," "testament/promise," or "agreement."[102] When διαθήκη ("covenant") appears in the New Testament, the Greek term can refer to the new covenant instituted by Jesus and his death even when the adjective "new" does not describe or appear with it (see Matt 26:28; Heb 7:22).

Διαθήκη ("covenant") in 1 Cor 11:25 should be understood as a "testament/promise" since Paul alludes to Jer 31:31–34 (LXX 38:31–34) where God promises (i.e., makes a covenant) to write

[95] Paul's account appears closer to Luke's than to the other Synoptic Gospels (see Luke 22:14–20) since Paul includes some of the same words and constructions as Luke. For the specific similarities, compare the Greek of Luke 22:14–20 with the Greek of 1 Cor 11:23–25.

[96] The substitutionary nature of Jesus' death is heightened in Luke since he attaches the phrase "for you" to the clause "which is given," which modifies "this is my body" (Luke 22:19), and to the clause "which is poured out," which modifies "this cup is the new covenant in my blood" (Luke 22:20).

[97] For additional examples where the preposition ὑπέρ ("for") conveys the idea of substitution in the Pauline corpus, see Rom 5:6–9; 8:32; 14:15; 1 Cor 1:13; 2 Cor 5:14–15,21; Gal 1:4; 2:20; 3:13; Eph 5:2,25; 1 Thess 5:10; 1 Tim 2:6; and Titus 2:14.

[98] The latter only occurs in Heb 12:24.

[99] See Matt 26:28; Mark 14:24; Luke 1:72; 22:20; Acts 3:25; 7:8; Rom 9:4; 11:27; 1 Cor 11:25; 2 Cor 3:6,14; Gal 3:15,17; 4:24; Eph 2:12; Heb 7:22; 8:6,8,9,10; 9:4,15,16–17,20; 10:16,29; 12:24; 13:20; Rev 11:19.

[100] E.g., Exod 24:7; Jer 31:31.

[101] Ibid.

[102] F. Brown, S. Driver, and C. Briggs, *The Brown-Driver-Briggs Hebrew and English Lexicon* (5th ed.; Peabody, MA: Hendrickson, 2000), 136; W. Bauer, F. Danker, W. F. Arndt, and F. W. Gingrich, *Greek-English Lexicon of the New Testament and Other Early Christian Literature* (3rd ed.; Chicago: University of Chicago Press, 2001), 183.

his law on the hearts of his people by the Spirit. In addition to Jer 31:31–34, Paul's words in 1 Cor 11:25 regarding Jesus' blood as the means by which the new covenant was ratified likewise alludes to Exod 24:8 when Moses both read the "book of the covenant" and sprinkled blood upon Israel to ratify the covenant. Blood ratified the covenant in MT Exod 24:8 according to Moses' statement after he sprinkled the blood upon the people: "Behold: the blood of the covenant which (i.e., the blood of the covenant) the Lord God cut."[103]

Paul also uses the phrase καινή διαθήκη ("new covenant") in 2 Cor 3:6 to describe the Spirit-empowered, new covenant ministry of which he is an ambassador. He contrasts this Spirit-empowered, new covenant ministry in 2 Cor 3:6 and 3:14 with the old covenant characterized by the letter of the law (see Exodus 20–24). Thus, Jesus' death fulfills God's old covenant promises made in the Old Testament (see Matt 26:28; Mark 14:24; Luke 22:19–20; Heb 7:1–8:13). Paul's use of καινὴ διαθήκη in 1 Cor 11:25 suggests, then, that Jesus' bloody death was sacrificial since it was the means by which God's covenant/promise to save a people from their sins and to empower them with the Spirit has been fulfilled and ratified.[104]

The "cup" (ποτήριον) in 1 Cor 11:25 suggests that Jesus' death was a sacrifice of atonement for sin since the cup represents Jesus' bloody death. He states in 1 Cor 11:25 that the cup is the covenant in Jesus' blood. Then in 1 Cor 11:27 he states that those who unworthily drink the cup of the Lord are guilty of the body and "blood of Christ." Other texts confirm that the cup represents Jesus' blood. Paul states in 1 Cor 10:16 that those who drink of the cup "share in the blood of Christ." Matthew 26:28 suggests that the cup was Jesus' blood offered for the forgiveness of sin.[105] Additionally, the cup also represents God's judgment/wrath against sin and thus suggests that Jesus' death was penal, for ποτήριον represents

---

[103] LXX Exod 24:8 places the emphasis upon the covenant, not the blood: "Behold: the blood of the covenant, which (i.e., the covenant) the Lord willed . . ." The relative pronoun ἧς ("which") agrees with διαθήκης ("covenant") in case, number, and gender. Since the relative pronoun only needs to agree with its antecedent in number and gender, the antecedent of the relative is covenant.

[104] According to Hebrews, the new covenant is not only new, but better (see Heb 7:1–8:13).

[105] Other New Testament texts suggest that Jesus' blood is the blood of the new covenant (see Matt 26:26–28; Mark 14:24; Luke 22:17–20; Heb 7:1–8:13).

God's judgment/wrath against sin in other texts (LXX Ps 10:6; Hab 2:16; Isa 51:17,22; Jer 30:6; 32:15,17,28–29; Ezek 23:32–33; Matt 20:22,23; 26:27,39; Mark 10:37–39; 14:23–24,36; Luke 22:17–20,22; John 18:11; Rev 14:10; 16:19; 18:6–19:4). Therefore, as a means of explaining to the Corinthians the appropriate manner by which they should conduct the Lord's Supper, Paul reminds them that the supper fundamentally represents the sacrificial nature of Jesus' death for sin, which he offered to deal with sin, to deal with God's judgment against sin, and to unite the body of Christ.

2 Corinthians 5:14–21

God made Jesus to be sin. Second Cor 5:14–21 suggests that Jesus' death was a sacrifice of atonement for sin.[106] Paul states in 2 Cor 5:14 that he endured sufferings for Christ because Christ's love compelled him. The phrase "love of Christ" echoes Paul's statement in Rom 5:8 regarding God's love since Paul connects both God's love and Christ's love to Jesus' death for the sins of others in both texts.[107] In 5:8, Paul states that God demonstrated his love for humanity in that Christ died for sinners. He likewise states in 2 Cor 5:14–15 that Jesus died for others to achieve life for them.[108]

The messages of Romans 5 and 2 Corinthians 5 differ. Nevertheless, in both texts Paul uses virtually the same vocabulary (e.g., ἀποθνήσκω, "to die" [Rom 5:6–8, 2 Cor 5:14–15]; the ὑπέρ-formula [Rom 5:6–9, 2 Cor 5:14–15]; καταλλάσσω, "to reconcile" [Rom 5:10, 2 Cor 5:18–20], and καταλλαγή, "reconciliation" [Rom 5:11; 2 Cor 5:18–19) to highlight the salvation that Jesus achieved by his sacrificial death for those for whom he died. In both Romans 5 and in 2 Corinthians 5, Paul states that a soteriological benefit that

---

[106] Second Corinthians 5:11–21 is part of a unit that consists of 1:12–7:1. Paul defends his apostolic ministry to the Corinthians in this unit. Second Corinthians 5:11–21 infers from 2 Cor 3:1–5:10 that he is minister of reconciliation. So M. J. Harris, *The Second Epistle to the Corinthians* (NIGTC; Grand Rapids: Eerdmans, 2005), 127.

[107] "Love of Christ" should be understood as a subjective genitive since Paul's focus is the love that Christ has shown to him by means of his death. See Harris, *Second Corinthians*, 418–19.

[108] Against C. Breytenbach, "Salvation of the Reconciled (with a Note on the Background of Paul's Metaphor of Reconciliation)," in *Salvation in the New Testament: Perspectives in Soteriology* (ed. J. G. der Watt; Leiden: Brill, 2005), 280–81. He rightly acknowledges that the dying formula so prominent in the Greek tradition influenced Paul here. Nevertheless, he went too far when he stated that the Greek tradition did not teach substitutionary atonement, but that a human died as a representative for the city-state or as someone who relieved a person or group from death.

Jesus achieved through his death for the ungodly is reconciliation with God.

Paul confirms in 2 Cor 5:19 and 5:21 that his statements in 2 Cor 5:14–15 should be read through a sacrificial lens. He states in 5:18–19 that God reconciled the world to himself in Christ and in 5:19 that he did not count the transgressions of those in the world against them.[109] Second Corinthians 5:14–15 confirms that Jesus' death was the basis of reconciliation in Christ. These verses also confirm that Jesus' death was the reason God did not count transgressions against the transgressors. Second Corinthians 5:21 especially supports that Jesus' death for others (5:14–15) and reconciliation in Christ (5:19) should be understood as sacrificial atonement since Paul states that God made Jesus sin for those for whom he died ("God made the one who did not know sin as sin for us").[110]

The preceding statement in 5:21 reflects the Old Testament cult since the statement suggests that Jesus identified in some manner with sin (see Rom 8:3).[111] In Leviticus, the author states that the priest should present a sin offering when he sins and brings guilt upon the people (Lev 4:2–3). Likewise, the people as a whole were commanded to sacrifice an animal as a sin offering when the sin of the people became known to the whole assembly (Lev 4:13–14). Once the people slaughtered the animal and once they sprinkled the blood in the appropriate places, God would forgive them through this atonement (see Lev 4:16,20).

Paul does not use the normal grammatical construction in the LXX (περὶ ἁμαρτίας, lit. "concerning sin") to convey the idea of *sin offering* (see LXX Lev 5:6–7; 5:11; 7:37; 9:2–3; 12:6,8; 14:13,22,31; 15:15,30; 16:3,5,9; 23:19; Num 6:11; et al.; NT Rom 8:3). Nevertheless, the concept of *sin offering* is present in 5:21 for at least four reasons. First, 2 Cor 5:14–15 suggests that Jesus died on behalf of others. Second, 2 Cor 5:17–18 suggests that Jesus brought about a new creation and reconciliation for all who are in him. Third, 2 Cor 5:19 suggests that because of the reconciliation Jesus' death achieved, God does not judge the transgressors for their

---

[109] I say more about this text in chapter 4.

[110] Scholars vigorously debate the meaning of 5:19–21. For a detailed discussion of the text, see Harris, *Second Corinthians*, 439–56.

[111] Against sin offering here, see M. E. Thrall, "Salvation Proclaimed: 2 Corinthians 5:18–21," *ExpTim* 93 (1982): 230; Breytenbach, "Salvation of the Reconciled," 276.

transgressions. Fourth, God made Jesus sin for others so that they would become God's righteousness in him. Therefore, Jesus' death for others was an offering for sin in 2 Cor. 5:14–15, 19, and 21 since his death was the manner by which God does not count the transgressions against the transgressors (5:19) and the reason for which they receive new creation, reconciliation, and the righteousness of God.[112]

Sacrificial Atonement in Galatians

Galatians 1:4 and 3:10–14

Jesus died for the sins of others. Galatians supports that Jesus died as a sacrifice of atonement for sin. Paul mentions Jesus' death in his salutation (Gal 1:4). In 1:4, Paul states that Jesus "gave himself for our sins so that he would deliver us from the present evil age." Galatians 1:4 depicts the sacrificial nature of Jesus' death in at least three ways: (1) Jesus voluntarily died ("who gave himself"). (2) Jesus died for sins ("for our sins"). (3) He died to deal with the problem of sin that enslaves humanity to the present evil age ("so that he would deliver us from the present evil age").

Jesus' Death, but God's Curse. The sacrificial nature of Jesus' death is especially evident in Gal 3:10–14. Paul continues the argument of 3:1–9 by grounding the latter in 3:10–14. Paul suggests in 3:1–9 that the Spirit came to the Galatians by faith and not by obedience to the law. In 3:10–14, he asserts that Jesus' death guaranteed the reception of the Spirit by faith and fulfilled the Abrahamic covenant, just as the Old Testament Scriptures promised (Deut 27:26): "for as many as are from the works of the law are under a curse" (Gal 3:10).[113] Those who seek to obtain the promise by yielding allegiance to the law are under a curse since "cursed is everyone who does not abide in all things which have been written in the book of the law in order to do them" (Gal 3:10).[114]

---

[112]Hooker ("Interchange," 349–61) broadens Paul's statement in 2 Cor 5:21 (that God made/appointed Jesus as sin) to include the incarnation. See Bell, "Sacrifice and Christology," 14–15.

[113]For the thesis that Paul used the theme of wisdom to reverse the Deuteronomistic curses, see C. M. Pate, *The Reverse of the Curse* (WUNT 114; Tübingen: Mohr Siebeck, 2000).

[114]Sanders (*Paul, the Law, and the Jewish People*, 22–23) rejects that the emphasis in Gal 3:10 should be placed on "all" perfectly obeying the law.

Determining whether Gal 3:10–14 refers to Jesus' death as a penal sacrifice for sin is crucial for defining the debated phrase "works of the law" (3:10) since those "from the works of the law are under a curse" (3:10).[115] N. T. Wright argues that because the phrase "works of the law" refers to Israel, 3:10 suggests that the people of the covenant are under a curse.[116] Dunn argues that the phrase "works of the law" refers to the boundary markers that demarcated Jews from Gentiles (i.e., food laws, Sabbath, circumcision, and purity laws).[117] Upon this reading, 3:10 suggests that Jews who were relying too much on boundary markers were missing that God had put an end to those ethnic distinctions through Christ. Recent exegesis demonstrates that the phrase "works of the law" in 3:10 specifically refers to the law itself as a personified entity since it occurs with the verb "to be."[118] Thus, the emphasis in 3:10 is on the curse that the *law brings* to those who do not obey it perfectly, not on the *works that one does*.[119]

I understand "works of the law" in 3:10 as a reference to works done in obedience to the law to attain right standing before God (see Rom 2:15; 3:20,28; Gal 2:16; 3:2,5, and DSS 1QS 5.8,21,24; 6.13–23; 8.4,10,20).[120] This reading suggests that Paul is reacting here against a legalistic understanding of the law in Second Temple Judaism.[121] Various texts in Second Temple Jewish literature support that Paul could have been reacting against a legalistic view of the law. A few examples should suffice.

---

[115] T. R. Schreiner, "Works of the Law," in *the Dictionary of Paul and His Letters* (ed. G. F. Hawthorne, R. P. Martin, and D. G. Reid; Downers Grove, IL: InterVarsity Press, 1993), 975–79.

[116] Wright, *Climax*, 137–51.

[117] J. D. G. Dunn, *A Commentary on the Epistle to the Galatians* (London: A&C Black, 1993), 172; idem, *New Perspectives on Paul* (Grand Rapids: Eerdmans, 2005).

[118] B. S. Davis, *Christ as Devotio: The Argument of Galatians 3:1–14* (New York: University Press of America, 2002), 72–74.

[119] Ibid., 74, 76.

[120] Against N. T. Wright, *The New Testament and the People of God* (Minneapolis: Fortress, 1992), 237–38; Dunn, *Galatians*, 172. Rightly, D. J. Moo, "Law, Works of the Law, and Legalism in Paul," *WTJ* 45 (1983): 73–100; T. R. Schreiner, "Is Perfect Obedience to the Law Possible? A Re-examination of Galatians 3:10," *JETS* 27 (1984): 151–60; idem, "Paul and Perfect Obedience to the Law: An Evaluation of the View of E. P. Sanders," *WTJ* 47 (1985): 245–78; idem, "Works of the Law," 975–79.

[121] This does not mean, however, that every segment of Second Temple Judaism (STJ) viewed the law in this way. My point is that Paul is reacting against a particular view of STJ that had a legalistic understanding of the law. See D. A. Carson, P. O'Brien, and M. A. Seifrid, eds., *Justification and Variegated Nomism: The Complexities of Second Temple Judaism*, 2 vols. (Grand Rapids: Baker, 2001); S. J. Gathercole, *Where Is Boasting? Early Jewish Soteriology and Paul's Response in Romans 1–5* (Grand Rapids: Eerdmans, 2002).

In LXX Ezra 7:26, doing the law refers to obeying the Mosaic law and the law of the king. This statement intends that they give complete (i.e., perfect) obedience to the command since disobeying the Lord and the king results in judgment (LXX Ezra 7:27; see LXX Lev 25:18; Wis 6:6; Sir 21:11). In Tobit 14, Tobias' father predicts Israel's exile, Jerusalem's destruction, and their future restoration. Before his death, Tobias's father urges Tobias and the rest of his children not to sin, but "to keep the law and the ordinances" (Tob 14:9). Since the book emphasizes that righteousness and obedience to the law of Moses provide atonement, Tobit's statements should be read as exhortations to his children to obey perfectly the stipulations within the Mosaic covenant in order to avoid Yahweh's judgment.

First Maccabees 1–2 records that Antiochus Epiphanes IV (henceforth Antiochus) wrote a letter and sent it throughout his entire kingdom, which included Jerusalem, ordering the residents to give up all of their customs (1 Macc 1:41). Along with the Gentiles within Antiochus's kingdom, many Jews obeyed Antiochus's edict, which led to their rejecting Yahweh, accepting Antiochus's religion, and practicing idolatry (1 Macc 1:42). Antiochus eventually informed all Jews that if they yielded to the law of Moses, he would kill them (1 Macc 1:43–50). Antiochus's edict and Israel's allegiance to it suggest that perfect disobedience to the ordinances of the law was expected since Antiochus expected Israel to forsake the entire law, not simply one aspect of it (e.g., Sabbath, circumcision, purity laws, etc.). For instance,1 Macc 1:48–49 suggests that he expected the Jews to forsake all of the ordinances in the law, and 1 Macc 2:21 states that some Jews refused to "forsake the law and the ordinances."

DSS 1QS (ca. 100 BC) is known as the Community Rule. In it the author discusses how those in the community should live in response to Yahweh's law. At various places in the scroll, the author emphasizes that the saints in the community must respond to God's precepts with absolute, perfect obedience as the children of the covenant. Observe the following excerpts:[122]

---

[122] The following translation of the scrolls comes from *The Complete Dead Sea Scrolls in English* (trans. Geza Vermes; rev. ed.; New York: Penguin Books, 2004), 98–110.

He shall admit into the Covenant of Grace all those who have freely devoted themselves to the observance of God's *precepts*, that they may be joined to the counsel of God and may *live perfectly before him in accordance with all* that has been revealed concerning their appointed times, and that they may love all the sons of light, each according to his lot in God's design, and hate all the sons of darkness, each according to his guilt in God's vengeance (1QS 1.5–10).

All those who freely devote themselves to his *truth* shall bring all their knowledge, powers, and possessions into the Community of God, that they may purify their knowledge in the truth of God's *precepts* and order their powers according to *his ways of perfection and all their possessions according to his righteous counsel. They shall not depart from any command of God* concerning their times; *they shall be neither early nor late for any of their appointed times; they shall stray neither to the right nor to the left of his true precepts.* All those who embrace the Community Rule shall enter into the Covenant before God *to obey all his commandments* so that they may not abandon him during the dominion of Belial because of fear or terror or affliction (1QS 1.11–18).

. . . And the priests shall bless all the men of the lot of God who *walk perfectly in all his way*, saying: May he bless you with all good and preserve you from all evil! May he lighten your heart with life-giving wisdom and grant you eternal knowledge! May he raise his merciful face towards you for everlasting bliss (1QS 2.1–4)!

But when a man enters the Covenant *to walk according to all these precepts* that he may be joined to the holy Congregation, they shall examine his spirit in community with respect to his understanding and *practice of the Law*, under the authority of the sons of Aaron who have freely pledged themselves in the Community to restore his Covenant and *to heed all the precepts commanded by him*, and of the multitude of Israel who have freely pledged themselves in the Community to return to his Covenant (1QS 5.20). . .

Every man who enters the Council of Holiness, *who walks in the way of perfection as commanded by God, and*

who deliberately or through negligence transgresses one
word of the Law of Moses, on any point whatever, shall be
expelled from the Council of the Community and shall
return no more (1QS 9.20–24).[123]

Finally, Paul uses the phrase "work of the law" in Rom 2:15 to
refer to obeying the Mosaic covenant perfectly since he pit doing
the law and transgressing (i.e, disobeying the law) side by side. The
latter suggests the collocation that to do the law is to obey the law
perfectly, but to transgress the law is to disobey a certain aspect of
the law. This interpretation is supported by Paul's reference to the
"righteous requirements of the law" in Rom 2:26, which refers to
obeying certain commands in the Mosaic covenant (see LXX Num
31:21; 36:13; Deut 4:1, 5; 1 Macc 2:21; Bar 2:12).

Again, Paul intends perfect obedience to the law with the
phrase "works of the law" because he states that circumcision (i.e.,
Jewishness) is equivalent to non-Jewishness (i.e., Gentileness) if
the law is disobeyed (Rom 2:25). Paul reiterates the latter point in
Rom 2:26 by asserting that if the uncircumcised obey the law, then
their uncircumcision will be counted as circumcision. That is, if
non-Jews yielded perfect obedience to the law, then God would
count them as his covenant people (i.e., as Jews). It follows, then,
that to be circumcised does not mean that one does/keeps the
law since a circumcised person who disobeys other aspects of the
Mosaic covenant was considered guilty of disobeying the law (see
Exod 20:2–Deut 31:22; Rom 10:5). Consequently, Gentiles who
obey the law would judge Jews, who do not obey the law, as transgressors of the law, if the Gentiles fulfill the law.

Likewise, Paul appears in Gal 3:10–14 to pit doing/obeying the
law against believing/faith as a means of receiving the fulfillment
of the Abrahamic promises (Gal 3:14). He primarily uses law here
and throughout his letters as a reference to the Mosaic covenant
(see Romans). Paul's point in 3:10 is that allegiance to the law does
not justify anyone (see Rom 3:20; Gal 2:16), because the righteous
one will inherit eschatological life by faith (Gal 3:11) since the law
requires obedience not faith (Gal 3:11; see Rom 3:20; DSS 1QS

---

[123] See also the Damascus Document (CD) 3:14–20; Pss Sol 3:11–12; 14:2,10; 5:17; 14:2–
3,10; 15:4; 4Q215a 2.2–7; 1Q22 2.7–10; 4Q171 2.13–14, and (although post AD 70) 4 Ezra
7:87–89.

5.8,21,24; 6.13–23; 8.4,10,20).[124] Thus, Gal. 3:13 confirms the sacrificial nature of Jesus' death because those who are from the works of the law are cursed since they do not (and even cannot) perfectly obey it. Nevertheless, "Christ freed us from the curse of the law in that He became a curse on behalf of us, because it has been written: 'cursed is everyone who hangs on a tree . . .'"[125]

An expressed connective is not present in 3:13 to explain how 3:13–14 relates to 3:10–12. Nevertheless, it is exegetically plausible to suggest that the entirety of 3:13–14 serves as an adversative to 3:10–12 since 3:13 provides the solution to the curse-pronouncements in 3:10–12. The main verb ἐξαγοράζω ("to set free") in 3:13 occurs only in Paul's letters in the New Testament (Gal 3:13; 4:5; Eph 5:16; Col 4:5). Both times in Galatians it refers to deliverance from the condemnation of the law through the work of Christ.[126]

The term ἐξαγοράζω occurs only once in the LXX in Dan 2:8. There it refers to buying time just as in Eph 5:16 and Col 4:5. Therefore, "to purchase/buy" is part of this word's semantic domain. In Gal 3:13, the term refers to the liberation/freedom from the curse of the law purchased by Jesus' death for others. Thus, the term conveys the idea of ransom since Paul states that Jesus became a "curse for us"[127] by his death and since he states that his death "for us" was the required price for Gentiles' reception of the Abrahamic blessing.[128]

---

[124] See S. J. Gathercole, "Torah, Life, and Salvation: Leviticus 18:5 in Early Judaism and the New Testament," in *From Prophecy to Testament: The Function of the Old Testament in the New* (ed. C. A. Evans; Peabody, MA: Hendrickson, 2004), 127–45.

[125] Against B. H. McLean, "Christ as Pharmakos in Pauline Soteriology," *JBL* (1991): 187–207; idem, "The Absence of an Atoning Sacrifice in Paul's Soteriology," *NTS* 38 (1992): 531–53; idem, *The Cursed Christ* (JSNTSup 126; Sheffield: Sheffield Academic Press, 1996). McLean argues that the *Pharmakos* rituals (rituals by which a curse was removed from the community in the Greco-Roman world) influenced Paul's comments in Gal 3:13 and that this ritual was not an atoning sacrifice for sin. Rather, it simply bore the curse of God and experienced divine rejection from the community.

[126] I understand the phrase "under the law" to be synonymous with being "under sin" in Paul, which entails that one is under condemnation. For the phrases "under the law" and "under sin" in Paul as synonyms, see Rom 3:9; 6:14–15; 7:14; Gal 3:22–23.

[127] The identity of the word "us" is debated. It could refer to only Jews or to both Jews and Gentiles. N. T. Wright (*Climax*, 14142) has argued that the statement "Christ redeemed us" means that Jesus redeemed Jews who were under the curse of the law (i.e., in exile) because of their sin. Nevertheless, when Paul asserts that "as many are from the works of the law are under a curse," he includes both Jews and Gentiles under this curse-pronouncement, especially since he wrote Galatians to Gentiles who were in danger of turning to Judaism for justification.

[128] A similar word (ἀγοράζω) also occurs in the New Testament. Each time it refers to some sort of buying back and thus conveys the idea of ransom. It refers to the buying back

In addition, 3:13 especially suggests that Jesus' death was a penal substitute.[129] The phrase "from the curse of the law," the clause "by becoming a curse for us," and the Old Testament citation "cursed is everyone who hangs on a tree" (Deut 21:23) all emphasize the penal nature of Jesus' death. The phrase "from the curse of the law" modifies the verb "to redeem" (ἐξηγόρασεν), and it conveys the idea of separation and liberation.[130] The phrase "by becoming a curse for us" is an adverbial participial clause (γενόμενος ὑπὲρ ἡμῶν κατάρα). The participle "becoming" (γενόμενος) should be understood instrumentally since it conveys the manner by which Christ "set us free" from the law's curse: "in that he became a curse for us" (see Phil 2:5). The citation from Deut 21:23 provides scriptural support for the penal nature of Jesus' death: "everyone who hangs on a tree is cursed."

The curse of Gal 3:13 results from one's inability to keep the law's demands prescribed in the Mosaic covenant. This situation is evident in four ways. (1) Paul uses the phrase "curse of the law" along with "works of the law" in the same context (see Gal 3:10–13). (2) He uses "curse of the law" to describe that the law produces or yields curse-pronouncements to those who disobey.[131] (3) He cites Deuteronomy, which is a recapitulation of the Mosaic covenant. (4) Deuteronomy 27 begins with an exhortation for Israel to "keep every commandment" that Moses prescribed for them in the law (Deut 27:1; see 27:10).

The law yields curse-pronouncements to those who disobey, for Paul cites Deut 27:26, Hab 2:4, and Lev 18:5.[132] Paul emphasizes that the law demands obedience and anything less results in a curse since the contexts of both Deut 27:26 and Lev 18:5 emphasize the importance of obedience to the covenant for the

---

of property (Matt 13:44,46) or food (Matt 14:15; Mark 6:36) with money and to the salvation that Jesus bought with his death (1 Cor 6:20; 7:23; 2 Pet 2:1; Rev 5:9; 14:3–4).

[129] S. Travis ("Christ as the Bearer of Divine Judgment in Paul's Thought about the Atonement," in *Atonement Today* [ed. J. Goldingay; London: SPCK, 1995], 21–38; esp. 24) doubts that Galatians 3:13 is about atonement in general or about the salvation of individuals.

[130] See D. B. Wallace (*Greek Grammar Beyond the Basics* [Grand Rapids: Zondervan, 1996], 371), who states that separation is an option for the preposition ἐκ ("from").

[131] I understand "of the law" (τοῦ νόμου) in the phrase "from the curse of the law" (ἐκ τῆς κατάρας τοῦ νόμου) as a genitive of production: the law produces curses/judgment.

[132] For thorough treatments of Paul's citation of Deuteronomy in Second Temple Judaism and in Galatians and specifically Lev 18:5 in Second Temple Judaism and in Paul, see, respectively, Pate, *The Reverse of the Curse*; P. M. Sprinkle, *Law and Life: The Interpretation of Leviticus 18:5 in Early Judaism and in Paul* (WUNT 241; Tübingen: Mohr-Siebeck, 2008).

purpose of remaining in the covenant and since Hab 2:4 emphasizes the importance of believing/faith versus doing (see DSS 1QS
5.8,21,24; 6.13–23; 8.4,10,20). Paul recalls Gal 3:10–12 in 3:13 with
his citation of Deut 27:26. His entire argument in 3:10–14 is that
the curse-pronouncements of the Mosaic covenant come upon
those who do not do the law (Gal 3:10–12), but Christ has freed
all who have faith from those curse-pronouncements by becoming
accursed himself on their behalf (3:12–13).

That Christ died a penal death for sin is confirmed by the
curse-formula of Paul's citations from Deuteronomy. The curses of
Deuteronomy 27 are the result of disobedience to God's commands
given through Moses (Deut 27:1). Moses prescribed for Israel
what they should and should not do when they crossed the Jordan
(Deut 27:2ff). If Israel disobeyed Yahweh's commands at one point,
the individual who disobeyed would be cursed (Deut 27:15–29:29;
see Lev 18:5; DSS 1QS 5.8,21,24; 6.13–23; 8.4,10,20). Deuteronomy 28:1–68 states that Yahweh is the author of the curses since he
promises to bless those who obey the covenant (Deut 28:1–14) and
to curse those who disobey the covenant (Deut 28:15–68).

Deuteronomy 21:23, which Paul quotes in Gal 3:13, specifically elucidates the penal nature of Jesus' death. Deuteronomy 21:22–
23 clarifies that those who commit sin worthy of death should be
put to death (i.e., should suffer the death penalty) and that Israel
should hang this person on a tree. Moses warns Israel not to leave
the dead body of this one on the tree throughout the night, "for a
curse of God is the one who is hanged" (Deut 21:23).[133] The hang-
ing promulgates to the entire nation that the one who hangs on a
tree has suffered divine judgment, that he is rejected by God, and
that he is accursed. Since God is the source of the law and of the
law's curse-pronouncements in Deuteronomy, God curses the one
who does not do the law since, according to Deuteronomy 27–28,
a violation of one of his commandments was worthy of judgment.
Jesus, therefore, by becoming a curse "for us" received God's divine death sentence and took upon himself God's curse that Jews
and Gentiles rightly deserved, so that Gentiles would be partakers
of the Abrahamic blessing (Gal 3:14–15). Jesus' death, then, was
penal because of God's curse on him, which is evident in that he

---

[133] R. Y. K. Fung (*Galatians* [NICNT; Grand Rapids: Eerdmans, 1988], 148) suggests that
Paul left out the words "of God" to avoid saying that Jesus was cursed by God in death.

was hanged upon a tree in fulfillment of Deut 21:23 (see DSS 11Q 64:7–12).

Sacrificial Atonement in Ephesians and Colossians

Ephesians 1–2 and Colossians 1–2

Redemption through Jesus' Blood. Ephesians 1–2 and Colossians 1–2 support the sacrificial nature of Jesus' death. Ephesians 1:3–14 is a doxology of praise. As Paul praises God for the spiritual blessings that believers inherit in Christ, he mentions redemption as one of those spiritual blessings. Paul states in 1:7, "In [Christ] we have redemption through his blood." With the exception of the different Greek nouns for the word "sin" in Eph 1:7 (παράπτωμα, "transgression") and Col 1:14 (ἁμαρτία, "sin"), Paul's statements in Eph 1:7 and Col 1:14 are the same. The phrase "in whom we have redemption" in the above respective contexts suggests that Jesus' redemption achieved salvation for the unredeemed.

The word that Paul uses for "redemption" (ἀπολύτρωσις) in Eph 1:7 (see 1:14) and Col 1:14 is the same term that he uses in Rom 3:24. In my discussion of Rom 3:24 above, I argued that this term conveys the idea of *ransom*. This meaning is also present here in Eph 1:7 since Paul states that Jesus' blood is the means by which, and thus the required price by which, the redemption was accomplished: "In [Christ] we have redemption through his blood" (see Isa 53:2–12; Rom 4:25).[134] The concept of ransom is also present in Col 1:14 since Paul states later that Jesus' blood provided peace and reconciliation for all things (Col 1:20) and that God forgave trespasses by means of Jesus' cross (Col 2:13–14). Paul defines more precisely the nature of the redemption that Jesus accomplished through his blood with the words "in [Christ] we have redemption through his blood, [i.e.], the forgiveness of transgressions" (Eph 1:7) and "in [Christ] we have redemption, [i.e.], the forgiveness of sins" (Col 1:14).[135]

---

[134]See I. H. Marshall, "The Development of the Concept of Redemption in the New Testament," in *Reconciliation and Hope: Essays in Honor of Leon Morris* (ed. R. J. Banks; Exeter: Paternoster, 1974), 153–69; H. W. Hoehner, *Ephesians* (Grand Rapids: Baker, 2002), 206. *Pace* A. T. Lincoln, *Ephesians* (WBC 42; Nashville: Nelson, 1990), 28.

[135]In Eph 1:7 and in Col 1:14, "forgiveness" and "redemption" are in the accusative case and thus are double accusatives. The second accusative "forgiveness" (ἄφεσιν) further de-

The term that Paul uses for forgiveness in Col 1:14 (ἄφεσις) occurs multiple times in the New Testament (Matt 26:28; Mark 1:4; 3:29; Luke 1:77; 3:3; 4:18; 24:47; Acts 2:38; 5:31; 10:43; 13:38; 26:18; Col 1:14; Heb 9:22; 10:19). When it occurs, it refers to the canceling out of sins since the term appears in conjunction with the phrase "of sins" or in a context in which the author is speaking of the wiping away of sins. The phrase "of sins" is not always attached to the term that Paul uses here for forgiveness (e.g., Matt 26:28; Heb 9:22). The only Pauline occurrences of ἄφεσις ("forgiveness") are in Eph 1:7 and Col 1:14. In both contexts, Paul mentions redemption, forgiveness, and Jesus' blood together (see Col 1:14–20; 2:1–13). The term mostly occurs in the New Testament with the phrase "of sins." Each time ἄφεσις occurs in the Greek text with the phrase "of sins," ἁμαρτία is the term used for sin except in Eph 1:7 (e.g., Matt 26:28; Mark 1:4; Luke 1:77; 3:3; 24:47; Acts 2:38; 5:31; 10:43; 13:38).

In Eph 1:7, Paul uses παράπτωμα ("transgression") in conjunction with "forgiveness" instead of ἁμαρτία ("sin"). Some overlap occurs between ἁμαρτία and παράπτωμα since Paul uses the latter in Eph 1:7 ("in whom we have redemption through his blood, the forgiveness of *transgressions*") and the former in Col 1:14 ("in whom we have redemption, the forgiveness of *sins*"), since he uses both terms together in Eph 2:1 and in Rom 5:12–21, and since he uses only παράπτωμα in Col 2:13 to describe the forgiveness that God has provided in Christ. This overlapping of the two terms in the Pauline corpus is especially significant in Eph 2:1 since Paul uses both terms together in Eph 2:1, but then uses a relative pronoun in Eph 2:2 that only modifies ἁμαρτία: "And you were dead in transgressions (παράπτωμα) and sins (ἁμαρτίαις)" (Eph 2:1), "*in which* (αἷς) you formerly walked (Eph 2:2). . ." The antecedent of the relative pronoun "which" (αἷς) in Eph 2:2 can *only* be ἁμαρτίαις in Eph 2:1 since the former agrees with the latter in number and gender.[136] Thus, that Paul groups ἁμαρτία and παράπτωμα together in Eph 2:1 and uses a relative pronoun in Eph 2:2 that only modifies the former suggests that overlap exists between these terms.

---

fines the first accusative "redemption" (ἀπολύτρωσιν) to suggest that the redemption that believers have through Jesus' blood is forgiveness of sins/trespasses.

[136] Here it agrees in case, number, and gender.

Nevertheless, ἁμαρτία ("sin") is Paul's preferred word for sin.[137] It is a general reference to sin's power (see Rom 5:12–6:14) and to sinful actions (see Rom 3:23). It does not necessarily refer to a violation of a specific command in Paul (as opposed to "transgression" [παράπτωμα] in Rom 5:15). Rather, it often refers to one's misstep or wrongdoing (see Rom 3:9,20; 4:7,8; 5:12–13,20; 6:1–2,6,7,10,11,12,13,14,16,17,18,20,22,23; 7:5,7,8,9,11,13,14,17,20,23, 25; 8:2–3,10; 11:27; 14:23; 1 Cor 15:3,17, 56; 2 Cor 5:21; 11:7; Gal 1:4; 2:17; 3:22; Eph 2:1; Col 1:14; 1 Thess 2:16; 1 Tim 5:22,24; 2 Tim 3:6). On the other hand, Paul often uses παράπτωμα ("transgression/trespass") to define sin more precisely: that is, a violation of a specific command (Rom 5:14,17,18,20; 11:11–12; see LXX Wis 10:1; Ezek 14:11; 18:22).[138] Thus, redemption through Jesus' blood in Eph 1:7 and in Col 1:14 (see 1:20; 2:13) confirms that Jesus' death was a sacrifice of atonement since his death wiped away sins and even canceled out the transgressions of those who violated God's specific commands.

Conclusion

Jesus' death was God's provision for racial reconciliation. I have argued that his death was a sacrifice of atonement for sin because his death was the basis upon which Paul states that Jews and Gentiles are justified before God by faith and reconciled to God. Jesus' death was the means by which God's wrath is appeased against sin, sins are forgiven, law-breakers are delivered from the law's curse, and the Abrahamic blessing comes to the Gentiles by faith. Chapter 4 will argue that Jesus' sacrificial death for sin achieves reconciliation for Jews and Gentiles.

---

[137] It occurs 53 times in Paul, whereas παράπτωμα occurs 16 times, παράβασις ("violation"), 5 times, and ἁμάρτημα ("sin/sinful deed"), 2 times.

[138] For further discussion of the terms for sin in Eph 1:7 and Col 1:14, see Hoehner, *Ephesians*, 207–8; P. T. O'Brien, *The Letter to the Ephesians* (PNTC; Grand Rapids: Eerdmans, 1999), 156–57.

4

the accomplishment of racial reconciliation

Chapters 2 and 3 focused on the reason and the provision for racial reconciliation. Chapter 2 argued that sin is the fundamental reason human beings need to be reconciled first to God and secondly to one another. Chapter 3 argued that Jesus' sacrificial death for humanity's sin is God's provision for racial reconciliation. I contend in this chapter that because Jesus died as a sacrifice of atonement for humanity's sin, he has accomplished reconciliation both for and between Jews and Gentiles. Although I discuss selected texts in the Pauline corpus in which Paul grounds God's reconciliatory act for Jews and Gentiles in Jesus' death, most of my discussion in this chapter focuses on Eph 2:11–22 since Paul states in this text that Jesus' death has reconciled Jews and Gentiles to God and one another.

Jesus' Death Reconciles Jews and Gentiles to God

Romans 5:1–11

Peace with God is reconciliation to God. In Rom 5:1, Paul turns to begin a new section (chaps. 5–8) that emphasizes the theme of hope.[1] Central to this hope is justification by faith in Christ. In fact, Paul's use of the word "therefore" in 5:1 closely connects chap.

---

[1] For other scholars who affirm this shift in theme in Romans 5–8, see chap. 3.

5 to 3:24–4:25. Paul argues in 3:21–4:25 that Jews and Gentiles are justified by their faith in Christ, who died for their sins. In 4:25, Paul concludes the argument with a reference to both Jesus' death for humankind's sin and Jesus' resurrection. He suggests in 4:24–25 that Jesus' death and resurrection together guarantee the future justification for those "who believe in him [God]."

Paul states, "Therefore, having been justified by faith, we have peace with God through our Lord Jesus Christ" (5:1). This statement provides the impetus for Paul's discussion of hope in Romans 5–8. It also suggests that the justification that comes by faith in Christ grants peace to all who are justified. The phrase "having been justified" (δικαιωθέντες) in 5:1 is a passive participle in the Greek text. It is likely a divine passive, which suggests that God is the theological subject, for Paul states earlier in Romans that God both reveals his righteousness (1:17, 3:21–22; see 9:30) and justifies those who believe by faith (3:26,30; see 8:30). As elsewhere in Romans, δικαιόω ("to justify") is forensic, that is, it is a legal term (see 2:13; 3:4,20,24,26,28,30; 4:2,5; 5:9; 6:7; 8:30). Moreover, since Paul has argued in 3:21–4:25 that Jews and Gentiles can be justified by faith, δικαιωθέντες should be understood as a causal participle ("because we have been justified").

The affirmation "because we have been justified by faith" is an extremely important theological one, but it is not Paul's main thought in 5:1 because it is a dependent clause. As such, the clause grammatically relies on the sentence "we have peace with God" in order to make grammatical sense. Since "have" is the main verb in the verse, the main thought is "we have peace with God through our Lord Jesus Christ."[2] The words "because we have been justi-

---

[2] An important textual variant occurs in 5:1. Scholars have noted that external evidence (various manuscripts from different locales) suggest that Paul uses a verb in the subjunctive mood (ἔχωμεν "let us have") instead of the indicative mood (ἔχομεν "we have") and that internal evidence (the argument of Romans) suggests that the latter verb is the correct reading. The former reading states a command ("let us have"). Thus, Paul is exhorting the Romans to pursue peace instead of stating that they have received it. V. D. Verbrugge ("The Grammatical Internal Evidence for ἔχομεν in Rom 5:1" [paper presented at the national meeting of the Evangelical Theological Society, Providence, RI, November 19, 2008], 1–4) offers a compelling piece of internal evidence that has been overlooked by scholars in support of the indicative reading "we have." He argues that if Paul had intended to use the hortatory subjunctive "let us have" (ἔχωμεν), he most likely would have begun 5:3 with the words μή μόνον ("not only") instead of οὐ μόνον ("not only") since μή normally negates verbs in moods other than those in the indicative mood. This argument is compelling since there is a correlative relationship between 5:1–2 and 5:3.

fied by faith," therefore, provide the reason those who have faith in Christ have peace with God.

Many people express a desire to have peace with God. This desire is indulged by the attempts our culture takes to outline the sure path of finding peace in this life. Paul says at least three noteworthy things in 5:1 about peace with God. First, those who have been justified by faith have peace with God. Second, faith is the means through which peace with God comes to the justified. Third, Jesus is the agent through whom peace with God comes to those justified. Nevertheless, the question of what is peace with God in 5:1 remains.

Paul refers to *peace* often in his letters. He either uses the term in a benediction by itself (Rom 15:33; 16:20; Eph 6:23; 1 Thess 5:23; 2 Thess 3:16) or in conjunction with grace (Rom 1:7; 1 Cor 1:3; 2 Cor 1:2; Gal 1:3; Eph 1:2: Phil 1:2; Col 1:2; 1 Thess 1:1; 2 Thess 1:2; Titus 1:4; Phlm 3), mercy (1 Tim 1:2), and joy (Rom 15:13). He uses *peace* to refer to eternal life (Rom 2:10; 8:6; Gal 6:16) and the gospel (Eph 2:17; 6:15). He uses *peace* as an attribute of God (Rom 15:33; 16:20; 1 Cor 14:33; 2 Cor 13:11) and to express how Jews and Gentiles ought to live in relation to one another in the world (Rom 3:17; 14:17,19; 1 Cor 7:15; 16:11; Eph 4:3; see Eph 2:14–15). He states that *peace* is a gift from God (Eph 1:2; Phil 4:7,9; Col 1:2; 1 Thess 5:23; 2 Thess 1:2; 1 Tim 1:2; Titus 1:4; Phlm 3) and from Christ (Eph 1:2; Col 3:15; 2 Thess 1:2; 3:16–17; 1 Tim 1:2; Titus 1:4; Phlm 3), and that it is a fruit of the Spirit (Gal 5:22).

In Rom 5:1, Paul uses *peace* as a relational term to refer to salvation since he states that the ones whom God justifies by faith "have peace with God" and that justification by faith is the basis for "peace with God." *Peace*, then, is an eschatological promise that has invaded the present age since Paul connects it with justification by faith (5:1,9) and with salvation (5:9), both of which are eschatological promises that have invaded the present age (see 3:20,24; 5:9). More specifically, "peace with God" suggests that hostility between God and humanity no longer exists for the justified ones. That is, the justified ones and God are no longer enemies, but they are friends, for God has reconciled them by faith on the basis of Jesus' sacrificial death for their sin (see Rom 5:6–11).

Romans 5:6–11 provides the reason for the hope that Paul discusses throughout Romans 5–8. "Peace with God" is part of this eschatological hope. The justified ones have this hope because Jesus died for their sins. Romans 5:6 states this point: "For Christ still died in time for the ungodly while we were still weak." The "weak" and the "ungodly" in 5:6 for whom Christ died are the same group, that is, "sinners," because Paul states in 5:8 that "Christ died for us while we were sinners." Romans 5:9–11 elucidates the nature of the hostile relationship that the "weak" and "ungodly" ones had with God before they were justified: they were God's enemies and subject to his eschatological wrath (see Rom 2:6–11). Romans 5:9 infers from 5:1–8 that Jesus' blood justifies ("having been justified by his blood") and that as a result, the justified will be saved from God's wrath. The phrase "having been justified" ($\delta\iota\kappa\alpha\iota\omega\theta\acute{\epsilon}\nu\tau\epsilon\varsigma$) in 5:9 provides the translation for the same form of the Greek participle in 5:1. In 5:9, Paul states what he merely assumes in 5:1: the foundation of justification by faith is Jesus' sacrificial death for sin.

In 5:10, Paul restates the premise of 5:8–9, but with more elaboration: "for if while we were enemies, we were reconciled to God through the death of his son, how much more we will be saved [from God's wrath] because we have been reconciled [to God through the death of his son]." Paul and all believers were God's enemies before they were justified since Paul states that the justified ones will be saved from God's eschatological wrath in the judgment on the basis of Jesus' blood (5:9) and since he states that God's enemies were reconciled to God by means of Jesus' death (5:9–10). But Jesus' death on their behalf justified them by their faith and reconciled them to God.

The verb "to reconcile" ($\kappa\alpha\tau\alpha\lambda\lambda\acute{\alpha}\sigma\sigma\omega$) in 5:10 is not used in the New Testament in a theological sense outside of Paul (see 2 Cor 5:18–19).[3] In the New Testament, neither the verb nor its cognate $\kappa\alpha\tau\alpha\lambda\lambda\alpha\gamma\acute{\eta}$ ("reconciliation") is applied to the sacrificial death of a human for the saving benefit of another except in Paul's letters.[4] Paul borrowed the concept of reconciliation from the Hellenistic

---

[3] Against C. Breytenbach, *Versöhnung: Eine Studie zur paulinischen Soteriologie* (WMANT 60; Neukirchener-Vluyn: Neukirchener Verlag, 1989), 40–83. J. Dupont (*La reconciliation dans la théologie de Saint Paul* [Paris: Desclée de Brouwer Universitaies de Louvain, 1953]) provided the most exhaustive investigation of reconciliation in Paul's theology prior to the work of Breytenbach and S. E. Porter (*Καταλλάσσω in Ancient Greek Literature, with Reference to the Pauline Writings* [Cordoba: Ediciones El Almendro], 1994).

[4] Against Breytenbach, *Versöhnung*, 40–83.

world in which he lived to speak of the reconciliation that Jesus accomplishes for those for whom he died.[5] He uses both the verb and the noun forms in 5:10–11 in the same manner as the author of 2 Macc 5:20 and 7:33 does since both 2 Maccabees and Paul suggest that righteous Jews vicariously died to achieve reconciliation for others (i.e., martyr traditions=Jewish martyrs and Paul=Jesus, a righteous Jew). That is, both the author of 2 Maccabees and Paul use the reconciliation motif to refer to the attainment of friendship between two parties by means of the sacrificial death of a human for the benefit of another person.[6]

The authors of 2 and 4 Maccabees suggest that the Jewish martyrs died vicariously as sacrifices of atonement for Israel's sin in order to reconcile the nation to God.[7] God was angry with Israel and judged the nation through Antiochus' persecution of them since many of the Jews had rebelled against Yahweh and heeded to Antiochus' pagan reforms (see 1 Maccabees 1–2 with 2 and 4 Maccabees). The author of 2 Maccabees confirms that the martyrs' deaths achieved reconciliation for Israel when he states (1) that the martyrs' deaths made peace between God and the martyrs who were otherwise at enmity with one another and (2) that after the martyrs' deaths Antiochus eventually made peace with Jews in the land (see 2 Macc 5:1–8:4, esp 7:33; 4 Macc 6:1–17:22).[8] Observe the following excerpts from 2 and 4 Maccabees that speak of the

---

[5] For reconciliation in the Greco-Roman world, see J. T. Fitzgerald, "Paul and Paradigm Shifts: Reconciliation and Its Linkage Group," in *Paul Beyond the Hellenism/Judaism Divide* (ed. T. Engberg-Pedersen; Louisville: Westminster John Knox Press, 2001), 241–62; idem, "Paul and Friendship," in *Paul in the Greco-Roman World: A Handbook* (ed. J. P. Sampley; Harrisburg, PA: Trinity Press International, 2003), 319–43. Fitzgerald especially argues that the concept of reconciliation is part of a linkage group: "a group of heredity characteristics which remain associated with one another through a number of generations. When applied to concepts, the expression 'linkage group' thus indicates certain terms and ideas that remain associated with one another through a number of generations" ("Paul and Friendship," 320, 331).

[6] This point is fiercely debated in scholarship. See my *Maccabean Martyr Traditions in Paul's Theology of Atonement: Did Martyr Theology Shape Paul's Conception of Jesus' Death?* (Eugene, OR: Wipf & Stock, 2010). Breytenbach's masterful work (*Versöhnung*, 118–19; 221) on reconciliation in Paul's soteriology argues that a Hellenistic military context was Paul's background for reconciliation. He posits that Paul merges the secular Hellenistic idea of reconciliation with Old Testament cultic vocabulary and thereby creatively interprets both reconciliation and atonement in light of the early Christian tradition of Jesus' death for others.

[7] Ibid.

[8] The sacrificial nature of the martyrs' deaths in 2 and 4 Maccabees is debated. For a discussion of Maccabean martyr theology's influence on Paul's atonement theology, see chaps. 2 and 3 in my *Maccabean Martyr Traditions*.

need for reconciliation between God and Israel and the use of the Jewish martyrs as the means by which God was reconciled to the nation and the nation was saved.

> May [God] hear your prayers and be reconciled (καταλλάσσω) to you, and may he not forsake you in time of evil (NRA, 2 Macc 1:5).
>
> . . . Therefore, [the temple] itself shared in the misfortunes that befell the nation and afterward participated in its benefits; and what was forsaken in the wrath of the Almighty was restored again in all its glory when the great Lord became reconciled (καταλλαγή) (NRA, 2 Macc 5:20).
>
> . . . For we ourselves suffer because of our own sins. But if our living Lord has been angered for a little while on account of rebuke and discipline, he will also again be reconciled (καταλλάσσω) to his own servants (2 Macc 7:32–33).
>
> Meanwhile Judas, who was also called Maccabeus, and his companions secretly entered the villages and summoned their kindred and enlisted those who had continued in the Jewish faith, and so they gathered about 6,000. They implored the Lord to look upon the people who were oppressed by all; and to have pity on the temple that had been profaned by the godless; to have mercy on the city that was being destroyed and about to be leveled to the ground; to hearken to the blood that cried out to him; to remember also the lawless destruction of the innocent babies and the blasphemies committed against his name; and to show his hatred of evil. As soon as Maccabeus got his army organized, the Gentiles could not withstand him, for the wrath of the Lord had turned to mercy (NRA, 2 Macc 8:1–5).
>
> After the Sabbath, they gave some of the spoils to those who had been tortured and to the widows and orphans, and distributed the rest among themselves and their children. When they had done this, they made common supplication and implored the merciful Lord to be wholly reconciled (καταλλάσσω) with his servants (NRA, 2 Macc 8:28–29).

[Lord], be merciful to your nation, and be satisfied with our judgment on behalf of them. Make my blood to be their purification, and receive my life as their ransom (4 Macc 6:28–29).

. . . the tyrant [Antiochus] was punished, and the homeland [Israel] purified—they having become, as it were, a ransom for the sin of our nation. And through the blood of those devout ones and their death as an atoning sacrifice, divine Providence preserved (διασῴζω) Israel that previously had been mistreated (NRA, 4 Macc 17:21–22).

Therefore, if Maccabean martyr traditions were the immediate background to Paul's reconciliation motif, then he makes the point in Rom 5:9–10 that Jesus' sacrificial death for humanity's sin befriends Jews and Gentiles to God and ends the hostility between God and the justified by providing salvation for them.[9] Thus, those who are justified by Jesus' blood are no longer subject to God's wrath. Jesus' sacrificial death (see Rom 5:12–21) has restored humanity's relationship with God, which had become broken because of Adam's and Eve's sin. Consequently, Paul can say in 5:11 that the justified ones hope in God through Christ, who is the very source of their justification and reconciliation with God. Reconciliation "marks the end of hatred and the inception or return of affection. Good will replaces ill will, and with that change, enemies are transformed into friends."[10] Therefore, peace with God in Rom 5:1 is reconciliation to God, and reconciliation to God equals friendship with God.[11] Peace, reconciliation, and friendship with God happen because of Jesus' sacrificial death for the sins of Jews and Gentiles.

---

[9] Although he does not connect Paul's reconciliation language with 2 Macc 5:20 and 7:33, Fitzgerald ("Paul and Friendship," 334–40) speaks of the connection between reconciliation and friendship terms in Greco-Roman literature.

[10] Ibid., 336.

[11] On reconciliation as friendship with God, see Fitzgerald, "Paul and Friendship," 337. I understand reconciliation in Pauline theology to be a result of justification by faith thereby making a distinction between these two soteriological categories. R. Bultmann (*Theology of the New Testament* [trans. K. Grobel; Waco, TX: Baylor University Press, 2007], 286–87, esp. 287), on the other hand, suggests that "peace with God unfolds the meaning of righteousness: as rightwised men, we have peace with God."

2 Corinthians 5:18–20 and 5:21

Reconciled to God. That Jesus' sacrificial death for sin reconciled humanity to God is exactly Paul's point in 2 Cor 5:18–19 and in 5:21.[12] Paul mentions Jesus' death for others in 5:14–15. Then, he states in 5:18 that God "reconciles us to himself through Christ" and that he gives "us a ministry of reconciliation." Thus, Jesus' death is the foundation of God's reconciliatory act for Jews and Gentiles in 5:18 since references to his death precede (5:14–15) and follow (5:21) Paul's references to God's reconciliatory act through Christ. Jesus' death is the foundation of reconciliation between God and human beings in this text since Paul states that God reconciles "us" to himself "through Christ."[13]

Second Corinthians 5:19 and 5:21 together support that Jesus' death reconciles Jews and Gentiles to God. Second Corinthians 5:19 further elaborates on 5:17–18 by stating how God has recreated all things in Christ.[14] Second Corinthians 5:19 and 5:21 suggest that Jesus' death for sin was the mechanism by which God reconciles Jews and Gentiles to himself. New creation, then, is God's reconciliatory act in Christ that he has accomplished through Jesus' sacrificial death for sin. This understanding is supported by God's not reckoning transgressions against those for whom Jesus died (5:19) and by Paul's stating that God "made Jesus sin" (5:21).

In light of the exegetical complexity of 5:19 and 5:21, I must note a few hermeneutical difficulties. Second Corinthians 5:19 presents two interpretive challenges. One is grammatical, and the other is exegetical. First, the syntax of 5:19 in the Greek text is difficult, which makes translating the verse a challenge. There are at least three translation options: (1) "It was God who in Christ was reconciling the world to himself." (2) "In Christ, God was reconciling the world to himself." (3) "God was in Christ reconciling

---

[12] 2 Cor 5:18–21 is part of a larger unit (chaps. 1–7) where Paul defends his apostolic ministry.

[13] M. J. Harris (*The Second Epistle to the Corinthians* [NIGTC; Grand Rapids: Eerdmans, 2005], 452) rightly suggests that being reconciled "through Christ" (διὰ Χριστοῦ) in 2 Cor 5:18 is equivalent to being reconciled "through the death of his son" (διὰ τοῦ θανάτου τοῦ υἱοῦ αὐτοῦ) in Rom 5:10 since 2 Cor 5:14–15 emphasizes Christ's death for all.

[14] In the Greek text of 2 Cor 5:19, v. 19 begins with the two adverbs ὡς ("as") and ὅτι ("because" or "that"). These two adverbs occur side by side elsewhere only two other times in Paul (2 Cor 11:21; 2 Thess 2:2). In both occurrences in 2 Corinthians, the statements that follow the two adverbs explain a preceding statement. Similarly Harris, *Second Corinthians*, 439–40, esp. 440.

the world to himself."[15] Option one should be dismissed on Greek grammatical grounds since it suggests that "God" is not the subject of the verb "was." Options 2 and 3 are both grammatically possible, and they essentially convey the same idea: God reconciled the world to himself. Nevertheless, option 3 is preferred here ("God was in Christ reconciling the world to himself") since it elevates Christ as God. Paul emphasizes Christ as God's agent through whom new creation and reconciliation are accomplished, and he thereby heralds Jesus as God's equal.[16] Paul uses this high Christology when he switches from Christ to God throughout 5:14–21 as he discusses God's love and Jesus' death (5:14–15,21), new creation (5:17), and reconciliation (5:18–20). According to 5:14–21, Christ and God cooperated in this reconciliatory activity for humanity.[17]

Second, 2 Cor 5:21 presents two exegetical challenges. Paul states that God made Jesus to be sin and that we become the righteousness of God in him. Three questions arise from this statement: (1) How did God make Jesus sin? (2) When did God make Jesus sin (i.e., at the incarnation or at the crucifixion)? (3) How do those for whom Jesus died become God's righteousness in him?

The verse, first of all, should be interpreted in the context of Paul's argument where he defends his apostolic ministry (see 3:1–5:21). In the context of 5:16–21, v. 21 likely explains v. 19, which explains v. 18. This interpretation seems right since 5:19 states that in addition to reconciling the world to himself, God does not count the transgressions against those who were reconciled, but instead God gave them a ministry of reconciliation. The three participles (καταλλάσσων ["reconciling"], λογιζόμενος ["counting"], and θέμενος ["placing"]) in 5:19, then, suggest at least three things that God in Christ provided: (1) reconciliation, (2) forgiveness of sins, and (3) a message of reconciliation.

Second Corinthians 5:21 states more specifically the reason that God does not count transgressions against those whom he reconciled to himself: He made Jesus (who knew no sin) to be sin for them (ἁμαρτίαν ὑπὲρ ἡμῶν). When Paul states that Jesus did not know sin, he possibly means that he was not acquainted with

---

[15] Each translation option comes from Harris, *Second Corinthians*, 440–41.

[16] For arguments in favor of the pre-existence of Christ in 2 Cor 5:21, see R. H. Bell, "Sacrifice and Christology in Paul," *JTS* 53 (2002): 14–16.

[17] For a recent work on Pauline Christology, see G. D. Fee, *Pauline Christology: An Exegetical-Theological Study* (Peabody, MA: Hendrickson, 2007).

sin nor had experience with it since Paul contrasts in 5:21 Christ's ignorance of sin with God's act of not counting transgressions against those for whom Christ died (5:14–15), that is, against those whom God reconciled (5:19) and against those whom he justified (5:21).[18] Yet, although Jesus had no personal experience with sin, God made him to be sin. Since Paul connects God's act of making Jesus sin in 5:21 with Jesus' death for others in 5:14–15 and with reconciliation in 5:18–19, it follows that God likely made Jesus to be sin by offering him to die *for* sin and *to bear its curse* for those who sinned, both of which were realized and culminated in Jesus' death on the cross (see LXX Isa 53:4–6,12; GNT Rom 3:25–26; 8:3; Gal 3:13).[19] Based on this reading, even if Paul is not calling Jesus a sin offering here,[20] he still suggests that Jesus bore the punishment of sin by his death for the transgressors.[21] His death should be viewed in 5:21 as both representative and substitutionary for others.[22]

The second exegetical difficulty is the meaning of the statement "so that we would become the righteousness of God in him."[23] The phrase "righteousness of God" (δικαιοσύνη θεοῦ) is the same exact phrase that Paul uses in Rom 1:17 and in 3:21–22 to refer to God's act of justification for those who have faith. As in Rom 1:17 and 3:21–22, Paul likewise uses the phrase here to refer to the salvation that Jesus has purchased by his death since he connects Jesus' death

---

[18] Ibid., 450. B. J. Vickers (*Jesus' Blood and Righteousness* [Wheaton: Crossway, 2004], 167 and 167 n. 4 and n. 5) suggests that the statement "who knew no sin" recalls the description that occurs often in the Old Testament cult in regard to the sacrificial offerings: "without defect."

[19] Harris (*Second Corinthians*, 454) suggests that God treated Christ as sin.

[20] Against Christ as a sin offering in 2 Cor 5:21, see Bell, "Sacrifice and Christology," 1–27, esp. 13–14. Bell (5–8) does not reject that Paul calls Jesus a sin offering elsewhere in his letters (e.g., Rom 8:3), but that Paul does not present him as such in 2 Cor 5:21. Some scholars (e.g., Breytenbach, *Versöhnung*, esp. 40–83) have been so ardent to demonstrate that 2 Cor 5:21 does not refer to Jesus' death as a sin offering that they have failed to see that 5:21 still conveys the idea that Jesus' death at least conceptually was a sin offering since 2 Cor 5:14–21 suggests that Jesus died for the sins of others.

[21] Vickers (*Jesus' Blood*, 162) makes a helpful observation when he asserts that "the link between 'made to be sin' and 'sin-offering' is stronger if one does not try to limit Paul's meaning to a particular sacrifice or aspect of a sacrifice. That is to say, perhaps there is a more general idea of Christ's being a sacrifice for sin in this verse, rather than a one-to-one correspondence with the Old Testament 'sin-offering.' It is what the sacrifice accomplished, not the particular sacrifice itself, that comes into focus." For further discussion of 5:21, see Vickers, 161–90.

[22] So Harris, *Second Corinthians*, 453.

[23] For recent discussion of the meaning of this statement and for an interaction with key scholars in the debate, see Vickers, 160–90.

(2 Cor 5:14–15,21) and reconciliation with the phrase "righteous-ness of God." Thus, "we" become "God's righteousness" in Christ by faith on the basis of Jesus' death and thereby are reconciled to God in that God declares the "we" for whom Christ died and who are in Christ to be in the right (2 Cor 5:19; see Rom 1:16–17; 3:21–5:1,9,10). The contrast between God making Jesus sin and "we" becoming God's righteousness in Jesus suggests that God imputed our sin to Jesus and he imputed his (God's) righteousness to those for whom he died.[24] Second Corinthians 5:21, then, states how God in Christ was reconciling the world to himself (5:19): namely, God judged sin in Jesus so that those for whom he died would be clothed with God's righteousness in Christ. As Brian J. Vickers states: "On the cross, God's saving righteousness and judging righ-teousness converge on Christ who vicariously bears the judgment for sin, proving the objective basis for the justification of sinners and the reconciliation of man to God" (see Rom 3:21–26).[25]

Be reconciled to God. Because of God's saving work of justi-fication and as a result of reconciliation to God, Paul states that he and others received a message of reconciliation from God by which they evangelistically announced, "Be reconciled to God" (5:20).[26] The command "be reconciled to God" does not contra-dict the assertion in 5:19 that God in Christ was reconciling the world to himself. Rather, it suggests that part of the content of the message of the "word of reconciliation" (5:19) was "be reconciled (καταλλάγητε) to God" (5:20). The divine act of reconciliation in Christ provides a means by which others can be drawn into this reconciliatory act, which is the proclamation that all should be reconciled to God. God's act of reconciliation through Christ is the foundation of one becoming reconciled to God and receiving

---

[24]So Harris, *Second Corinthians*, 455. Against N. T. Wright, "On Becoming the Righ-teousness of God: 2 Corinthians 5:21," in *Pauline Theology* (ed. D. M. Hay; Minneapolis: Fortress, 1993), 1:205–06. Wright argues that "righteousness of God" here refers to God's covenantal faithfulness: "God made him who knew no sin to be sin so that we would be-come God's covenantal faithfulness." Nevertheless, Wright's view hardly seems defensible since Paul's point in 5:14–21 pertains to God's reconciliatory action for humanity in Christ by his sacrificial death for sin.

[25]Vickers, *Jesus' Blood*, 182–83.

[26]Harris (*Second Corinthians*, 448) rightly understands the command "be reconciled to God" in 5:20 as an evangelistic appeal to any audience that Paul (and his colleagues) would address as ambassadors of Christ. For interaction with alternative readings of 5:20, see Har-ris, *Second Corinthians*, 447–49.

the righteousness of God in him, and Jesus' sacrificial death for sin is the foundation of the message of reconciliation.[27]

Jesus' Death Reconciles Jews and Gentiles to One Another

Ephesians 2:11–22

Jesus' death also reconciles Jews and Gentiles to one another. This truth is seen in Eph 2:11–22 where Paul argues that Jesus' death reconciles Jews and Gentiles to God and to one another by making the two groups into one new man. As I discuss reconciliation in Eph 2:11–22, the reader should remember that Ephesians is about the church. Paul's statements in Eph 2:11–22 are not isolated from the message of the letter. He writes this letter to churches in Asia Minor to discuss the spiritual blessings that the church has in Christ.[28] He mentions some of those spiritual blessings in 1:3–14 (e.g., predestination, election, and redemption). Paul also discusses in this letter (1) Jesus as the head of the church (Eph 1:22; 4:15), (2) unity in the church (Eph 4:1–16), (3) the sort of people who make up the church (Eph 2:11–22), (4) the human family and the church (Eph 5:6–33), and (5) spiritual warfare and the church (Eph 6:10–20). In Eph 2:11–22, Paul especially emphasizes the new relationship that Jews and Gentiles have with one another as a result of Jesus' sacrificial death for them.

Gentiles Were Excluded from God's Promises to Israel

As a means of discussing reconciliation between Jews and Gentiles, Paul urges his Gentile audience to remember what had separated Jews and Gentiles from one another.[29] They were former-ly "without Christ, separated from the commonwealth of Israel, strangers of the covenants of promise, without hope, and without

---

[27] This point is especially seen by the relationship between the verses in 2 Cor 5:19–21. Second Cor 5:20 is bilateral to 2 Cor 5:19 and 2 Cor 5:21. That is, the inference of 5:20 relates both to the assertion in 5:19 and in 5:21, so that Paul's ambassadorial ministry results from God in Christ reconciling the world to himself and making Jesus sin.

[28] The cyclical nature of Ephesians is commonplace in New Testament scholarship. E.g., A. T. Lincoln, *Ephesians* (WBC 42; Nashville: Thomas Nelson, 1990), xl–xli; H. W. Hoehner, *Ephesians: An Exegetical Commentary* (Grand Rapids: Baker, 2002), 141.

[29] Since Paul addresses his comments to Gentile Christians in Eph 2:11–22, R. P. Martin (*Reconciliation: A Study of Paul's Theology* [Atlanta: John Knox, 1981], 166) suggests that these Gentile Christians could have been in danger of forgetting the Jewish heritage of their faith. Paul, thus, wants to oppose any Gentile arrogance (see Rom 11:18–36).

God in the world" (2:11–12). The call to remember in 2:11–12 reveals a connection with 2:1–10 since the word "therefore" precedes the exhortation in 2:11–12.[30] Paul urges these Gentiles to remember on the basis of what he has previously discussed. In the latter text, he argues that these Gentiles were formerly dead in trespasses and sins (2:1) and therefore were void of spiritual life and utterly incapable of doing anything to generate this life (2:1–5; see Ezekiel 36–37). Instead, God himself took the initiative and saved these Gentiles by grace through faith, not by their works, so that they would have no reason to boast in themselves before God (2:6–9; see Rom 3:27–31).

Paul concludes his discussion of 2:1–9 in 2:10 by saying that God's work of salvation is the reason believers should produce good works (2:10). Then, in 2:11, Paul urges the Ephesians: "Therefore remember!" What should they remember? They should remember that before their conversion to faith in Christ they were outside of God's promises of salvation to Israel. In fact, everything that Paul mentions in 2:12 pertains to Jewish privileges (e.g., Messiah, citizenship in the commonwealth, the covenants of promise, and hope).

Gentiles were the uncircumcised. The term "Gentiles" (ἔθνη) in 2:11 is the first place in 2:11–22 where Paul distinguishes between Jews and Gentiles. This distinction is accentuated in 2:11 when Paul calls his readers "Gentiles in the flesh, who are called uncircumcised by those who are called the physical circumcision." One of the many aspects that distinguished Jews from Gentiles in the ancient world was circumcision. Yet, circumcision was also the fundamental sign that the Israelites were the people of God and, thus, were part of the covenant that God made with his people. Circumcision as a covenantal sign goes back to Abraham in Genesis 17. God tells Abraham that circumcision serves as a sign that God has made a covenant with him and that everyone who became a part of this covenant and participated in the covenantal sign would receive the covenantal blessings (Gen 17:11–14; see 17:10–14). This commandment of circumcision becomes part of the Mosaic covenant, and it is the fundamental sign whether a

---

[30] So Lincoln, *Ephesians*, 135.

male is a child of the covenant that God made with Abraham (Lev 12:3; Jos 5:2–9).

The adverb "formerly" in 2:11 and the phrase "in that time" in 2:12 express the time when the Gentiles were excluded from God's promises of salvation to Israel: when they were dead in trespasses and sins (see 2:1–10). This interpretation is sustained by the "therefore" in 2:11, which links 2:1–10 with 2:11–22. That the noun "Gentiles" (ἔθνη) is in apposition to the term "you" (ὑμεῖς) and that the statement "those who are called uncircumcised" (οἱ λεγόμενοι ἀκροβυστία) is an attributive participial construction describing "you" demonstrate my point. Circumcision was one sign that revealed that the Jews were people of the covenant and that the Gentiles were not since they were uncircumcised. Thus, Paul states in 2:11 that these Gentiles were formerly not God's covenantal people since they were Gentiles and since they were called Gentiles by the circumcised people of the covenant.[31]

The Gentiles were without Christ. In Eph 2:12 Paul elaborates that the Gentiles were not the people of the covenant by stating that they "were without Christ in that time." Paul mentions in 2:12 exactly what he wants the Gentiles to remember. They should remember that when they were dead in trespasses and sins, they had no access to Christ. But why were the Gentiles "without Christ" before their conversion? The answer is simple. From the Jewish perspective in the ancient world, since Gentiles were not Jewish, they were not part of God's covenantal people (see Rom 9:4–5; Phil 3:4–6), and, therefore, had no part in Israel's messianic hope.

The Old Testament speaks often about Israel's promised Christ. The term "Christ" (Χριστός) means "anointed one." In the LXX, the term translates from the Hebrew משיח ("Messiah," "anointed one," "king"; see MT and LXX Ps 2:2). In MT and LXX Ps 2:2, David is referred to as God's anointed. God anointed David (i.e., installed him and set him apart) as king over his people (1 Sam 16:13). Thus, both משיח and Χριστός carry royal and kingly connotations.

Throughout 1 and 2 Samuel, 1 and 2 Kings, and 1 and 2 Chronicles, the authors discuss the various successes and (mainly) the shortcomings of Israel's earthly kings and the destruction of their earthly kingdoms. The story of those six books is simply that all

---

[31] So Hoehner, *Ephesians*, 352.

of Israel's earthly kings—from the first king to the last one—have failed and Israel's earthly dynasty is ruined. The narratives where the kings' sins divide the kingdom into northern and southern territories, force both kingdoms into exile, and result in the temple's destruction especially display the kings' failures and ruin. Throughout Israel's darkened history, God constantly promised through the prophets that he would send the Messiah (the perfect king) who would save his people and whose kingdom would never end (see 2 Sam 7; Isa 40–66).

The New Testament authors, applying the term Χριστός to Jesus, state that God anointed Jesus as king over an eternal kingdom, that is, one whose reign and kingdom would never end (Acts 2:36; Rev 11:15; 12:10; 20:4,6). The failures of Israel's kings and their kingdoms anticipate a greater king and an eternal kingdom (2 Sam 7:12–16). Although God's promise of salvation in the Old Testament through a Messiah did anticipate an ingathering of Gentiles (see Gen 12:1–3; Isa 42:6) and although all unbelieving Jews are separated from Jesus (see Rom 9:1–5), the promise of a Messiah to save God's people was fundamentally given to Israel, not to the Gentiles (see Gen 49:10; Deut 18:15; Pss 2; 45:3–5,17; Isaiah 40–66).[32] The Jewishness of God's messianic promises is elucidated by 2 Sam 7:12, which states that the king who would succeed David would be from his seed (see LXX 2 Sam 7:12); that is, he would be a Jewish descendant of David (see Matt 1:1). Thus, since the Gentiles were not children of the covenant, God's messianic promises to Israel did not apply to them, and consequently "they were without Christ."

In Eph 2:12 Paul states the reason Gentiles were formerly without Christ: "having been separated from the commonwealth of Israel, and [you were] strangers of the covenants of promise." The statement "having been separated" (ἀπηλλοτριωμένοι) is a participle in the Greek text. Its function here is possibly causal since in context Paul appears to offer a reason the Gentiles were without Christ. A causal understanding of the participle would require the translation "because you were separated."[33]

---

[32] Similarly, P. T. O'Brien, *The Letter to the Ephesians* (PNTC; Grand Rapids: Eerdmans, 1999), 188.

[33] Against Hoehner, *Ephesians*, 356.

The verb "separate" (ἀπαλλοτριόω) occurs only 3 times in Paul (Eph 2:12; 4:18; Col 1:21; but see LXX Josh 22:25; Pss 57:4; 68:9: Job 21:29; Hos 9:10; Jer 19:4; 27:8; Ezek 14:5,7). The verb suggests that the Gentiles had absolutely no association with Israel's religious heritage and thereby were excluded from God's saving promises to the nation (see 3 Macc 1:3) since Paul coalesces the ideas of the Gentiles being "without Christ" and "separated from Israel's citizenship" along with their being "strangers of the covenants of promise" (see Philo, *On Special Laws*, 1.9.51).[34] The "covenants of promise" from which the Gentiles were separate at least refer to the promised covenants that God made with Abraham regarding land, seed, and universal blessing (Gen 12:1–4; 13:14–18; 15:1–21, and 17:1–21), with David regarding a promised seed to succeed his place on the throne and whose kingdom would never end (2 Sam 7:12–17; 23:5, Ps 89:3,27–37,49), and with Israel and Judah regarding the new covenant of a future restoration (Jer 31:31–34; Ezekiel 36–37) since Paul connects "the covenants of promise" with messiah (Eph 2:12).[35] Thus, the "covenants of promise" refer to God's salvation-historical promises to Israel, which began with Abraham, continued with David and the prophets, and culminated in Jesus' cross and resurrection (see Acts 2, 7–8, 13). Therefore, when the Gentiles were without Christ, they were hopeless and without God in the world because they had no part in the salvation-historical promises that God gave to Israel during the old covenant (Eph 2:12; see Pss Sol 18:1–12).[36]

Jesus' Sacrificial Death and God's Promises to the Gentiles

Jesus' blood extends God's promises to the Gentiles. With the words "but now" in 2:13, Paul offers an emphatic antithesis to his statements in 2:11–12. Everything in the text dramatically changes. Although Gentiles were formerly without Christ, alienated from Israel, hopeless, and without God (2:11–12), their union with Jesus changes their status and includes them in God's promises of salvation. With the words "but now," Paul does something similar in Rom 3:21–26 to what he does in Eph 2:13. In Rom 1:18–3:20, Paul

[34] Ibid., 356–57.
[35] Ibid., 358–59.
[36] Ibid., 359.

argues that Jews and Gentiles are both guilty before God in the judgment since both groups fail to honor God to the degree that he deserves (see Rom 3:23). Then, in 3:21, he says "but now" God has chosen to justify Jews and Gentiles by faith in Christ on the basis of his death (see Rom 3:21–26).

In Eph 2:13 Paul emphasizes that Christ Jesus was the agent through whom the Gentiles have been brought near God's salvation-historical promises to Israel with his repetition of "by means of Christ Jesus" (Eph 2:13*a*) and "by means of Christ" (Eph 2:13*b*). To be brought near here must mean that God extends his saving promises to the Gentiles (see Acts 22:21), for Paul states in Eph 2:11–12 they were excluded from these promises since they were not Jewish. To be brought near "by the blood of Christ" refers to Jesus' death.[37] His death was necessary for these Gentiles to be included in God's salvation-historical promises since they had no ethnic connection with the Jewish Messiah. So, Christ himself had to act on behalf of both Israel and the Gentiles in order to fulfill those saving promises to Jews and also make Israel a light to the Gentiles (see Isaiah 40–66).[38] That is, the very Messiah with whom the Gentiles had no ethnic connection was the One who has included them into God's promises of salvation to Israel. Paul emphasizes here not that Gentiles become ethnic Jews and surrender their ethnic identity by being connected to Israel's Jewish Messiah, for Paul calls them Gentiles in 2:11. Rather, Paul emphasizes that God includes them as Gentiles into his saving promises to Israel through the blood of Israel's Jewish Messiah (see 2:13 with 2:16).

Jesus' death shattered ethnic boundary markers. Paul states how God included the Gentiles into his saving promises in Eph 2:14–22: Jesus' death shattered all ethnic boundary markers between Jews and Gentiles. He reconciled by his death both groups into one new man, and he is building them up into the temple of God as one body.[39] When Paul states that Jesus is "our peace" (Eph

---

[37] Against D. C Smith ("Jewish and Greek Traditions in Eph 2:11–22" [Ph.D. diss., Yale University, 1970], 44–50), who argues that the blood in 2:13 refers to Jesus' circumcision since the author mentions circumcision in 2:11. This thesis has absolutely no textual warrant since Paul refers to Jesus' death in 2:16 as the means through which God includes Gentiles into his promises to Israel.

[38] See Martin, *Reconciliation*, 178.

[39] A former trend in German scholarship found a Jewish Gnostic redeemer myth in Eph 2:14–18. E.g., H. Schlier, *Christus und die Kirche im Epheserbrief* (BHT 6; Tübingen: Mohr, 1930); idem, *Der Brief an die Epheser* (2nd ed.; Düsseldorf: Patmos-Verlag, 1958), 118–45;

2:14), he echoes his statement in Rom 5:1: "We have peace with God." As in Rom 5:1, "peace" in Eph 2:14 is reconciliation since Paul argues in 2:14–22 that God has recreated Jews and Gentiles into one new man and thereby shattered their hostility between one another.[40] In distinction from Rom 5:1, Paul states here that Jesus does not simply provide peace for Jews and Gentiles, but that he is "our peace."

Paul offers in 2:13–18 a Christological exegesis of Isa 9:6; 52:7; and 57:19 (see Mic 5:5).[41] "Peace" in 2:14 and the proclamation of peace to "those far" and to "those near" in 2:17 link Eph 2:13–18 with Isaiah.[42] In the above texts from Isaiah, this "peace" refers to Israel's Messiah (Isa 9:6) and to the salvation that he would bring to the nation through him (Isa 52:7; 57:19; see Isaiah 40–66). Some within Israel were "far off" in that they had turned away from faithful devotion to Yahweh (see Isaiah 1), but others within Israel were "near" in that they were serving Yahweh. Nevertheless, Yahweh sent Israel and Judah into exile because of the disobedience of some in both parts of the kingdom (see 1 Kings–2 Chronicles). Paul suggests that these texts from Isaiah are fulfilled in Jesus and that the Gentiles have been included in these messianic promises of salvation through him.[43] Therefore, since Paul specifically mentions Messiah in 2:12–13 and since 2:14 explains that Messiah brought the Gentiles near God's promises to Israel by Messiah's blood, "our peace" most likely refers to Messiah. The emphasis in Eph 2:14–22 (unlike Romans 5) is not God's act of reconciling Jews and Gentiles to himself, but his act of reconciling Jews and Gentiles to one another. The latter becomes clear by considering other statements throughout the text.[44]

Paul states that Jesus "made both to be one" (2:14) and that "he created the two into one new man" (2:15). He declares that

---

E. Käsemann, *Leib und Leib Christi* (BHT 9; Tübingen: Mohr, 1933); idem, "The Theological Problem Presented by the Motif of the Body of Christ," in *Pauline Perspectives* (Philadelphia: Fortress, 1969), 102–21, esp. 109–110. Against such a theory, see Stuhlmacher, *Reconciliation*, 182–94. Stuhlmacher convincingly argues that Paul offers a Christological exegesis of Isa 9:5–6; 52:7; and 57:19 in Eph 2:13–18.

[40] Similarly, Stuhlmacher, *Reconciliation*, 188; Hoehner, *Ephesians*, 367.

[41] So Stuhlmacher, 187. Similarly, O'Brien, *Ephesians*, 194. Against Lincoln, *Ephesians*, 126–27.

[42] Stuhlmacher, *Reconciliation*, 187.

[43] Ibid., 188.

[44] The Greek syntax of Eph 2:14b–18 is difficult. For a detailed discussion of the syntax, see Hoehner, *Ephesians*, 371–74.

Jesus made peace between Jews and Gentiles (2:15) and that he reconciled both in one body to God through the cross by killing the enmity between them (2:16). He states that Jesus preached the gospel to both Jews and Gentiles (2:17; see Isa 52:7) and that both groups have access to God by the Spirit (2:18). Finally, he claims that Gentile Christians (along with Jewish Christians) are fellow citizens in God's family (2:19), are built upon the same apostolic and messianic foundation as Jewish Christians (2:20), and are growing together with fellow Jewish Christians into a holy temple in the Lord (2:21–22).

Paul's main thought in Eph 2:14–16 is that Jesus is peace for Jews and Gentiles.[45] The pronoun "our" in "our peace" most likely includes both Jews and Gentiles since Paul's entire discussion in Eph 2:14–22 highlights that the two groups are reconciled into one body. The way that Paul explains that Jesus provides peace for Jews and Gentiles is particularly pertinent to my thesis. He states that Jesus "made both [Jews and Gentiles] to be one." As stated above, this result does not mean that Gentiles become ethnic Jews when they become Christians, no more than it means that one surrenders his gender when he becomes a Christian (see Gal 3:28). Rather, Paul emphasizes that although the two groups (Jews and Gentiles) fundamentally differ from one another and although they were once hostile toward one another, God through Christ's sacrificial death shattered the boundary markers that distinguish them from one another and preclude them from fellowship.

The above interpretation fits with 2:14b–22. After stating that Jesus made Jews and Gentiles into "one new man," Paul states that "he destroyed by his flesh the dividing wall, [i.e.], the fence" and that this "dividing wall" caused enmity between Jews and Gentiles. The language of the "dividing wall" alludes to the walls of Jerusalem (LXX 3 Kgs 10:22; 11:27; 2 Esd 9:9) and to the courtyards of the temple (see DSS 11QT 36–40; Jos *Ant.* 15.5.417).[46] But the allusion

---

[45] See the Greek text.

[46] Some take Paul's reference to refer to actual inscriptions on the temple that warn Gentiles from entering the partitions erected to keep them out. As Hoehner (*Ephesians*, 369 n. 3) notes, "two inscriptions have been uncovered. The first one was found in 1871 and it measures 57 centimeters (22 ½ inches) high, 85 centimeters (33 ½ inches) long, and 37 centimeters (14 ½ inches) thick." Hoehner continues, saying, "The inscription reads: Let no foreigner enter within the partition and enclosure surrounding the temple. Whoever is arrested will himself be responsible for his death which will follow." The second inscription, which is only fragmentary, was discovered in 1935.

is only metaphorical since when Paul wrote this letter both the walls of Jerusalem and the Second Temple were standing. Thus, Jesus' death did not literally destroy the dividing walls of Jerusalem that protected Israel from its enemies nor did his death destroy the walls that separated the Gentiles from the inner courts of the temple. Rather, Jesus' death destroyed the wall between Jews and Gentiles that was erected by the law.[47] That is, the wall that separated Jews and Gentiles and caused enmity between them was the law itself, but Jesus' death abolished the law and thereby destroyed the enmity between Jews and Gentiles.[48] The phrases "by means of the blood of Christ" (ἐν τῷ αἵματι τοῦ Χριστοῦ, 2:13), "by means of his flesh" (ἐν τῇ σαρκὶ αὐτοῦ, 2:14), and "through the cross" (διὰ τοῦ σταυροῦ, 2:16), and the reference to Jesus' "killing" the enmity in him, that is, in his flesh (2:16), support that Jesus' sacrificial death destroyed the enmity between Jews and Gentiles.[49]

"Law" in Eph 2:15 refers to the Mosaic covenant as a whole, not simply to ceremonial aspects of the law, since the entire Mosaic system was the fence that divided Jews and Gentiles from one another (see Eph 2:15 with *Ep. Arist.* 142). The law and all of its ordinances served as a fence of protection around Israel in order to protect the nation from the pollution of the Gentiles (see 3 Macc 1:3). This interpretation is supported by one Jewish perspective of the law in Second Temple Judaism (STJ). Observe the following excerpt from the *Letter of Aristeas* (ca. 170 BC):

> In his wisdom, the legislator, in a comprehensive survey of each particular part, and being endowed by God for the knowledge of universal truths, surrounded us with unbroken palisades and iron walls to prevent our mixing with any of the other peoples in any matter, being thus kept pure in body and soul, preserved from false beliefs, and worshipping the only God omnipotent over all creation (*Let. Arist.* 139, Charlesworth II, 22). . . . So, to prevent our being perverted by contact with others or by mixing with

---

[47] For other arguments against a reference to the temple in 2:14, see Hoehner, *Ephesians,* 369–71.

[48] Although my understanding of the syntax differs from Hoehner's (*Ephesians,* 373), if I correctly understand his view, we both interpret the text to mean that Jesus' death was the means by which God ended the hostility, erected by the law, between Jews and Gentiles.

[49] So Hoehner, *Ephesians,* 374.

bad influences, he hedges us in on all sides with strict observances connected with meat and drink and touch and hearing and sight, after the manner of the Law (*Let. Arist.* 142, Charlesworth II, 22). . . .[50]

Thus, the law and its ordinances (i.e., the Mosaic covenant) were the dividing wall between Jews and Gentiles. But Jesus by his blood shattered the wall erected by the Mosaic covenant along with all of its ordinances, "so that he would create the two in him into one new man by making peace" (Eph 2:15).[51] God's new creation of Jews and Gentiles into one new man is regeneration and conversion since the Gentiles were formerly dead in trespasses and sins and since Jesus' blood was the foundation to God's recreation of this new race.[52]

Paul expresses that Jesus ended the hostility between them "by destroying the law, i.e., the commandments, with the ordinances."[53] Christ destroyed the enmity between Jews and Gentiles by destroying the source of its enmity. Harold Hoehner thinks translating the verb καταργέω ("to destroy, to nullify") as "to destroy" in Eph 2:15 is incorrect since the verb consistently means "to render inoperative," "to nullify," or "to invalidate" in Paul's letters.[54] Instead, Jesus' death made the law inoperative and nullified it for the believer.[55]

Nevertheless, in response to Hoehner, I offer three reasons this verb should be translated as "to destroy" in Eph 2:15. First, Hoehner states that the verb occurs in Paul 26 times and consistently means "to render inoperative," "to nullify," or "to invalidate," but he

---

[50] Martin (*Reconciliation*, 185) pointed me to the above texts.

[51] Rightly, O'Brien, *Ephesians*, 196–99, esp. 199.

[52] In support of conversion, Philo (*On Special Laws*, 1.9.51) and the love story of Joseph and Asenath (chaps. 49–50) suggest that Gentile converts to Judaism are freshly created. Philo (*On Special Laws*, 1.9.51) especially states that proselytes become joined to Israel's commonwealth.

[53] So Lincoln, *Ephesians*, 142. I understand τὸ μεσότοιχον ("the dividing wall") and τήν ἔχθραν ("the enmity") as a compound direct object construction of the participle λύσας ("the one who destroyed"). I also understand τὸν νόμον ("the law") as the direct object of the participle καταργήσας ("having destroyed"), which is instrumental. Finally, I understand "the dividing wall" and "the enmity" as a nominal hendiadys. Thus, Paul is stating that Jesus' death destroyed what separated them in that he abolished the law. For alternative readings of the syntax, see Lincoln, *Ephesians*, 141–44; Hoehner, *Ephesians*, 368–74. For a Pauline theology of law, see T. R. Schreiner, *The Law and Its Fulfillment: A Pauline Theology of Law* (Grand Rapids: Baker, 1993).

[54] Hoehner, *Ephesians*, 375.

[55] Ibid.

only cites six texts to support this assertion.[56] Four of the six texts that he cites could easily be translated as "to destroy" in their given contexts (e.g., Rom 3:3,31; 4:14; 6:6; see Gal 3:17; 5:11). Second, other uses of the verb in Paul could only be translated as "to destroy" (1 Cor 1:28; 6:13; 15:24,26; 2 Thess 2:8; 2 Tim 2:10). Third, the translation "to destroy" fits best in Eph 2:15a since Paul speaks of new creation in 2:15b. Jesus destroyed the old so that he could recreate a new humanity that is free from the restrictions in and the exclusivity of the Mosaic covenant. Fourth, "to render inoperative," "to destroy," and "to nullify" are synonymous verbs (compare Matt 5:17; Rom 14:20; 2 Cor 5:1; and Gal 2:18 with Rom 3:3,31; 6:6; 1 Cor 1:28; 6:13; 15:24; Eph 2:15).[57]

Paul further explains Eph 2:15 with another purpose clause found in 2:16. In 2:16, he states both the purpose and the means by which Jesus made Jews and Gentiles into one new man: "so that he would reconcile both in one body to God through the cross having put to death the enmity by means of him." To achieve reconciliation for and between Jews and Gentiles was the purpose of making them into one new man. Jesus' death for them was the means by which this reconciliation was accomplished. Here, Paul uses a word for reconciliation (ἀποκαταλλάσσω) different from the one in Rom 5:9 and 2 Cor 5:18–19 (καταλλάσσω). Nevertheless, the meaning is the same: two parties who were once at enmity with one another now have peace with one another (see Col 1:22).

In general, hatred between Jews and Gentiles was fierce and reciprocal in the ancient world.[58] In many respects, it was more vitriolic than the hatred that African-Americans and Caucasians have expressed toward one another in the United States since the days of slavery. The greatest difference was that the Jews' and Gentiles' hatred toward one another was not based on skin color, but on religion. Disputes regarding religion were the impetus behind the great war between the Jews and the Seleucids (Gentiles) years earlier (1 Maccabees). Simply put, in their mindset the Jews hated

---

[56] Ibid.

[57] Hoehner (*Ephesians*, 377) demonstrates this point when he states regarding Eph 2:15 that "Paul's progression in the argument is that Christ has destroyed the symptom, that is, enmity between Jews and Gentiles, by making inoperative the root cause, namely, the law of commandments in decrees."

[58] For important works on Jew-Gentile relations in Second Temple Judaism, see M. Hengel, *Judaism and Hellenism*, 2 vols. in one (trans. John Bowden; Minneapolis: Fortress, 1974); L. Feldman, *Judaism and Hellenism Reconsidered* (Leiden: Brill, 2006).

and despised Gentiles because they were not God's people and did not honor Yahweh with their lives. Similarly, Gentiles hated Jews since they thought that the Jews had odd religious customs and a misanthropic attitude toward other nations (see Tacitus, *Hist.* 5.1–13).

Observe the following examples that demonstrate Jewish national pride and the hostility and hatred of Jews and Gentiles toward one another:

> The conventional picture (based on comments by writers such as Juvenal and Seneca) is that Jews were perceived [by Gentiles] as arrogant and foolish: they refused to work on the Sabbath (which was a sign of laziness); they circumcised their sons (which was revolting); they had strict food laws and they kept themselves to themselves and rejected the gods (which was misanthropy).[59]

> [Ptolemy] proposed to inflict public disgrace on the Jewish community, and he set up a stone on the tower in the courtyard with this inscription: None of those who do not sacrifice shall enter their sanctuaries, and all Jews shall be subjected to a registration involving poll tax and to the status of slaves. Those who object to this are to be taken by force and put to death. Those who are registered are also to be branded on their bodies by fire with the ivy-leaf symbol of Dionysus, and they shall also be reduced to their former limited status (NRA, 3 Macc 2:27–29).

> When the impious king comprehended this situation, he became so infuriated that not only was he enraged against those Jews who lived in Alexandria, but was still more bitterly hostile toward those in the countryside; and he ordered that all should promptly be gathered into one place, and put to death by the most cruel means (NRA, 3 Macc 3:1).

> While these matters were being arranged, a hostile rumor was circulated against the Jewish nation by some who conspired to do them ill, a pretext being given by a report

---

[59] For the above quote, see D. R. de Lacey, "Gentiles," in *Dictionary of Paul and His Letters* (ed. G. F. Hawthorne, R. P. Martin, and D. G. Reid; Downers Grove, IL: InterVarsity Press, 1993), 335. Lacey's comments are from the perspective of certain Greco-Roman authors; they are not his own views of the Jews.

that they hindered others from the observance of their customs. The Jews, however, continued to maintain goodwill and unswerving loyalty toward the dynasty; but because they worshiped God and conducted themselves by his law, they kept their separateness with respect to foods. For this reason, they appeared hateful to some; but since they adorned their style of life with the good deeds of upright people, they were established in good repute with everyone. Nevertheless, those of other races paid no heed to their good service to their nation, which was common talk among all; instead they gossiped about the differences in worship and foods, alleging that these people were loyal neither to the king nor to his authorities, but were hostile and greatly opposed to his government. So they attached no ordinary reproach to them (NRA, 3 Macc 3:2–7; see 3 Macc 4–6).

And when we had granted very great revenues to the temples in the cities, we came on to Jerusalem also, and went up to honor the temple of those wicked people, who never cease from their folly. They accepted our presence by word, but insincerely by deed, because when we proposed to enter their inner temple and honor it with magnificent and most beautiful offerings, they were carried away by their traditional arrogance, and excluded us from entering. . . (NRA, 3 Macc 3:16–18).

. . . This moreover explains why we are distinct from all men. The majority of other men defile themselves in their relationships, thereby committing a serious offense, and lands and whole cities take pride in it: they not only procure the males, they also defile mothers and daughters. We are quite separated from these practices (Ep. Arist. 152–53, Charlesworth II, 23). . . .

Happy are we, O Israel, for we know what is pleasing to God (NRA, Bar 4:4).

These are some of our teachings [ ] which are [the] works which w[e think and a]ll of them concern [ ] and the purity of . . . [And concerning the offering of the wh] eat of the [Gentiles which they. . .] and they touch it . . . and de[file it . . . One should not accept anything] from the wheat [of the Gen]tiles [and none of it is] to enter the Sanctuary. [And concerning] {the sacrifice} which they cook in a vessel. . . {in it} the meat of their sacrifices and that they . . . in the courtyar[d. . .] {it} with the broth of their sacrifice. And concerning the sacrifice of the Gentiles . . . [we consider that] they {sacrifice} to [an idol and] that is [like] a woman fornicating with him (DSS 4Q394 3–7 i. conflated with 4Q395).

Separate yourself from the Gentiles, and do not eat with them, and do not perform deeds like theirs, because their deeds are defiled, and all of their ways are contaminated and despicable and abominable. They slaughter their sacrifices to the dead, and to the demons they bow down. And they eat in tombs. And all their deeds are worthless and vain. And they have no heart to perceive, and they have no eyes to see what their deeds are, and where they wander astray, saying to the tree 'you are my god,' and to a stone 'you are my lord, and you are my savior,' and they have no heart (Jub 22:16–18, Charlesworth II, 98).

. . . For Israel is the portion and inheritance of God (Pss Sol 14:5, Charlesworth II, 663). . . .

O Lord, your mercy is upon the works of your hands forever. (You show) your goodness to Israel with a rich gift. Your eyes (are) watching over them and none of them will be in need. Your ears listen to the hopeful prayer of the poor. Your compassionate judgments (are) over the whole world, and your love is for the descendants of Abraham, an Israelite (Pss Sol 18:1–3, Charlesworth I, 669). . . . May God cleanse Israel for the day of mercy in blessing, for the appointed day when Messiah will reign (Pss Sol 18:5, Charlesworth I, 669). . . .

The blessing of Enoch: with which he blessed the elect and the righteous who would be present on the day of tribulation at (the time of) the removal of all the ungodly ones . . . (1 Enoch 1:1, Charlesworth I, 13).

. . . But when you pray, do not use thoughtless chatter as the Gentiles . . . (Matt 6:7).

. . . Men of Israel, help! This is the man who is teaching everyone everywhere against the people and the law and this place. Moreover, he even brought Greeks into the temple and has defiled this holy place (ESV, Acts 21:27; see Jos *Ant*. 15.5.417).

I could wish myself to be accursed from Christ on behalf of my brother, my fleshly relatives, who are Israelites, with whom is the adoption and the glory and the covenants and the giving of the law and the service and the promises, of whom are the fathers, and from whom is the Christ . . . (Rom 9:4–5).

. . . Even if someone has confidence in the flesh, I have more: [I was] circumcised on the eighth day, from the race of Israel, from the tribe of Benjamin, a Hebrew from the Hebrews, a Pharisee according to the law, persecutor of the church according to zeal, [and with respect to] the righteousness that is by means of the law I was blameless . . . (Phil 3:4b–6).

By means of Jesus' death, the hostility between Jews and Gentiles has ceased, and the boundary markers that distinguish them have been shattered.

With reconciliation in view, Eph 2:15–16 is quite amazing for at least two reasons: (1) Paul uses violent, warlike language (destruction, death through a cross, and the killing of enmity) to describe the hostility that existed between Jews and Gentiles and the peace Jesus achieved for them, and (2) he states that both Jews and Gentiles were reconciled to God through Jesus' cross. Ephesians 2:16 is the key verse of my thesis: Jesus' death is the foundation of Paul's theology of racial reconciliation. Paul does not state here that Jesus' death hypothetically achieved or can possibly assist in the endeavor of reconciliation between Jews and Gentiles.[60] Instead, he emphatically states that Jesus' death has accomplished it for the believing community of faith (see 1:15; 2:8–9)!

This accomplishment does not mean that Jesus' death "brought a universal redemption so that all Jews and Gentiles are reconciled" to God and to one another apart from faith in Christ.[61] Rather, Paul's argument in Eph 2:15 assumes that believing Jews and Gentiles are in view. First, Paul commends the Ephesians for their

---

[60] Against Breytenbach, *Versöhnung*, 158–59, 165, 169, 215, 221, 223.
[61] Rightly. Hoehner, *Ephesians*, 380–81.

faith in Jesus (1:15; 3:12).[62] Second, Paul states in the preceding context that Gentiles were saved by grace through faith (2:8–10).[63] Third, Jesus' blood was the means by which God created this new humanity (2:13–14,16). Fourth, Paul states that Jesus preached the gospel to both Jews and Gentiles (2:17). Therefore, the union is not between Jews and Gentiles *per se*, but between believing Jews and believing Gentiles who have been redeemed by Jesus' blood (see 1:7; 2:12,16; 3:12).[64]

Paul highlights in 2:17–18 Jesus' reconciliatory ministry. He states in 2:17 that Jesus "preached peace to those who were far off and peace to those who were near." In light of the argument in 2:11–15, "peace" here refers to reconciliation. When did Jesus proclaim this peace: during the first advent, after the resurrection, or after the resurrection through his prophets and apostles? Since Paul states that "Jesus preached peace to Jews and Gentiles after he came" (ἐλθὼν εὐηγγελίσατο εἰρήνην ὑμῖν τοῖς μακρὰν καὶ εἰρήνην τοῖς ἐγγύς), this preaching could refer to his earthly ministry.[65] Jesus' gospel message of reconciliation did not discriminate against Gentiles. Certainly, Jesus is Israel's Messiah, who came to save the lost sheep of Israel (see Matt 1:1,21). Moreover, he primarily took the gospel to Jews (Matt 10:5–14). Nevertheless, Jesus did not limit his ministry to Jews (see Matt 4:15; 12:18,21; 21:43; 24:13; 28:19; Luke 2:32; John 4). He also preached the good news of reconciliation to Gentiles (John 4). But after the resurrection, he universally proclaims peace to Gentiles through his prophets and apostles empowered by the Holy Spirit (Eph 3:5–8).[66]

Ephesians 2:18 in the Greek text begins with the word ὅτι. The normal meaning of this word is "because" or "that," but neither of these definitions makes sense in 2:18. Paul does not say here that Jesus preached peace to Jews and Gentiles (2:17), "because we both have access through him . . ." (2:18).[67] He also does not mean

---

[62] So Hoehner, *Ephesians*, 381.

[63] Ibid.

[64] Ibid.

[65] Against Hoehner, *Ephesians*, 385; K. O. Sandnes, *Paul: One of the Prophets?: A Contribution to the Apostle's Self-Understanding* (WUNT 43; Tübingen: Mohr, 1991), 229. Hoehner (*Ephesians*, 385) suggests that no evidence exists that Jesus ever preached to Gentiles, but that "it is better to assume that on the basis of the peace he accomplished, it was proclaimed by him to Jews and Gentiles by means of the Holy Spirit through his apostles (cf. Eph 3:5–6)."

[66] O'Brien, *Ephesians*, 206–08, esp. 207–08.

[67] Against Lincoln, *Ephesians*, 149.

that Jesus preached peace to Jews and Gentiles (2:17) "that we both have access through him . . ." (2:18). Instead, the word ὅτι is most likely resultant.[68] Thus, 2:18 states the result of 2:17 so that the two verses should be read in the following manner: Jesus preached peace to both Jews and Gentiles [with the result that] "we both have access in one Spirit to the Father" (2:18). Again, Paul assumes faith in the preached gospel is a means by which Jews and Gentiles have access to God (see 3:6).

As in 2:15–16, 2:18 emphasizes the unity between Jews and Gentiles. Paul states in 2:15 that God created Jews and Gentiles (two groups) "into one new man." In 2:16, he states that God reconciled both groups into "one body" through Jesus' cross. Then, in 2:18, he states that both groups have equal access to the Father "by means of one Spirit." The latter suggests that God has given the Gentiles the same Holy Spirit that he poured out on Jews (see Acts 2), the same Spirit that was promised and anticipated during the old covenant (see Jer 31:31–37; Joel 2; Ezekiel 36–37). The Gentiles who were once alienated from God's covenantal promises simply because they were not Jewish (2:11–12) now through Christ's death have equal access to the Father by his Spirit along with Jewish Christians (2:18).

That Jews and Gentiles have equal access to God is truly profound since Paul states in 2:12 that they were without Christ, without God, and hopeless in the world prior to their faith in Christ. Additionally, Paul's statements are even more incredible if he alludes here to the temple. The Jews had access to God through their priests who entered into the holy place on their behalf where God appeared over the mercy seat (see Leviticus 16). Gentiles were forbidden to enter the temple since their uncleanness would have defiled the holy place (see 1 Maccabees 1–2; 3 Maccabees; Acts 21:28; Acts 24–25). Israel fought against Gentile nations on various occasions when they sought either to enter or to take over the temple (see 1, 2, and 3 Maccabees). The Gentiles' inability to enter the temple impeded their ability to have access to God's presence since he appeared to the high priest, who offered atonement for the people, over the mercy seat in the temple in the most holy

---

[68] So Hoehner, *Ephesians*, 388. Admittedly, this is an abnormal function of ὅτι. In his detailed exegesis of the Greek text, Hoehner does not cite even one text to support the resultant usage. Such a usage seems present in John 7:35.

place. Now in this new age of salvation-history, Jews and Gentiles through Christ by the Spirit stand together as one new man, and together they have equal access to God.[69]

Ephesians 2:19–22 further emphasizes the unity that Jews and Gentiles have with one another because of Jesus' death. Ephesians 2:19 begins with an emphatic inference: "therefore then" (ἄρα οὖν).[70] The latter refers back to 2:11–12 and thus includes the unit of 2:11–18 since 2:14–18 forms part of the argument in 2:11–13 and since 2:19 states that Gentiles through Christ are recipients of God's salvation-historical promises to Israel, whereas in 2:11–12 he states that they were excluded from them. Paul, therefore, concludes the argument of 2:11–18 in 2:19–21. The terms "therefore then" in 2:19 accentuate the result of Jesus' sacrificial death for Jews and Gentiles, and the reconciliation that it accomplished between both groups: "Therefore, now, you are no longer strangers and aliens, but you are fellow-citizens, [i.e.,] saints, and [you are] members of God's family."

The Gentiles are no longer foreigners or second-class citizens in God's economy (see contra DSS 4Q279).[71] To the contrary, Jesus' sacrificial death for sin has reconciled both groups to God and to one another in such a way that both groups have equal access to God's covenantal promises that he originally gave to Israel. Ephesians 2:19 especially emphasizes the Gentiles' covenantal status. They, along with Jewish Christians, are "saints." Through Christ they are now members of God's family—spiritually united and related to Christian Jews—so that they have equal access to Israel's messianic promises (see Rom 2:28–29).

Paul elaborates this latter point in Eph 2:20–22. He metaphorically uses temple imagery in these verses to explain further the Gentiles' part in God's salvation-historical promises and to emphasize the unity between Jews and Gentiles through Christ. This point is fascinating since an inscription on the temple wall forbade Gentiles from entering beyond the second gate of the temple

---

[69] See G. D. Fee, *God's Empowering Presence* (Peabody, MA: Hendrickson, 1994), 683; O'Brien, *Ephesians*, 210.

[70] So M. E. Thrall, *Greek Particles in the New Testament: Linguistic and Exegetical Studies* (Leiden: Brill, 1962), 10–11. The combination of the above particles in the New Testament only occurs in Paul (Rom 5:18; 7:3,25; 8:12; 9:16,18; 14:12,19; Gal 6:10; Eph 2:19; 1 Thess 5:6; 2 Thess 2:15). See also O'Brien, *Ephesians*, 210.

[71] So O'Brien, *Ephesians*, 211.

(Jos *Ant.* 15.5.417) and since years earlier the Jews ardently fought against Gentiles who sought to sack their temple (see 1, 2, and 3 Maccabees).

Paul states in 2:20–21 the reason the Gentiles are fellow citizens with the Jews: namely, their faith was built on the same apostolic and prophetic foundation as the faith of the Christian Jews, a foundation with Jesus, the Christ, as its cornerstone. He states in 2:21 that the entire structure of the foundation is held together in Christ, and it will grow into a "holy temple" in the Lord. Finally, he states in 2:22 that the Gentiles are being built up together into a house of God by the Spirit. Since Paul mentions earlier that Jews and Gentiles have the same Holy Spirit (2:18) and since 2:14–21 emphasizes that God has reconciled Jews and Gentiles to one another and has incorporated Gentiles into God's family with Jews through Christ's death, Paul most likely suggests in 2:22 that believing Jews and Gentiles (not only believing Gentiles) are being built up together into a holy temple of God, that is, a heavenly city (see Rev 3:12; 7:15; 11:1–2,19; 14:7; 15:5; 21:22). The Gentiles formerly could not enter the Jewish temple, but now through Christ's cross Jews and Gentiles together are the temple (see Jer 31:31–37; Ezekiel 36–37).

Paul's statements in Eph 2:11–22 were revolutionary for a first-century Jew. Any devout Jew would have been considered scandalous and antagonistic toward the law and the temple (see Acts 21–26), for in Eph 2:11–22, Paul emphasizes not that ethnic distinctions no longer exist between Jews and Gentiles, but that these distinctions no longer matter since Jesus' death "killed" the boundary markers that divided them (see Acts 13; 22; 26:19–23; 27:28). To discern the depth of Paul's comments, observe the following statements that Jews made about Gentiles in selected excerpts from Second Temple Jewish Literature (STJL).

> Separate yourself from the Gentiles, and do not eat with them, and do not perform deeds like theirs, because their deeds are defiled, and all of their ways are contaminated and despicable and abominable. They slaughter their sacrifices to the dead, and to the demons they bow down. And they eat in tombs. And all their deeds are worthless and vain. And they have no heart to perceive, and they have no eyes to see what their deeds are, and where they

wander astray, saying to the tree 'you are my god,' and to a stone 'you are my lord, and you are my savior,' and they have no heart (Jub 22:16–18; Charlesworth II, 98).

And if there is any man in Israel who wishes to give his daughter or his sister to any who is from the seed of the Gentiles, let him surely die, and let him be stoned because he has caused shame in Israel. And also the woman will be burned with fire because she has defiled the name of her father's house and so she will be uprooted from Israel (Jub 30:7; Charlesworth II, 112–13).

Gentile foreigners went up to your place of sacrifice; they arrogantly trampled [it] with their sandals (Pss Sol 2:2; Charlesworth II, 652).

For the Gentiles insulted Jerusalem, trampling [her] down; he dragged her beauty down from the throne of glory. . . . Do not delay, O' God, to repay them on [their] heads; to declare dishonorable the arrogance of the dragon (Pss Sol 2:19,25; Charlesworth II, 653).

The Lord plucks up the roots of the Gentiles and plants the humble in their place. The Lord always lays waste the land of the Gentiles and destroys them to the foundation of the earth. He removes some of them and destroys them and erases the memory of them from the earth (NRA, Sir 10:16–17).

[Lord], lift up your hand against foreign nations (NRA, Sir 36:2).

Ephesians 2:11–22 radically contrasts with the above texts from STJL. Paul asserts that in Christ, Jewish boundary markers erected by the Mosaic covenant such as circumcision, food laws, purity laws, and the Sabbath, no longer drive a wedge between believing Jews and Gentiles. Rather, by means of Christ's sacrificial death for sin, God's salvation-historical promises of new creation have been fulfilled by the inclusion of the Gentiles into these promises, and God has thereby reconciled Jews and Gentiles to himself and to one another through Jesus' cross.

Conclusion

Because Jesus died as a sacrifice of atonement for Jews and Gentiles, his death reconciles both groups to God and to one another when they place faith in Jesus. Jesus' death shattered all ethnic boundary markers between the two groups, and then recreated them into one new man. This reconciliatory act of God has power not because it has made Jews and Gentiles no longer different or has caused them to surrender their ethnic identities, but because both groups (though different) are one and their differences are overcome by the power of the cross since God has reconciled them by faith through Jesus' death. Therefore, notwithstanding their ethnic distinctions and individual idiosyncrasies, God recreates Jews and Gentiles into one new man in Christ. Chapter 5 will next discuss some practical ramifications of this racial reconciliation.

5

conclusion: the practice of racial reconciliation

Chapter 1 introduced the thesis and the method used for arguing the thesis. My study has involved a two-fold demonstration: (1) that sin is the fundamental reason humanity needs to be reconciled first to God and second to one another and (2) that Jesus' sacrificial death for humanity's sin is God's only provision for racial reconciliation. Chapters 2, 3, and 4, the major sections of the book, support these viewpoints. Chapter 2 presented the reason for reconciliation. Sin is the reason that human beings need to be reconciled first to God and second to one another. Chapter 3 presented the provision for racial reconciliation. Jesus' sacrificial death for the sins of Jews and Gentiles was God's only provision for racial reconciliation. Chapter 4 presented the accomplishment of racial reconciliation. Jesus' sacrificial death for humanity's sin actually—not hypothetically—accomplished reconciliation for Jews and Gentiles who exercise faith in Christ, both reconciliation with God and with one another. In this chapter, I outline some practical ramifications and also discuss some ways in which Christians can practice racial reconciliation in their church and communities.

Ethnic Diversity Versus Racial Reconciliation

Ethnic diversity is not racial reconciliation. As I briefly explained in chapter 1, ethnic diversity and racial reconciliation are not the same. Racial reconciliation leads to more than a multi-ethnic church, a diverse work environment, or a multiracial community. A particular church or community could theoretically be ethnically diverse, but racial reconciliation could be absent from both entities if love is absent. Different races can attend the same church, but a family from one race might not desire to associate with families from another race, or parents from one race might not want their children to date or marry children from another race. Moreover, the Grand Dragon of the Ku Klux Klan and a Black Muslim could live in the same community, but their mutual hatred for each other's race would inevitably preclude them from associating with each other. One might work in an ethnically diverse environment or in an environment where ethnic diversity is strongly encouraged and even pursued, but various people in the work environment—even the boss who may champion affirmative action—might deeply despise others because of their race. In all of these cases, *ethnic diversity* is present, but *racial reconciliation* is not, because love is absent.

Ethnic diversity is not enough. Because of the above examples and especially because of the thesis argued in this book, Christians, the Christian church, and Christian organizations should not merely pursue ethnic diversity. If Christian churches, universities, high schools, businesses, and other Christian places of business are only concerned with implementing affirmative action, they have greatly fallen short of living out what Jesus has achieved by his death and what he expects his followers to pursue regarding racial reconciliation. In other words, I think affirmative action was originally created and implemented for a good purpose since it leveled the playing field for minorities and women who applied for the same jobs as those from the predominant race or gender. As our culture has increasingly changed over the years, many work environments have used affirmative action as a means by which to employ someone exclusively because of his or her race or gender. Many organizations, even Christian ones, have hired employees only because of their race or gender in order to diversify the work environment, even when that person might not have been the most qualified for the position. As a result, these organizations show favoritism toward one group and discriminate against another because of race or gender, while they simultaneously justify this discrimination in the name of diversity or equal opportunity. Christian churches and organizations who express this favoritism greatly misunderstand the Pauline concept of *racial reconciliation.*

According to Paul, racial reconciliation does not mean that a certain number of races should be in a work environment or that all churches should be multiethnic. In fact, all of the churches that Paul established were Gentile congregations with very few, if any, Jews in them. Rather, for Paul, racial reconciliation requires more direct and continued involvement than ethnic diversity does. It requires more than an African-American congregation participating in a joint worship service with a Caucasian congregation on Dr. Martin Luther King Jr.'s birthday or during Black History Month. It requires more than just including different races in certain activities, functions, and jobs, and it involves more than celebrating and crusading in favor of racial diversity.

According to Paul, racial reconciliation suggests that because of Jesus' death for humanity's sin, Jews and Gentiles who have faith in Christ are recreated into one new man. From Paul's perspective racial reconciliation expresses that the boundary markers once separating Jews and Gentiles from one another do not matter anymore because Christ's death destroyed them. That Gentiles are not circumcised does not matter anymore. That Jews are circumcised does not matter anymore. That Caucasians and Africans enslaved Africans does not matter anymore. That Africans sold their own people into slavery does not matter anymore. That Palestinians and Arabs hate each other does not matter anymore. No ethnic boundary marker or cultural idiosyncrasy matters anymore since Jesus' death ends the hostility between Jews and Gentiles who believe, and then makes both groups into one new man (see Gal 3:27–4:7).

Ethnic diversity only means that people from various backgrounds worship, work, or live in the same environment. To the contrary, racial reconciliation means that different races are now members of the same spiritual family by their faith in Christ because of his death for sin, and they have equal access to God by the same Spirit since Jesus recreated all who believe into one new man. This new man is the new race in Christ. This new race transcends our old ethnic identities and our old man in Adam (see Rom 6:6).

Thus, regardless of whether a church, a community, or a work environment is ethnically diverse, racial reconciliation can still be a reality, that is, if ethnic diversity is not absent in those environments because of racist ideologies. Racial reconciliation can still be a reality when the members in those environments demonstrate the same type of selfless and Christlike love to believers from different races as they would those believers from their own race and when they universally pray for and minister to their brothers and sisters in Christ in their communities and in the world regardless of ethnic distinctions. Indeed, Paul's gospel calls for a mixing and inclusion of different races in the church (i.e., ethnic diversity [see Gal 3:28]), but it especially calls for Jews and Gentiles to live with one another in love as God's family even if a church might not be able to be ethnically diverse because everyone in the community is from the same homogeneous unit.

Practicing racial reconciliation means that I regard a white Christian as my brother (remember that I am an African-American), but not an African-American who is a non-Christian. Hence, my love and service to my Christian brothers and sisters should transcend any love, affection, favoritism, devotion, and service that I offer someone from my race, because Christians are part of the family of God. Membership in the Christian family is much more important than association with any ethnic group or club. Churches that are located in ethnically diverse communities should reach out to those ethnic groups in their communities, and churches that are not located in diverse communities should think of and pray about practical ways by which they can live out the reconciling power of the gospel both in their community and throughout the world.

Racist Churches Are Unacceptable

Paul's theology of racial reconciliation suggests that racist churches are unacceptable. Paul calls Christians to love one another (Rom 12:10; 13:8; 1 Thess 3:12; 4:9–10), to live in harmony with one another (Rom 12:16; 14:19; 15:5; 1 Cor 12:25), not to judge one another (Rom 14:13), to receive one another (Rom 15:7), to greet one another with affection (Rom 16:16; 1 Cor 16:20; 2 Cor 13:12), to share the Lord's Supper with one another in the appropriate manner (1 Cor 11:33), to serve one another (Gal 5:13), and not to consume one another with insidious actions (Gal 5:15). Also, Paul calls Christians to bear the burdens of one another (Gal 6:2), to be patient with one another (Eph 4:2; Col 3:12–13), to be kind to one another (Eph 4:32), to submit to one another with reverence for Christ (Eph 5:21), to treat one another as more valuable than oneself (Phil 2:3), to live sacrificially for one another (Phil 2:5–9), not to lie to one another (Col 3:9), to encourage one another with the truths of God (1 Thess 4:18; 5:11), and to do good to one another (1 Thess 5:15). Finally, he states that Jews and Gentiles hated one another before their faith in Christ, but God's work of regeneration in their lives converted their hatred toward one another into love (Titus 3:3–7). He never simply urges believers to recruit minorities in order to diversify the ministry or the church. Rather, he emphatically exhorts his Christian congregations to live out the power of the cross by striving "to keep the unity of the Spirit in the bond of peace" (Eph 4:3).

Furthermore, the above Pauline exhortations are not autochthonous or limited to a specific homogenous unit. That is, Paul does not say that black Christians should only love or serve black Christians or white Christians should only love or serve white Christians. Rather, the above exhortations are universal and should be universally practiced by all Christians toward all Christians. Genuine, sincere, Christlike love for brothers and sisters in Christ that transcends one's love for and allegiance to one's race and ethnic traditions is the essence of what it means to live out racial reconciliation.

That so many churches are segregated because of racism absolutely disgraces the gospel and Jesus' death. Many pastors and parishioners attempt to appease their racist consciences and to justify their segregated congregations by appealing to the various cultural differences between, for example, African-Americans, Caucasians, Hispanics, and Koreans, as an excuse for segregation. Thus, the preceding excuse, they think, justifies the presence of an entirely African-American congregation across the street from an entirely Anglo congregation or an entirely Korean congregation down the block from a Hispanic congregation. Paul would quickly reject this notion.

More specifically, many African-American and Anglo pastors work to appease their racist consciences and to justify their segregated congregations by participating in joint worship services on Dr. Martin Luther King Jr.'s birthday or during Black History Month. Some of these same pastors find repulsive even the thought of someone from a different race either attending or joining their churches. Joint worship services between different ethnic groups during special days do not come close to practicing the heart of Paul's theology of racial reconciliation. Such services are also insufficient in light of Jesus' sacrificial death for Jews and Gentiles and in light of the reconciliation that his death has accomplished for them so that they will live as one new man as the new community. If pastors and parishioners truly grasped the reconciling power of the gospel, churches composed of a single ethnicity in close proximity of a church from a different ethnicity would merge and become one congregation, especially if these churches agreed theologically and one or both of these churches had dying congregations. Pastors and church members who understand the reconciling power of the gospel would also speak against all forms of racism in the church, would discipline their members for practicing racism, just as they would discipline them for committing sexual sin, and would work hard to ensure that the membership of the church looks like the people who live in the community where the church is located, regardless of how many different ethnic groups are in the particular community.

Other Christians might appeal to the differences in worship style or preaching in certain ethnic traditions to support the establishment and maintenance of ethnically segregated congregations. Christians must avoid making generalizations regarding race. For example, since African-Americans worship and express themselves differently than Caucasians, black Christians and white Christians should have segregated congregations.

Paul's theology of racial reconciliation categorically demolishes the above argument. Different people, though not necessarily different races, do express themselves differently when they worship, but these liturgical differences do not justify the establishment of segregated congregations any more than cultural or political differences justify ecclesiological segregation. The notion of segregated congregations based on different worship styles assumes that congregational unity can be achieved only if the parishioners in a particular congregation are from the same race. I (but most importantly Paul) reject such a premise. It simply is not true, for example, that all

African-Americans, Anglos, or Hispanics expect to hear the same preaching style or to worship the same way. To suggest otherwise is both ignorant and racist. For example, I recently visited a Southern Baptist church in Louisville, Kentucky, whose multiethnic congregation consists of African-Americans, Anglos, Hispanics, and a few Native Americans. The lead pastor is Anglo, the worship pastor is an African-American, and the worship pastor's team consists of two African-Americans and three Anglos. To my great delight, the congregational worship is God-centered because it focuses on the Scriptures. The congregation expresses great unity in its corporate worship, notwithstanding that the congregation consists of members from different ethnic backgrounds.

Church members should focus more on listening to the careful biblical exposition in their minister's preaching and teaching, singing the Bible, and praying the Bible in their worship services than on desiring emotionally driven worship that is more concerned with entertainment, mass media, and the newest or most relevant cultural movement or that is more informed by cultural preferences than the Holy Spirit and the biblical text. If, regardless of their ethnic identity, church members made those activities their focus, then biblical worship would cultivate in those churches a God-exalting and Christ-honoring environment that would attract all people from different races who hunger and thirst to worship the one and true living God in Spirit and in truth. Christ-exalting worship that is biblically driven and thoroughly saturated in and empowered by the Holy Spirit is the worship that pleases God. This type of worship transcends the boundary markers and the limitations that ethnic distinctions place on Christians. Furthermore, in light of Paul's argument in Eph 2:11–22, the argument that different races cannot worship together because they are different does not stand. Jewish worship and Gentile worship were utterly different in the ancient world. The former was monotheistic, but the latter was polytheistic. In Christ Jesus, however, Jews and Gentiles have united to become "one new man" who worships the same God by faith in Christ, regardless of the distinctions that once divided them.

Many churches are more committed to their ethnic heritage than to the gospel. This misplaced commitment is evident in those churches whose worship experiences exclusively focus on the particular ethnic heritage of the church, either intentionally or unintentionally, and thereby exclude other races, either directly or indirectly, from joining and participating in the worship experiences. Labeling worship as "black" or "white" and calling a church "black" or "white" also erect fences around worship. Such expressions are superficial, generic, and unbiblical. More importantly, God despises and rejects them. In Paul's day, there were three classes of people: Jews, Samaritans, and Gentiles. There was one type of church: a body of Jews and Gentiles redeemed by Jesus' blood and reconciled to God and to one another by faith in Christ (see Acts 20:28; Eph 2:1–22).

Paul's theology of racial reconciliation demands that churches stop being and calling themselves black churches, white churches, or Korean churches. Paul's theology of racial reconciliation demands that churches that have been purchased by Jesus' blood simply call themselves churches that are seeking to glorify God in Christ and to reach out to those in their respective communities, regardless of the ethnicity of the church or of the people within its community. When Christians and, even worse, pastors label their churches as black churches or white churches, they use unbiblical language that was absolutely foreign to Paul and the early church. Moreover, they use language as part of their Christian vocabulary that the apostle Paul and the other apostles, especially Peter, would have relentlessly endeavored to suppress since the Mosaic covenant, ethnic identity, and various boundary markers separated Jews and Gentiles from one another. Unlike Paul, some Jewish Christians used these distinctions as a means by which to exclude Gentile Christians from Christian fellowship in the church (see Acts 13–15; Gal 2:11–21). Paul's theology of racial reconciliation, however, demands that the church that Jesus purchased with his own blood should be focused on the glory of God in Christ and the edification of the body, so that those who belong to the body of Christ—Jews and Gentiles—can participate in a unified ecclesiological experience. His theology of racial reconciliation categorically rejects all notions of a segregated body of Christ and all forms of racism and discrimination in the body of Christ (Eph 4:1–5).

What about Racial Slurs or Jokes?

Racial slurs and ethnic jokes are inconsistent with the Pauline message of racial reconciliation. Since Jesus has shattered all boundary markers between Jews and Gentiles and since he has made the two groups into one new man by his sacrificial death for their sin, Christians should never under any circumstances participate in any form of racist speech, which includes racial slurs and ethnic jokes. A racial slur or an ethnic joke is intended to degrade one race and uplift another. In essence, this sort of speech reflects the unregenerate mentality that Jews and Gentiles experienced before their faith in Christ when they were dead in trespasses and sins (see Eph 2:1–22). Racist speech or rhetoric disobeys Paul's exhortation to put off the old man, to walk in a manner worthy of Christ, not to give Satan a place in one's life, and to be filled with God's Spirit (Eph 4:17–5:20).

Racist catchphrases that the culture applies to specific ethnic groups should not be part of a Christian's speech. For instance, a Christian should not utter disrespectful language such as "cracker," "half-breed," "honky," "nigger," "porch monkey," "spic," "Uncle Tom," and "wetback" toward any person—Christian or non-Christian—who belongs to the race in which these types of racist words have been traditionally applied. The preceding point equally requires that Christians not use the racist vocabulary toward those of their own ethnic group, which they had used before they professed faith in Christ.

For example, I cannot imagine any circumstance in which Paul would be pleased to hear black Christians calling each other "nigger," two white Christians calling each other "cracker" or "honky," and a black Christian calling another black Christian an "Uncle Tom." Neither can I imagine that Paul would ever be pleased to hear a black Christian call a white Christian "honky" or a white Christian call a black Christian "nigger" since historically these words have been used to wound and to disrespect these two races. This language is not cute, funny, or cool. It is simply racist and therefore opposes the gospel and racial reconciliation. This sort of speech disregards and misunderstands the reconciliation that Jesus has achieved for all races who believe that his sacrificial death has paid for their sin.

Moreover, jokes and rhetoric that disrespect the ethnic group of a fellow believer in Christ are fundamentally unacceptable. A Christian who is filled with the Spirit, is redeemed by Christ's blood, and has been reconciled by Christ into one body of all believers regardless of their races should speak of, to, and about different races in ways that are consistent with the reconciling power of the Pauline gospel. Thus, one way Christians live out the reconciling power of the gospel is by refusing to accept or participate in speech that degrades any one race below another or that elevates any one race above another.

What about Interracial Relationships?

Contrary to the racist worldviews in many cultures, interracial relationships are not displeasing to God. Unfortunately, many Christians in the United States of America have allowed their racist cultures or history to convince them otherwise by appropriating as the biblical worldview a position that rejects interracial relationships or interracial marriages. To the contrary, a white Christian's marriage pleases God only if that person's spouse is a Christian regardless of whether that person is white, black, or of some other race. On the other hand, if two people from the same race marry each other and if one spouse is a Christian and the other is not, this relationship displeases God.

Paul's theology of racial reconciliation shatters the racist ideology that interracial or crosscultural marriages are wrong. Jews and Gentiles who have faith in Christ have been reconciled to God and to one another through Christ and have been created into one new man. Christians who forbid their children from marrying a fellow Christian from a different race reveal that they do not fundamentally understand the gospel or the racial reconciliation Jesus' death has achieved. They do not understand that their actions at their core are racist and are just as offensive to God as any other sin. Paul's theology of racial reconciliation suggests that Jews and Gentiles who have been justified by faith in Christ are free to love God and Christ together, to love one another, to marry one another in Christ, and to worship together. In Christ Jesus, the dividing wall has been broken down, and ethnic distinctions no longer matter. All who have been redeemed by Christ's blood and reconciled to God and to one another are one in Christ (Gal 3:28). Therefore, all Christians must live their lives as though they have been reconciled both to God and to another because Jesus' death has reconciled all believing Jews and Gentiles into one new man.

bibliography

Primary Sources

Aland, Barbara, Kurt Aland, Johannes Karavidopoulos, Carlo M. Martini, and Bruce Metzger, eds. *The Greek New Testament.* 4th rev. ed. Stuttgart: Deutsche Bibelgesellschaft, 1998.

Charlesworth, James H., ed. *The Old Testament Pseudepigrapha.* 2 vols. New York: Doubleday, 1983.

The Complete Dead Sea Scrolls in English. Translated by Geza Vermes. New York: Penguin Books, 2004.

The Dead Sea Scrolls: Study Edition. 2 vols. Translated by Florentino Garcia Martinez and Eibert J. C. Tigchelar. Vol. 1. Leiden: Brill, 1997.

Martinez, Florentino Garcia, ed. *The Dead Sea Scrolls Translated: The Qumran Texts in English.* Translated by Wilfred G. E. Watson. 2nd ed. Leiden: Brill, 1994.

Rahlfs, A., ed. *Septuaginta.* Stuttgart: Deutsche Bibelgesellschaft, 1979.

Schenker, A., ed. *Biblia Hebraica Stuttgartensia.* Stuttgart: Deutsche Bibelgesellschaft, 1967/77.

Schiffmann, Lawrence, ed. *Texts and Traditions: A Source Reader for the Study of Second Temple and Rabbinic Judaism.* Hoboken, NJ: Ktav Publishing House, 1998.

Stone, Michael E., ed. *Jewish Writings of the Second Temple Period: Apocrypha, Pseudepigrapha, Qumran Sectarian Writings, Philo, and Josephus.* Philadelphia: Fortress, 1984.

Secondary Sources

Books

Hebrew Lexicon and Grammars

Brown, F., S. Driver, and C. Briggs. *The Brown-Driver-Briggs Hebrew and English Lexicon.* Peabody, MA: Hendrickson, 2000.

Joüon, Paul, and T. Muraoka. *A Grammar of Biblical Hebrew:* Pt. 3, *Syntax.* Rome: Editrice Pontificio Instituto Biblico, 2003.

Kautzsch, E., and A. E. Cowley. *Gesenius' Hebrew Grammar.* 2nd ed. Oxford: Clarendon Press, 1909.

Merwe, H. J. van der, Jackie Naudé, and Jan H. Kroeze. *A Biblical Hebrew Reference Grammar.* Sheffield: Sheffield Academic Press, 2002.

Waltke, Bruce K., and M. O'Connor. *An Introduction to Biblical Hebrew Syntax.* Winona Lake, IN: Eisenbrauns, 1990.

Greek Lexicon and Grammars

Danker, Frederick William. *A Greek—English Lexicon of the New Testament and Other Early Christian Literature.* 3rd ed. Chicago: University Press, 2000.

Mounce, William. *An Analytical Lexicon to the Greek New Testament.* Grand Rapids: Zondervan, 1993.

Wallace, Daniel B. *Greek Grammar Beyond the Basics.* Grand Rapids: Zondervan, 1996.

Commentaries

Barth, Karl. *The Epistle to the Romans.* Translated by Edwyn C. Hoskyns. 6th ed. London: University of Cambridge Press, 1950.

Bruce, F. F. *The Epistle of Paul to the Romans.* The New Testament Commentary. Grand Rapids: Eerdmans, 1963.

_____. *Galatians.* New International Greek Testament Commentary. Grand Rapids: Eerdmans, 1982.

Burton, Ernest De Witt. *Galatians.* International Critical Commentary. 2nd ed. Edinburgh: T&T Clark, 1975.

Byrne, Brendon. *Romans*. Sacra Pagina 6. Collegeville, MN: Liturgical Press, 1996.

Calvin, John. *Commentary on the Epistle of Paul to the Romans*. Edited and Translated by John Owen. Grand Rapids: Eerdmans, 1947.

_____. *The Epistles of Paul to the Romans and to the Thessalonians*. Translated by R. McKenzie. Grand Rapids: Eerdmans, 1960.

Cranfield, C. E. B. *Romans 1–8*. International Critical Commentary. Edinburgh: T&T Clark, 1975.

Delitzsch, F. *A New Commentary on Genesis*. Edinburgh: T&T Clark, 1888.

Dodd, C. H. *The Epistle of Paul to the Romans*. Moffatt New Testament Commentary. New York: Harper and Brothers, 1932.

Dunn, James D. G. *A Commentary on the Epistle to the Galatians*. London: A & C Black, 1993.

_____. *Romans 1–8*. Word Biblical Commentary 38. Dallas: Word Books, 1988.

Fitzmyer, Joseph A. *Romans*. Anchor Bible Commentary. New York: Doubleday, 1993.

Fung, R. Y. K. *Galatians*. New International Commentary of the New Testament. Grand Rapids: Eerdmans, 1988.

Garland, David E. *1 Corinthians*. Baker Exegetical Commentary of the New Testament. Grand Rapids: Baker, 2003.

Haacker, Klaus. *Der Brief des Paulus an die Römer*. Leipzig: Evangelische Verlagsanstalt, 1999.

Harris, Murray J. *The Second Epistle to the Corinthians*. New International Greek Testament Commentary. Grand Rapids: Eerdmans, 2005.

Hoehner, Harold W. *Ephesians*. Grand Rapids: Baker, 2002.

Jewett, Paul K. *Romans*. Hermeneia. Minneapolis: Fortress, 2007.

Käsemann, Ernst. *Commentary on Romans*. Translated by Geoffrey W. Bromiley. Grand Rapids: Eerdmans, 1980.

Lincoln, Andrew T. *Ephesians*. Word Biblical Commentary 42. Nashville: Thomas Nelson, 1990.

Longenecker, Richard N. *Galatians*. Word Biblical Commentary 41. Nashville: Thomas Nelson, 1990.

Metzger, Bruce M. *A Textual Commentary on the Greek New Testament*. 2nd ed. Stuttgart: Deutsche Bibelgesellschaft, 1994.

Moo, Douglas J. *The Epistle to the Romans*. New International Commentary on the New Testament. Grand Rapids: Eerdmans, 1996.

Nygren, Anders. *Commentary on Romans*. Translated by C. C. Rasmussen. Philadelphia: Muhlenburg Press, 1949.

O'Brien, Peter T. *The Letter to the Ephesians*. Pillar New Testament Commentary. Grand Rapids: Eerdmans, 1999.

_____. *Philippians*. New International Greek Testament Commentary. Grand Rapids: Eerdmans, 1991.

Origen. *Commentary on the Epistle to the Romans: Books 1–5*. Translated by Thomas P. Scheck. Washington, DC: The Catholic University of America, 2001.

Sanday, W., and A. C. Headlam. *The Epistle to the Romans*. International Critical Commentary. Edinburgh: T&T Clark, 1896.

Schlatter, Adolf von. *Romans: The Righteousness of God*. Peabody, MA: Hendrickson, 1995.

Schlier, H. *Der Brief and die Epheser*. 2nd ed. Dusseldorf: Patmos-Verlag, 1958.

Schreiner, Thomas R. *Romans*. Baker Exegetical Commentary of the New Testament. Grand Rapids: Baker, 1998.

Seifrid, Mark. "Romans." Pages 618–22 in *Commentary on the New Testament Use of the Old Testament*. Edited by G. K. Beale and D. A. Carson. Grand Rapids: Baker, 2007.

Stuhlmacher, Peter. *Paul's Letter to the Romans: A Commentary*. Translated by Scott J. Hafemann. Louisville: Westminster/John Knox, 1994.

Talbert, Charles H. *Romans*. Macon: Smyth and Helwys, 2002.

Wilckens, U. *Der Brief an die Römer*. Evangelisch-Katholischer Kommentar zum NeuenTestament 6/1. Zürich: Benziger/Neukirchen-Vlyun: Neukirchener Verlag, 1980.

Wright, N. T. *The Letter to the Romans: Introduction, Commentary, and Reflections*. The New International Interpreter's Bible Commentary 10. Nashville: Abingdon Press, 2002.

Monographs

Alexander, T. D. *From Paradise to the Promised Land: An Introduction to the Pentateuch*. 2nd ed. Grand Rapids: Baker, 2002.

Anayabwile, Thabiti M. *The Decline of African American Theology: From Biblical Faith to Cultural Captivity*. Downers Grove, IL: InterVarsity Press, 2007.

Beker, J. C. *Paul, the Apostle: The Triumph of God in Life and Thought*. Philadelphia: Fortress, 1980.

Ben Ezra, Daniel Stökl. *The Impact of Yom Kippur on Early Christianity*. Wissenschaftliche Untersuchungen zum Neuen Testament. Tübingen: Mohr Siebeck, 2003.

Boersma, Hans. *Violence, Hospitality, and the Cross: Reappropriating the Atonement Tradition*. Grand Rapids: Baker, 2004.

Boureux, Christophe, and Christoph Theobald, eds. *Original Sin: A Code of Fallibility*. London: SCM Press, 2004.

Breytenbach, Cilliers. *Versöhnung: Eine Studie zur paulinischen Soteriologie*. Wissenschaftliche Monographien zum Alten und Neuen Testament 60. Neukirchener-Vluyn: Neukirchener Verlag, 1989.

Brondos, David A. *Paul on the Cross: Reconstructing the Apostle's Story of Redemption*. Minnesota: Fortress, 2006.

Bultmann, Rudolph. *Theology of the New Testament*. Translated by Kendrick Grobel. 2 vols. New York: Charles Scribner's Sons, 1951.

Calvin, John. *Institutes of the Christian Religion*. Translated by Henry Beveridge. Grand Rapids: Eerdmans, 1997.

Campbell, Douglas A. *The Rhetoric of Righteousness in Romans 3:21–26*. Journal for the Study of the New Testament 65. Sheffield: Sheffield Academic Press, 1992.

Chalke, Steve. *The Lost Message of Jesus*. Grand Rapids: Zondervan, 2003.

Childs, Brevard S. *Myth and Reality in the Old Testament*. London: SCM Press, 1960.

Cousar, Charles B. *A Theology of the Cross: The Death of Jesus in the Pauline Letters*. Minneapolis: Augsburg Fortress, 1990.

Dahl, Nils. *Studies in Paul: Theology for the Early Christian Mission*. Minneapolis: Augsburg, 1977.

Das, A. Andrew. *Solving the Romans Debate*. Minneapolis: Fortress, 2007.

Davis, Basil S. *Christ as Devotio: The Argument of Galatians 3:1–14*. Lanham, MD: University Press of America, 2002.

Deissmann, Adolf. *Bible Studies*. Translated by A. Grieve. Edinburgh: T&T Clark, 1895.

_____. *Light from the Ancient East*. New York: Harper, 1927.

Dodd, C. H. *The Bible and the Greeks*. 2nd ed. London: Hodder and Stoughton, 1954.

Dunn, James D. G. *Jesus, Paul, and the Law*. London: SPK, 1990.

_____. *The New Perspective on Paul*. Wissenschaftliche Untersuchungen zum Neuen Testament 185. Tubingen: Mohr-Siebeck, 2005.

Dupont, Jacques. *La reconciliation dans la théologie de Saint Paul*. Paris: Desclée deBrouwer, Universitaies de Louvain, 1953.

Elliott, Neil. *The Rhetoric of Romans: Argumentative Constraint and Strategy and Paul's Dialogue with Judaism*. Journal for the Study of the New Testament Supplemental Series 45. Sheffield: Sheffield Academic Press, 1960.

Ellul, J. *The Meaning of the City*. Translated by D. Pardee. Grand Rapids: Eerdmans, 1970.

Erickson, Millard J. *Christian Theology*. 2nd ed. Grand Rapids: Baker, 1998.

Fee, Gordon D. *God's Empowering Presence*. Peabody, MA: Hendrickson, 1994.

_____. *Pauline Christology: An Exegetical-Theological Study*. Peabody, MA: Hendrickson, 2007.

Feldman, Louis H. *Judaism and Hellenism Reconsidered*. Supplemental Journal for the Study of Judaism 107. Leiden: Brill, 2006.

Finlan, Stephen. *The Background and Content of Paul's Cultic Atonement Metaphors*. Atlanta: SBL, 2004.

_____. *Problems with Atonement*. Minnesota: Liturgical Press, 2005.

Friedrich, Gerhard. *Die Verkündigung des Todes Jesu im Neuen Testament*. Biblischetheologische Studien. Neukirchener-Vluyn: Neukirchener Verlag, 1982.

Gathercole, Simon J. *Where Is Boasting? Early Jewish Soteriology and Paul's Response in Romans 1–5*. Grand Rapids: Eerdmans, 2002.

Gorringe, Timothy. *God's Just Vengeance*. Cambridge: Cambridge University Press, 1996.

Green, Joel B. *The Death of Jesus: Tradition and Interpretation in the Passion Narrative.* Wissenschaftliche Untersuchungen zum Neuen Testament 2. Tubingen: Mohr, 1988.

Green, Joel B., and Mark D. Baker. *Recovering the Scandal of the Cross: Atonement in New Testament and Contemporary Contexts.* Downers Grove, IL: InterVarsity Press, 2000.

Hafemann, Scott J. *Paul, Moses, and the History of Israel: The Letter/Spirit Contrast and the Argument from Scripture in 2 Corinthians 3.* London: Paternoster, 2005.

Hanson, A. T. *The Wrath of the Lamb.* London: SPK, 1957.

Hays, Richard B. *The Faith of Jesus Christ: An Investigation of the Narrative Substructure of Gal. 3:1–4:11.* 3rd ed. Grand Rapids: Eerdmans, 2002.

Hengel, Martin. *The Atonement: A Study of the Origins of the Doctrine in the New Testament.* London: SCM, 1981.

_____. *Judaism and Hellenism: Studies in Their Encounter in Palestine in the Early Hellenistic Period.* Translated by John Bowden. Minneapolis: Fortress, 1990.

Hill, David. *Greek Words and Hebrew Meanings: Studies in the Semantics of Soteriological Terms.* Society for the New Testament Monograph Series 5. Cambridge: Cambridge University Press, 1967.

Holland, Tom. *Contours of Pauline Theology: A Radical New Survey of the Influences on Paul's Biblical Writings.* Scotland, UK: Mentor, 2004.

Hooker, Morna D. *Not Ashamed of the Gospel: New Testament Interpretations of the Death of Christ.* Grand Rapids: Eerdmans, 1994.

Hultgren, Arnold J. *Paul's Gospel and Mission: The Outlook from His Letter to the Romans.* Philadelphia: Fortress, 1985.

Janowski, Bernd. *Sühne als Heilsgeschehen.* 2nd ed. Wissenschaftliche Monographien zum Alten und Neuen Testament. Neukirchener-Vluyn: Neukirchener Verlag, 2000.

Jeffery, Steve, Michael Ovey, and Andrew Sach. *Pierced for Our Transgressions: Rediscovering the Glory of Penal Substitution.* Wheaton, IL: Crossway, 2007.

Jersak, Brad, and Michael Hardin, eds. *Stricken by God?: Nonviolent Identification and the Victory of Christ.* Grand Rapids: Eerdmans, 2007.

Käsemann, Ernst. *Leib und Leib Christi*. Beiträge zur historischen Theologie 9. Tubingen: Mohr, 1933.

Knöppler, Thomas. *Sühne im Neuen Testament*. Wissenschaftliche Monographien zum Alten und Neuen Testament 88. Neukirchener-Vluyn: Neukirchener Verlag, 2001.

Kraus, Wolfgang. *Der Tod Jesu als Heiligtumsweihe: Eine Untersuchung zum Umfeldder Sühnevorstellung im Römer 3:25–26a*. Wissenschaftliche Monographien zum Alten und Neuen Testament 66. Neukirchener-Vluyn: NeukirchenerVerlag, 1991.

Kurtz, J. H. *Offerings, Sacrifices, and Worship in the Old Testament*. Translated by James Martin. Peabody, MA: Hendrickson, 1998.

Lyonnet, Stanislas, and Léopold Sabourin. *Sin, Redemption, and Sacrifice: A Biblical and Patristic Study*. Rome: Biblical Institute Press, 1970.

Marshall, I. Howard. *Aspects of the Atonement: Cross and Resurrection in the Reconciling of God and Humanity*. London: Paternoster, 2008.

Martin, Ralph. *Reconciliation: A Study of Paul's Theology*. 2nd ed. Atlanta: John Knox, 1981.

Mathews, Kenneth A. *Genesis 1–11:26*. New American Commentary. Nashville: Broadman & Holman, 2002.

McGavran, Donald A. *Understanding Church Growth*. Rev. ed. Grand Rapids: Eerdmans, 1980.

McKnight, Scot. *A Community Called Atonement*. Nashville: Abingdon, 2007.

_____. *Jesus and His Death: Historiography, the Historical Jesus, and Atonement Theory*. Waco, TX: Baylor University Press, 2005.

McLean, Bradley H. *The Cursed Christ*. Journal for the Study of the New Testament 126. Sheffield: Sheffield Academic Press, 1996.

Morgan, Edmund S. *American Slavery, American Freedom: The Ordeal of Colonial Virginia*. New York: Norton, 1975.

Morris, Leon. *The Apostolic Preaching of the Cross*. 3rd ed. Grand Rapids: Eerdmans, 1965.

_____. *The Cross in the New Testament*. Grand Rapids: Baker, 1965.

Noll, Mark A. *A History of Christianity in the United States and Canada*. Grand Rapids: Eerdmans, 1992.

_____. *The Old Religion in a New World: The History of North American Christianity*. Grand Rapids: Eerdmans, 2002.

Packer, J. I., and Mark Dever. *In My Place Condemned He Stood*. Wheaton: Crossway, 2008.

Pate, C. Marvin. *The Reverse of the Curse*. Wissenschaftliche Untersuchungen zum Neuen Testament 114. Tübingen: Mohr Siebeck, 2000.

Piper, John. *Counted Righteous in Christ: Should We Abandon the Imputation of Christ's Righteousness?* Wheaton: Crossway, 2002.

_____. *The Future of Justification: A Response to N. T. Wright*. Wheaton: Crossway, 2007.

Porter, Stanley E. *Καταλλάσσω in Ancient Greek Literature, with Reference to the Pauline Writings*. Cordoba: Ediciones El Almendro, 1994.

Rashdall, Hastings. *The Idea of Atonement in Christian Theology: Being the Bampton Lectures for 1915*. London: Macmillan, 1925.

Ridderbos, Herman. *Paul: An Outline of His Theology*. Grand Rapids: Eerdmans, 1966.

Ross, A. *Creation and Blessing: A Guide to the Study and Exposition of the Book of Genesis*. Grand Rapids: Baker, 1988.

Sanders, E. P. *Paul and Palestinian Judaism*. Philadelphia: Fortress, 1977.

_____. *Paul, the Law, and the Jewish People*. Minneapolis: Fortress, 1983.

Sandnes, Karl Olav. *Paul: One of the Prophets?: A Contribution to the Apostle's Self-Understanding*. Wissenschaftliche Untersuchungen zum Neuen Testament 43. Tubingen: Mohr, 1991.

Schlier, H. *Christus und die Kirche im Epheserbrief*. Beiträge zur historischen Theologie 6. Tubingen: Mohr, 1930.

Schmithals, W. *Paul and the Gnostics*. Nashville: Abingdon, 1972.

Schreiner, Thomas R. *The Law and Its Fulfillment: A Pauline Theology of Law*. 2nd ed. Grand Rapids: Baker, 2001.

_____. *New Testament Theology: Magnifying God in Christ*. Grand Rapids: Baker, 2008.

Seeley, David. *The Noble-Death: Greco-Roman Martyrology and Paul's Concept of Salvation*. Journal for the Study of the New Testament 28. Sheffield: Sheffield Academic Press, 1990.

Sprinkle, Preston M. *Law and Life: The Interpretation of Leviticus 18:5 in Early Judaism and in Paul*. Wissenschaftliche Untersuchungen zum Neuen Testament 241. Tubingen: Mohr-Siebeck, 2008.

Stowers, Stanley K. *A Rereading of Romans: Justice, Jews, and Gentiles*. New Haven: Yale University Press, 1994.

Stuhlmacher, Peter. *Der Brief and die Romer*. Das Neue Testament Deutsch 6. Gottingen: Vandenhoeck & Ruprecht, 1989.

_____. *Reconciliation, Law, and Righteousness: Essays in Biblical Theology*. Philadelphia: Fortress, 1986.

Thielman, Frank. *Paul and the Law: A Contextual Approach*. Downers Grove, IL: InterVarsity Press, 1994.

_____. *Theology of the New Testament: A Canonical and Synthetic Approach*. Grand Rapids: Baker, 2005.

Thrall, Margaret H. *Greek Particles in the New Testament: Linguistic and Exegetical Studies*. Leiden: Brill, 1962.

Tidball, Derek. *The Message of the Cross*. Bible Themes Series. Downers Grove, IL: InterVarsity Press, 2001.

Tidball, Derek, David Hilborn, and Justin Thacker, eds. *The Atonement Debate: Papers from a London Symposium on the Theology of Atonement*. Grand Rapids: Zondervan, 2008.

Van Landingham, Chris. *Judgment and Justification in Early Judaism and the Apostle Paul*. Peabody, MA: Hendrickson, 2006.

Vickers, Brian J. *Jesus' Blood and Righteousness*. Wheaton: Crossway, 2006.

Ware, Bruce A. *God's Greater Glory*. Wheaton: Crossway, 2004.

_____. *God's Lesser Glory*. Wheaton: Crossway, 2000.

Waters, Guy Prentiss. *Justification and the New Perspectives on Paul: A Review and Response*. Phillipsburg, NJ: P&R, 2004.

Wengst, K. *Christologische Formeln und Lieder des Urchristentums*. Gütersloh: Gerd Mohn, 1972.

Westerholm, Stephen. *Perspectives Old and New on Paul: The Lutheran Paul and His Critics*. Grand Rapids: Eerdmans, 2004.

Williams, David J. *Paul's Metaphors: Their Context and Character*. Peabody, MA: Hendrickson, 1999.

Williams, Jarvis J. *Maccabean Martyr Traditions in Paul's Theology of Atonement: Did Martyr Theology Shape Paul's Conception of Jesus' Death?* Eugene, OR: Wipf & Stock, 2009.

Williams, Sam K. *Jesus' Death as Saving Event: The Background and Origin of a Concept.* Harvard Dissertation Review. Missoula: Scholars Press, 1975.

Wright, N. T. *Climax of the Covenant: Christ and the Law in Pauline Theology.* Minneapolis: Fortress, 1991.

_____. *The New Testament and the People of God.* Minneapolis: Fortress, 1992.

_____. *What Saint Paul Really Said: Was Saul of Tarsus the Real Founder of Christianity?* Grand Rapids: Eerdmans, 1997.

Ziesler, J. A. *The Meaning of Righteousness in Paul: A Linguistic and Theological Enquiry.* Society for New Testament Studies Monograph Series. Cambridge: Cambridge University Press, 1972.

Essays

Bailey, Daniel P. "Concepts of Stellvertretung in the Interpretation of Isaiah 53." Pages 223–50 in *Jesus and the Suffering Servant: Isaiah 53 and Christian Origins.* Edited by William H. Bellinger and William R. Farmer Jr. Harrisburg, PA: Trinity Press International, 1998.

Breytenbach, Cilliers. "Salvation of the Reconciled (with a Note on the Background of Paul's Metaphor of Reconciliation)." Pages 271–86 in *Salvation in the New Testament: Perspectives in Soteriology.* Edited by J. G. der Witt. Leiden: Brill, 2005.

Bultmann, Rudolph. "Adam and Christ according to Romans 5." Pages 143–65 in *Current Issues in New Testament Interpretation: Essays in Honor of Otto A. Piper.* Edited and translated by W. Klassen and G. F. Snyder. New York: Harper & Brothers, 1962.

Cone, James H., and Gayraud S. Wilmore, eds. *Black Theology: A Documentary History, Volume 1: 1966–1979.* 2nd ed. New York: Orbis, 1993.

Dunn, James D. G. "Paul's Understanding of the Death of Jesus as Sacrifice." Pages 35–56 in *Sacrifice and Redemption: Dur-*

ham Essays in Theology. Edited by S.W. Sykes. Cambridge: Cambridge University Press, 1997.

Fitzgerald, John T. "Paul and Friendship." Pages 319–43 in *Paul in the Greco-Roman World: A Handbook.* Edited by J. Paul Sampley. Harrisburg, PA: Trinity Press International, 2003.

————. "Paul and Paradigm Shifts: Reconciliation and Its Linkage Group." Pages 241–62 in *Paul Beyond the Judaism/Hellenism Divide.* Edited by Troels Engberg-Pedersen. Louisville: Westminster/John Knox, 2001.

Gathercole, Simon J. "Justified by Faith, Justified by His Blood: The Evidence of Romans 3:21–4:25." Page 168 in *The Paradoxes of Paul.* Edited by D. A. Carson, Peter O'Brien, and Mark A Seifrid. Vol. 2 of *Justification and Variegated Nomism: A Fresh Appraisal of Paul and Second Temple Judaism.* Grand Rapids: Baker, 2004.

————. "Torah, Life, and Salvation: Leviticus 18:5 in Early Judaism and the New Testament." Pages 127–45 in *From Prophecy to Testament: The Function of the Old Testament in the New.* Edited by Craig A. Evans. Peabody, MA: Hendrickson, 2004.

Henten, Jan Wilhem van. "The Tradition-Historical Background of Romans 3:25: A Search for Pagan and Jewish Parallels." Pages 101–28 in *From Jesus to John: Essays on Jesus and New Testament Christology in Honour of Marinus De Jonge.* Journal for the Study of the New Testament: Supplement Series 84. Edited by Martinus C. de Boer. Sheffield: JSOT Press, 1993.

Hofius, Otfried. "The Fourth Servant Song in the New Testament Letters." Pages 172–83 in *The Suffering Servant: Isaiah 53 in Jewish and Christian Sources.* Edited by Bernd Janowski and Peter Stuhlmacher. Translated by Daniel P. Bailey. Grand Rapids: Eerdmans, 2004.

————. "The Lord's Supper and the Lord's Supper Tradition: Reflections on 1 Corinthians 11:23b-25." Pages 75–115 in *One Loaf, One Cup: Ecumenical Studies of 1 Cor 11 and Other Eucharistic Texts.* Edited by B. F. Meyer. New Gospel Studies 6. 115. Macon, GA: Mercer University Press, 1993.

Käsemann, Ernst. "The Saving Significance of the Death of Jesus in Paul." Pages 32–59 in *Perspectives on Paul.* Translated by M. Kohl. Philadelphia: Fortress, 1971.

_____. "The Theological Problem Presented by the Motif of the Body of Christ." Pages 102–21 in *Pauline Perspectives*. Philadelphia: Fortress, 1969.

Lacey, D. R. de. "Gentiles." Page 335–39 in *Dictionary of Paul and His Letters*. Edited by Gerald F. Hawthorne, Ralph P. Martin, and Daniel G. Reid. Downers Grove, IL: InterVarsity Press, 1993.

Lampe, Peter. "Human Sacrifice and Pauline Christology." Pages 191–209 in *Human Sacrifice in Jewish and Christian Tradition*. Edited by Kain Finterbusch, Armin Lange, and K. F. Deithard. Leiden: Brill, 2007.

Lincoln, Andrew T. "From Wrath to Justification." Pages 130–59 in *Pauline Theology: Romans*. Edited by David M. Hay and E. Elizabeth Johnson. Vol. 3. Atlanta: SBL, 2002.

Marshall, I. Howard. "The Development of the Concept of Redemption in the New Testament." Pages 153–69 in *Reconciliation and Hope*. Edited by Robert J. Banks. Exeter: Paternoster, 1974.

Morris, Leon. "Redemption." Pages 784–86 in *Dictionary of Paul and His Letters*. Edited by Gerald F. Hawthorne, Ralph P. Martin, and Daniel G. Reid. Downers Grove, IL: InterVarsity Press, 1993.

Muller, Hans-Peter. "Eva und Das Paradies." Pages 501–10 in *Ex Mesopotamia et Syria Lux*. Munster: Ugarit-Verlag, 2002.

Peterson, David. "Atonement in the New Testament." Page 40 in *Where Wrath and Mercy Meet: Proclaiming the Atonement Today*. Edited by David Peterson. Carlisle, UK: Paternoster, 2001.

Schreiner, Thomas R. "The Penal Substitution View." Pages 67–98 in *The Nature of the Atonement: 4 Views*. Ed. James Beilby and Paul R. Eddy. Downers Grove, IL: InterVarsity Press, 2006.

_____. "Works of the Law." Pages 975–79 in *The Dictionary of Paul and His Letters*. Edited by Gerald F. Hawthorne, Ralph P. Martin, and Daniel G. Reid. Downers Grove, IL: InterVarsity Press: 1993.

Seifrid, Mark A. "Paul's Use of Habakkuk 2:4 in Romans 1:17: Reflections on Israel's Exile in Romans." In *History and Exegesis: New Testament Essays in Honor of Dr. E. Earle Ellis for*

His 80th Birthday, ed. Sang-Won (Aaron) Son, 133–49. New York: T&T Clark, 2006.

Soggin, J. Alberto. "And You Will Be Like God and Know What Is Good and What Is Bad: Genesis 2–3." In *Sefer Moshe*, 191–93. Winona Lake, IN: Eisenbrauns, 2004.

Stuhlmacher, Peter. "Zur neueren Exegese van Romer 3:24–26." In *Versohnung, Gesetz, und Gerechtigkeit*, ed. Earle Ellis and Erich Grasser, 117–35. Gottingen: Vandengoeck & Ruprecht, 1981.

Thielman, Frank S. "The Atonement." Pages 102–27 in *Central Themes in Biblical Theology: Mapping Unity in Diversity*. Edited by Scott Hafemann and Paul R. House. Grand Rapids: Baker, 2007.

_____. *From Plight to Solution: A Jewish Framework for Understanding Paul's View of the Law in Romans and Galatians*. Leiden: Brill, 1989.

Travis, Stephen H. "Christ as Bearer of Divine Judgment in Paul's Thought about the Atonement." Pages 21–38 in *Atonement Today*. Edited by John Goldingay. London: SPK, 1995.

Warfield, Benjamin B. "The New Testament Terminology of Redemption." Pages 327–98 in *Bible Doctrines: The Works of Benjamin B. Warfield*. vol. 2. Grand Rapids: Baker, 2003.

Wedderburn, A. J. M. "Adam in Paul's Letter to the Romans." Pages 413–30 in *Studia Biblica* 3. Edited by E. A. Livingstone. Journal for the Study of the New Testament: Supplemental Series 3. Sheffield: JSOT Press, 1980.

Wenin, Andre, and John Bowden. "The Serpent and the Woman, or the Process of Evil according to Genesis 2–3." Pages 41–48 in *Original Sin: A Code of Fallibility*. Edited by Christophe Boureux and Christoph Theobald. London: SCM Press, 2004.

Wright, N. T. "On Becoming the Righteousness of God: 2 Corinthians 5:21." Pages 205–6 in *Pauline Theology*. Vol. 1. Edited by David M. Hay. Minneapolis: Fortress, 1993.

Articles

Ansell, Nik. "The Call of Wisdom/The Voice of the Serpent: A Canonical Approach to the Tree of Knowledge." *Christian Scholar's Review* 31 (2001): 31–57.

Bechtel, Lyn M. "Genesis 2:4*b*–3:24: A Myth about Human Maturation." *Journal for the Study of the Old Testament* 67 (1995): 3–26.

Bell, Richard. "Sacrifice and Christology in Paul." *Journal of Theological Studies* 53 (2002): 1–27.

Branick, Bell V. P. "The Sinful Flesh of the Son of God (Rom 8:3): A Key Image in Pauline Theology." *Catholic Biblical Quarterly* 47 (1985): 246–62.

Breytenbach, Cilliers. "Versohnung, Stellvertretung und Suhne: Semantische untraditionsgeschichtliche Bemerkungen am Beispiel der paulinischen Briefe." *New Testament Studies* 39 (1993): 59–79.

Burns, Sherard. "A Practical Theology for Racial Harmony." *Southern Baptist Journal of Theology* 8, no. 2 (2004): 34–54.

Cambier, J. "Peches des homes et peches d' Adam en Rom v. 12." *New Testament Studies* 11 (1964–65): 246–53.

Collins, John C. "What Happened to Adam and Eve? A Literary-Theological Approach to Genesis 3." *Presbyterion* 27 (2001): 12–44.

Danker, Frederick W. "Rom V.12: Sin under Law." *New Testament Studies* 14 (1967–68): 428.

Dennis, John. "Jesus' Death in John's Gospel: A Survey of Research from Bultmann to the Present with Special Reference to the Johannine Hyper-Texts." *Currents in Biblical Research* 4.3 (2006): 331–63.

Dumbrell, William. "Genesis 2:1–3: A Biblical Theology of Creation Covenant." *Evangelical Review of Theology* 25 (2001): 219–30.

Eckstein, Hans-Joachim. "Deen Gottes Zorn wird Himmel her offenbar warden: Exegetisch Erwagungen zu Rom 1:18." *Zeitschrift für die neutestamentliche Wissenschaft und die Kunde der älteren Kirche* 78 (1987): 82–89.

Ekem, John D. K. "A Dialogical Exegesis of Romans 3:25*a*." *Journal for the Study of the New Testament* 30 (2007): 75–93.

Emmrich, Martin. "The Temptation Narrative of Genesis 3:1–6: A Prelude to the Pentateuch and the History of Israel." *Evangelical Quarterly* 73 (2001): 3–20.

Fitzmyer, Joseph. "The Consecutive Meaning of *eph hō* in Romans 5.12." *New Testament Studies* (1993): 321–39.

Fryer, Nico S. L. "The Meaning and Translation of *Hilastērion* in Romans 3:25." *Evangelical Quarterly* 59 (1987): 99–116.

Garlington, D. B. "The Obedience of Faith in the Letter to the Romans: Part 3, The Obedience of Christ and the Obedience of the Christian." *Westminster Theological Journal* 55 (1993): 87–112.

Gellman, Jerome I. "Gender and Sexuality in the Garden of Eden." *Theology and Sexuality* 12 (2006): 319–335.

Gemeren, W. A. van. "The Sons of God in Genesis 6:1–4: (An Example of Evangelical Demythologization?)." *Westminster Theological Journal* 43 (1981): 320–48.

Gosse, Bernard. "L' ecriture de Genesis 3, Le Serpent Dualite de la femme et L' home." *Biblische Notizen* 98 (1999): 19–20.

Gruber, M. I. "Was Cain Angry or Depressed?" *Biblical Archaeology Review* 6 (1980): 35–36.

Hanson, T. W. "ἱλαστήριον." *Journal of Theological Studies* 46 (1945): 1–10.

Hartman, Louis Francis. "Sin in Paradise." *Catholic Biblical Quarterly* 20 (1958): 26– 40.

Higgins, Jean M. "Myth of Eve: The Temptress." *Journal of the American Academy of Religion* 44 (1976): 639–47.

Hooker , Morna D. "Adam in Romans 1." *New Testament Studies* 6 (1959–60): 297–306.

_____. "A Further Note on Romans 1." *New Testament Studies* 13 (1966–67): 181–83.

_____. "Interchange and Atonement." *Biblical Journal of Religious Literature* 60 (1978): 462–81.

_____. "Interchange in Christ." *Journal of Theological Studies* 22 (1974): 349–61.

Joy, Donald M. "Toward A Symbolic Revival: Creation Revisited." *Religious Education* 80 (1985): 399–412.

Käsemann, Ernst. "Zum Verständis von Römer 3:24–26." *Zeitschrift für die neutestamentliche Wissenschaft* 43 (1950–1951): 150–54.

Kenneth, Craig M. "Misspeaking in Eden or Fielding Questions in the Garden (Genesis 2:16–3:13)." *Perspectives in Religious Studies* 27 (2000): 235–47.

Klein, G. "Exegeisch Probleme in Rom 3:21–25." *Evangelical Theology* 24 (1964): 678–83.

Kümmel, Werner G. "Paresis and Endeixis: A Contribution to the Understanding of the Pauline Doctrine of Justification." *Journal for Theology and the Church* 3 (1967): 1–13.

Lyonnet, Stanlis. "De notione expiationis." *Vetus Testamentum* 37 (1959): 336–52.

MacGregor, G. H. C. "The Concept of the Wrath of God in the NT." *New Testament Studies* 7 (1960–1961): 101–9.

McIntyre, John. "The Real Adam and Original Sin." *Perspectives on Science and Christian Faith* 58 (2006): 90–98.

McKinlay, Judith E. "To Eat or Not to Eat: Where Is Wisdom in This Choice?" *Semeia* 86 (1999): 73–84.

McLean, Bradley H. "The Absence of Atoning Sacrifice in Paul's Soteriology." *New Testament Studies* 38 (1992): 531–53.

_____. "Christ as a Pharmakos in Pauline Soteriology." *Society of Biblical Literature Seminar Papers* (1991): 187–206.

Meyer, B. F. "The Pre-Pauline Formula in Rom 3:25–26a." *New Testament Studies* 29 (1983): 198–208.

Moo, Douglas J. "Law, Works of the Law, and Legalism in Paul." *Westminster Theological Journal* 45 (1983): 73–100.

Morgan, F. A. "Romans 6:5a: United to a Death like Christ's." *Ephemerides theologicae lovanienses* 59 (1983): 267–302.

Morris, Leon. "The Biblical Use of the Term Blood." *Journal for Theological Studies* 3 (1952): 216–27.

_____. "The Meaning of ΗΙΛΑΣΤΗΡΙΟΝ in Romans 3:25." *New Testament Studies* (1955–1956): 39–43.

Nicole, Roger. "C. H. Dodd and the Doctrine of Propitiation." *Westminster Theological Journal* 17 (1954–55): 117–57.

Parker, Kim Ian. "Mirror, Mirror on the Wall, Must We Leave Eden, Once and for All?: A Lacanian Pleasure Trip through the Garden." *Journal for the Study of the Old Testament* 83 (1999): 73–84.

Phillips, Elaine A. "Serpent Intertexts: Tantalizing Twists in the Tales." *Bulletin for Biblical Research* 10 (2002): 233–45.

Schreiner, Thomas R. "Is Perfect Obedience to the Law Possible? A Re-examination of Galatians 3:10." *Journal of the Evangelical Theological Society* 27 (1984): 151–60.

_____. "Paul and Perfect Obedience to the Law: An Evaluation of the View of E. P. Sanders." *Westminster Theological Journal* 47 (1985): 245–78.

Stordalen, Terje. "Man, Soil, Garden: Basic Plot in Genesis 2–3 Considered." *Journal for the Study of the Old Testament* 53 (1992): 3–25.

Swain, William C. "For Our Sins: The Image of Sacrifice in the Thought of the Apostle Paul." *Interpretation* 17 (1963): 131–39.

Swallow, Frederick R. "Redemption in St. Paul." *Sacrament* 10 (1958): 21–27

Talbert, Charles H. "A Non-Pauline Fragment at Romans 3:24–26?" *Journal of Biblical Literature* 85 (1966): 287–96.

Thrall, Margaret E. "Salvation Proclaimed: 2 Corinthians 5:18–21." *Expository Times* 93 (1982): 230.

Townsend, Wayne P. "Eve's Answer to the Serpent: An Alternative Paradigm for Sin and Some Implications in Theology." *Calvin Theological Journal* 33 (1998): 399–420.

Vogels, Walter. "Like One of Us, Knowing Good and Evil (Gen 3:22)." *Semeia* 81 (1998): 144–57.

Walsh, Jerome T. "Genesis 2:4b–3:24: A Synchronic Approach." *Journal of Biblical Literature* 96 (1977): 161–77.

Wilckens, Ulrich. "Zu Romer 3:21–25." *Evangelical Theology* 24 (1964): 584–610.

Williams, Garry J. "Penal Substitution: A Response to Recent Criticisms." *Journal of the Evangelical Theological Society* 50 (2007): 71–86.

Williams, Jarvis J. "Penal Substitution in Romans 3:25–26?" *The Princeton Theological Review* 13 (2007): 73–81.

Williams, Jay G. "Genesis 3." *Interpretation* 35 (1981): 274–70.

Yee, Gale A. "Gender, Class, and the Social-Scientific Study of Genesis 2–3." *Semeia* 87 (1999): 177–92.

Yoder, Perry B. "Will the Real Adam Please Stand Up!" *Perspectives on Science and Christian Faith* 58 (2006): 99–101.

Dissertations

Bailey, Daniel P. "Jesus as the Mercy Seat: The Semantics and Theology of Paul's Use of *Hilastērion* in Romans 3:25." Ph.D. diss., Cambridge University, 1999.

Smith, Derwood Cooper. "Jewish and Greek Traditions in Ephesians 2:11–22." Ph. D. diss., Yale University, 1970.

Yong, Kukwah Philemon. "The Faith of Jesus Christ: An Analysis of Paul's Use of Pistis Christou." Ph.D. diss., The Southern Baptist Theological Seminary, 2003.

Unpublished Paper

Verbrugge, Verlyn D. "The Grammatical Internal Evidence for ἔχωμεν in Romans 5:1." Paper presented at the national meeting of the Evangelical Theological Society. Providence, RI, November 19, 2008.

author index

Scripture index

ancient writings index

Apocrypha

Old Testament Pseudepigrapha

Dead Sea Scrolls and related texts